Elusive Equality

Constitutional Guarantees and Legal Regimes in South Asia, Malaysia and China

edited by

INDIRA JAISING

women
UNLIMITED
an associate of
kali for women

Elusive Equality
Constitutional Guarantees and Legal Regimes in South Asia, Malaysia and China
was first published in India in 2011
by
Women Unlimited
(an associate of Kali for Women)
K-36, Hauz Khas Enclave
New Delhi 110016

ISBN: 81-88965-70-7

Cover design: Neelima Rao

Printed at De Unique, A-62 DSIDC Work Center, Tilak Vihar,
New Delhi 110018 and typeset by Gopalakrishnan, New Delhi 110029

Contents

Acknowledgements

We are grateful to Ford Foundation, China for funding the Asia Cause Lawyers Network (ACLN) project and this publication.

The ACLN Steering Committee Members – Zarizana Abdul Aziz, Salma Ali, Savitri Goonesekere, Rowena Guanzon, Akiko Ito, Guo Jianmei, Hina Jilani, Rita Kalibonso, Sapana Pradhan Malla, Ramamurti Vaigai and Anna Wu – have provided their valuable guidance and steady support to help ensure the success of this project. We especially thank Rangita deSilva for her work in setting up the ACLN network.

The contributors to this volume generously shared with us their insights gained over years of academic scholarship and grassroots activism, enabling us to compile a volume that poses important theoretical questions and strategic challenges regarding substantive equality and gender justice in South Asia.

UNIFEM South Asia Sub Regional Office kindly granted permission to reprint Savitri Goonesekere's paper in this volume.

Ritu Menon at Women Unlimited has been both patient and prompt as she shepherded this project from start to completion.

Sonal Makhija and Ratna Menon provided diligent and dedicated editorial support for this publication.

1 Introduction

Indira Jaising

This volume of essays is envisaged as a companion volume to an earlier publication, *Men's Laws, Women's Lives* that examined the impact of religion, custom and tradition on the right to equality and non-discrimination for women. The earlier compilation was primarily dedicated to locating the right to equality in the familial setting and was viewed through the constitutional lens of the different countries of South Asia including India, Pakistan, Bangladesh and Sri Lanka. At the heart of the problem examined in that compilation is the existence and efficacy of the plural legal systems that these countries have inherited from their shared colonial legacy. A plural legal system indicates a political formation where more than one system of laws finds application. One system is secular in nature, uniformly applicable in matters relating to the public domain such as administration, trade, commerce, crime, etc. A system of courts with access open to all has been established to implement these laws. The other is a codified system of religious laws that relates to the domain of the personal/private/family: i.e., matters of marriage, divorce, guardianship and inheritance. These religious laws may be enforced either through the same system of courts that administer secular laws or by religious heads who administer personal law.

The current volume, however, focuses on conceptions of equality, per se, and does not limit itself to any particular sphere of equality as did the first volume on family. It deals with how different constitutional systems—whether plural, secular, theocratic or socialist—approach the issue of equality in different spheres of activity. The question then is: what does the right to equality mean for women in these different situations?

An analysis of certain countries in the Asian region across a spectrum of constitutions provides a key to answering that question. Located on the theocratic end of the spectrum is Malaysia, a country which has what can be called a hybrid constitution: one that is neither Islamic nor secular. It recognises Islam as the state religion and shows tolerance towards other religions. On the other end of the spectrum, one finds China, a country with a secular socialist constitution, having no recognition of religious or personal laws. Located somewhere in between on this spectrum is India with a secular constitution that recognises personal laws. And Nepal presents an intriguing case study of a country in transition; at present engaged in shifting from being a Hindu monarchy to a democracy with a secular constitution. It is our hope that by examining these countries together in one volume, we will be able to evaluate the relevance that a particular constitution has to the status of women and their right to equality and non-discrimination. Indeed, this compilation makes a noteworthy suggestion: that the outcome of an interpretive understanding of the right to equality will depend more on what one understands by notions of 'equality' rather than by constitutional provisions in themselves.

It may be appropriate then to chronologically map the evolving concept of equality under international law and to deal with the meaning of equality and non-discrimination in CEDAW and in constitutional texts. The Universal Declaration of Human Rights (UDHR) was the first international document to deal with human rights, and inherently accords that status to equality. The International Covenant on Civil and Political Rights (ICCPR) concretised notions of formal equality.[1] Under Article 26 of the ICCPR, "all persons are equal before the law and are entitled without any discrimination to the equal protection of the law. In this respect, the law shall prohibit any discrimination, and guarantee to all persons equal and effective protection against discrimination on any ground such as race, colour, sex, language, religion, political or other opinion, national or social origin, property, birth or other status."

Historically, the right to equality produced strangely unequal results for women. In the USA, which guarantees the right to equality for women, the Supreme Court held that women cannot practice law, as their primary role is that of procreators and care-givers, and the role of men to protect them.[2] This strange interpretation proceeded from understanding equality as the right to treat likes alike; since women and men were not alike, treating them differently was no denial of equality. This is a formal conception of equality, entailing that likes should be treated in a similar manner, and unlikes should be treated differently, according to their differences. As Sandra Fredman argues in her paper, such an understanding is based on the premise that individuals should be treated on the basis of merit, rather than gender. However, feminism and struggles for non-discrimination based on race, shifted radically from this formal understanding of equality to one based on the notion of 'substantive equality'. This development can surely be described as revolutionary; it rejects the need for a male comparator and looks instead at the context in which the demand is made to evaluate whether the right to equality has been denied, per se. To quote Sandra Fredman, "Rather than the abstract individual of formal equality, substantive equality focuses on disadvantage; it aims to break the cycle of disadvantage associated with women, rather than to treat gender as irrelevant to decision-making." It is the CEDAW that comes closest to taking a substantive view of equality for women.[3] All countries selected for comment in this volume have signed the CEDAW with or without reservations. We can, therefore, say that they have a shared definition of equality.

It is possible to achieve formal equality in law-making and yet not reach the goal of equality when viewed from the impact of a seemingly equal measure on rights and when the outcome for women is evaluated. This shift from form to substance marks a reliance on evidence-based judgements on the question of whether equality has been achieved. It is no longer sufficient for governments to argue, for example, that they have in place laws to ensure equal pay for equal work. Figures for the payout to women will have to be looked at so as to judge whether equality has been attained as a constitutional goal. The status of women when viewed by the human development index on literacy, land ownership, participation in public life or any other such factor clearly places them at a disadvantage compared to men. This is the gap that substantive equality requires the state to fill with policy and action plans in order to attain the goal of substantive equality.

The contribution made by CEDAW to the improvement in the status of women worldwide is that it has given us a definition of equality which addresses both direct and indirect discrimination, and evaluates the attainment of the goal of equality by looking at *impact* and *outcome* rather than looking at the *form* of the law. Direct and indirect discrimination are both required to be banned, as pointed out by both Sandra Fredman and Savitri Goonesekere. While Fredman points to the limitations of CEDAW itself, Goonesekere focuses on policy changes at the national level in the Asia region to comply with the requirement to "promote, protect and respect" the right to equality. These duties enjoined on states require them to not only respect the right to non-discrimination by not violating it, but to provide protection against others, in particular, the private non-state sector, violating this right. This has profound implications for women as it requires the state to, for instance, prevent violence against women by the family or by private individuals. Governments can no longer see their duty purely in a negative sense; they will have to proactively prevent private actors from violating the rights of women to equality and non-discrimination.

It is thus appropriate that this volume begins by clarifying what we mean by equality and non-discrimination. Savitri Goonesekere gives us a blueprint for action in the Asia region. She points out that the concept of equality requires a combination of formal and substantive equality measures to eliminate discrimination. Reservations and quotas for women in electoral bodies is a tried and tested strategy in some countries of the Asia region such as Pakistan, Bangladesh and India. Protective legislation, though much criticised by feminists, may be necessary when one considers available resources in a country and its state of preparedness for preventing violence in public spaces. Such legislation should however be phased out; for example, countries in the Asian subcontinent have abolished the ban on night work for women on the ground that it is likely to restrict employment opportunities for them.

Zarizana Abdul Aziz, in her study of Malaysia, endorses the concept of substantive equality, despite two almost insurmountable obstacles prevailing in that country. One is the declaration of Islam as the state religion, apparently circumvented by confining its operation to observing Islamic ceremonies by the state on ritual occasions, and leaving citizens free to practice a religion of their choice. A closer examination however reveals that this right to practice is an empty formality. First, it is the Sharia courts which alone have the jurisdiction to interpret rights relating to inheritance, marriage, divorce, child custody, adoption and guardianship. Thus Islamic law governs a woman throughout her life, and is immune from constitutional challenge on the ground that it violates the right to equality. When it comes to a change of religion the situation is the same; religion cannot be renounced without the declaration of the Sharia court that it has been renounced. The right to profess any religion is a virtual mirage and a woman is confined to the religion into which she is born. The second insurmountable obstacle is the narrow and formal understanding of equality which demands that it is nothing more than treating likes alike, as the case of Beatrice indicates.[4] Beatrice was discharged from her job as an air hostess because of her pregnancy. The court did not see this as a violation of her right to equality as the condition was imposed on her not because of her sex but because of the nature of work, which was arduous and required long hours of night duty. The comparison with ground staff who did not have to retire on account of pregnancy was not considered discriminatory, as they did not do the same work. This indicates that the court had a flawed understating of equality, and that CEDAW, which Malaysia signed with no reservations in the field of employment, had no impact on its understanding of it. What this suggests is that courts in Malaysia have not necessarily imbibed the ethos of the advances made in our understanding of women's rights as human rights. Nor were they willing to impose constitutional obligations on private actors such as the airline which discriminated against its female employee. This decision must be seen as a failure of justice in a secular field of employment for women and has the effect of undoing constitutional guarantees of equality and non-discrimination based on sex. No clearer case can be found of discrimination based on sex, as pregnancy is a condition specific to women. A protectionist approach was adopted with the court ruling that the employer was justified in not assigning arduous work to a woman during pregnancy. This case galvanised women who then realised how precarious their constitutional guarantee of equality was, and made them lobby for legislation that would accept the basis of substantive equality and ban all discrimination, direct and indirect. The law drafted by civil society has not yet been enacted. A comparison with a similar case decided in India is befitting here. *Nargesh Mirza*[5] was decided several decades earlier in a similar manner. Air hostesses were forced to retire on pregnancy and their age of retirement was determined at being much earlier than that of men. This was justified on the basis that they were not similarly situated: their job functions were different. This was not discrimination based on sex but sex-plus! What this tells us is that seemingly different countries on the constitutional scale of secularism have a common understanding, or rather a lack of understanding, of 'equality' and demonstrate the devastating impact it has on the rights of women not only in matters of personal law but also where secular employment laws are concerned. Here it is the understanding of rights itself that is flawed.

The core issue in the case of Malaysia is not just its Islamic constitution but its inability to internalise the mandate of equality and CEDAW. This is symptomatic of many countries who sign international treaties, with or without reservations, but without understanding what it takes to make equality a living reality for women. The battleground in such cases moves to the legislature with demands for a statute which defines discrimination, direct and indirect, and which emphasises results and outcomes; such a statute would be binding on both the public and private sectors, thereby redeeming the promise of CEDAW to "promote, protect and respect" the right to equality. The need of the day is to spell out the duties of the state, and this is true of both India and Malaysia.

Moving to Nepal, what we see here is a constitution in the making. The challenge now lies in the need to dismantle the structure of Hinduism and translate the secularism of the transitional constitution and the proposed new constitution into rights for women. The process is most interesting, and is perhaps without precedent. It consists of repealing more than 200 pieces of legislation. Ordinarily, the process of repeal happens very slowly, if indeed it happens at all. Parliaments are not known to pay attention to unconstitutional statutes, leaving this to a case-by-case decision by courts. It is only the political process which has enabled repeal, by identifying statutes which are Hindu and allowing subjects such as marriage, inheritance and guardianship to be governed by equitable laws. The courts possess no such magic wand but people, in the exercise of their sovereign power, do. This is not to say that the process was magical; women's groups tirelessly undertook a sanitation process, ruthlessly eliminating religion from the public sphere. Nepal's transitional constitution represents a case study in secular constitution-making and allows us a glimpse of what it may be like to work on a clean slate. It is too early to predict the impact of this process; however, statistics are available about the numbers of women engaged in constitution-making, and the number of those elected to the constituent assembly is substantially higher than before the process began. Thanks to affirmative action endorsed by the transitional constitution, there is a reservation of one-third of all seats in the assembly for women. Sapana Malla, in her paper, attributes this to the participation of women in the constituent body; but the political process that brought them there, changes on the judicial front, and international developments have all contributed to the process of guaranteeing equality to women. We are inclined to think of the process of legislating as one which fills a vacuum; in Nepal, however, the process has been one of dismantling an existing legal structure. While it has been relatively easy to dismantle laws because of a recognition of the need to guarantee equality for women, entrenched customary practices may not be quite so easy to dislodge. The task has been facilitated partly by the fact that Nepal is a monist country and that, in the absence of a constitution, the international treaties it has signed can be seen as reflecting its constitutional obligations. The deadline for formulating the constitution by March 2010 has been extended, as a substantial amount of work remains to be done. At the same time, courts were extraordinarily active before the process of constitution-making began. Public interest litigation, as we know it in the subcontinent, took birth in India but has flourished in Nepal. Several unjust laws have been struck down, inheritance laws and marital rape have all been declared unconstitutional. One is tempted to say that the discrimination under Hindu law was so patent that it was just waiting to be struck down. However, similar provisions in India have not been dealt with similarly, and we must look elsewhere for explanations. The repeated references in judgements to international obligations establishes that Nepal's monist position on international law enables the judiciary to depart from the Hindu law and invoke international treaties in order to grant relief to women.

Nevertheless, Nepal has yet to come up with a constitution and adopt it. This is clearly indicative of an absence of consensus in the constitution-making process. The contentious and unaddressed issues include: what is to be done with Maoist activists in the refugee camps; reparations and compensation for the disappeared and their families; how to deal with the violence perpetrated by non-state actors; and with the thin dividing line between non-state and state actors. It will not be enough for women to sit on sub-committees drafting the women's charter; rather, they will have to deal with all these issues and the inter-sectorality of rights will have to be actively addressed. Sharp differences between civil and political rights and social and economic rights will need to be resolved, and gender will be a cross-cutting issue across these guaranteed rights.

Discussing the Indian context, Poonam Saxena takes us through Articles 14 and 15 to demonstrate how fundamental rights of non-discrimination based on sex have been used to strike down discriminatory legislation. This brings us to a discussion on the secular constitution of India which nevertheless recognises personal law, and in that sense cannot be said to be truly secular. Personal laws exist, attaching to women by virtue of the religion to which they belong; once born a Hindu you are always a Hindu, and once born a Muslim, you are always a Muslim. The Special Marriages Act of 1954 permits inter-religious marriages, but they are not the norm. Both in form and content marriage is governed by the law of the religion to which you belong. This has resulted in a large hangover of discriminatory laws in place for women in matters relating to marriage, divorce, inheritance, child custody and guardianship.

In contrast to Malaysia, Indian high courts and the Supreme Court have the power to strike down any law, secular or religious, on the ground that, in theory, it violates fundamental rights. In this respect, India stands apart from all the other countries in the region. Moreover, Sharia laws are administered by regular courts in India, not by Sharia courts. In most other countries there is a strict separation of Sharia courts which are supposed to be manned by religious experts, and regular civil and constitutional courts which do not opine on any religious question. This accords India its unique position in the region and provides limitless opportunity for challenging laws on the ground that they violate women's right to equality. Poonam Saxena demonstrates that this power has not been generously invoked. She contends that courts, though empowered to do so, do not often use this power. Rather, they have tended to sustain them on several grounds. These include reliance on tradition and custom; the need to be cautious while dealing with social reform; and, most importantly, relying on the doctrine of separation of power. It is the job of the legislature to make changes, not theirs. Thus, the difference between the power of the courts under a secular constitution and an Islamic one is not as great as it appears at first glance. Secularism and equality do not necessarily tilt the balance in favour of non-discrimination. One can only conclude that differences in constitutions in those countries which prohibit personal laws do not determine the outcome of a case as they should, notwithstanding the power to strike down a discriminating statute. And yet it is not possible to say that a constitution has no relevance to laws.

At this juncture, it is relevant to recall the now famous *Shah Bano* case[6] and its companion, *Daniel Latifi,*[7] both remarkable for the jurisprudence that evolved as a result. Faced with a demand for maintenance by a divorced Muslim woman, the court had to contend with an argument that

Muslim personal law dealt with marriage as a contract, a "clean break", with no obligation to pay post-divorce maintenance except for the three-month iddat period. Skilfully avoiding a perceived and actual conflict between a secular law which grants post-divorce maintenance and a personal law which limits it, the court held that the two rights operated in different fields; the secular law envisaged a situation not contemplated by personal law, i.e., one in which a woman could not maintain herself, while her divorced husband had the means to do so. This was a secular social obligation to prevent vagrancy, was not based on religion and was expressly made applicable to *all* women. The relief was granted. A major political backlash broke out and the Muslim Personal Law Board, demonstrating its electoral clout, managed to mobilise and get the Muslim Women's (Protection of Rights on Divorce) Act, 1986 passed, with the ostensible object of limiting post-divorce maintenance to three months. This law was challenged and the consequent judgement established that there was an understanding by the court of substantive equality while interpreting the law; specific observations indicate that the *judges took the view that a woman's contribution to the development of the marital assets could not be ignored when a divorce takes place.* This was the first time that a woman's contribution to matrimonial assets through her domestic work and home-based labour were valorised in a judgement. The judges' observations have the potential of developing active equality jurisprudence for women of *all* religions, as the letter of the law to "make reasonable and fair provision" was interpreted to create a standalone right to receive a lumpsum settlement. This could be a provision for life, in addition to a claim for maintenance for three months; *the court held that to do otherwise would clearly violate the right to equality for Muslim women, as women of all other communities were entitled to post-divorce maintenance.* These cases illustrate the role of the constitutional court in advancing the agenda of substantive equality. India stands at a mid-point between Islamic countries and secular ones by recognising personal and customary laws, but subjecting them to constitutional scrutiny on grounds of non-discrimination based on sex.

Finally, China takes us to a purely secular and socialist constitution where there is no mention of religious laws, much less an enforcement of them. The basic law on the rights of women guarantees equality; yet China lacks an enforcement mechanism for this constitutional law, leading to the conclusion that it is merely a statement of intent. The obvious need for a statutory law on equality and non-discrimination cannot be overstated to ensure enforceability. It is here that the true test of substantive equality is made and is seen to be wholly missing from the legal regime; women are dependent on local administrations for enforcement and declarations of intent. Guo Jianmei and Li Ying document the laws in discussion and then go on to discuss the strategies used to bridge the gap. Activism by women's groups has led local administrations to address issues such as domestic violence and sexual harassment at the workplace. Evidence-based reports on denial of land rights to married women led to the granting of relief to them, thus underlining the supremacy of activism as a primary agent of social change.

Together these essays present case studies of different routes taken towards achieving substantive equality. At one end of the spectrum are constitutions that enshrine religious laws; in these countries women strive to interpret religious texts in a gender-sensitive manner to keep them in harmony with the times and with international commitments. In the middle are countries like India which recognise religious laws but permit an open challenge to them on the ground that they discriminate against women on the basis of sex alone. It is noteworthy that the battles against discrimination in India have been fought by women from within their respective communities, giving the lie to the belief that the community is not ready for change. At the other end is China with a perfectly secular constitution and framework but with no enforcement mechanisms, asserting the primacy of politics over law enforcement. Nepal is an example of a society in dramatic transition from Hindu monarchy to secular democracy, a most unusual development in the subcontinent.

What this volume illustrates is that equality is not a closed category in legal thought, but a living and evolving concept that needs constant interpretation and reinterpretation in keeping with the rising aspirations of women to shake off the historic and ancient inferior status ascribed to them, at least before the law.

Notes

1 Article 3 of the ICCPR lays down the obligation of state parties to ensure the equal right of men and women to the enjoyment of all civil and political rights enshrined in the covenant. Article 14 refers to the equality of all persons before courts and tribunals.

2 *Bradwell* v. *Illinois* 83 US 130 (1872).

3 Article 1, CEDAW states: "For the purposes of the present Convention, the term *'discrimination against women'* shall mean any distinction, exclusion or restriction made on the basis of sex which has the effect or purpose of impairing or nullifying the recognition, enjoyment or exercise by women, irrespective of their marital status, on a basis of equality of men and women, of human rights and fundamental freedoms in the political, economic, social, cultural, civil or any other field."

4 *Beatrice Fernandez* v. *Sistem Penerbangan Malaysia* [2004] 4CLJ 403 (Court of Appeal) and [2005] 2 CLJ 173 (Federal Court).

5 *Air India* v. *Nargesh Mirza* (1981) 4 SCC 335.

6 *Mohd. Ahmed Khan* v. *Shah Bano Begum & Others* (1985) AIR SC 945.

7 *Danial Latifi & Anr.* v. *Union of India* 2001 (7) SCC 746.

2 Substantive Equality for Women

Sandra Fredman

Introduction

Equality for women is an ideal for which we all fervently strive, yet it remains as elusive as ever. For many women, equality before the law is still by no means guaranteed, and even when we do have it there remain deeply ingrained inequalities between men and women. This has led us to seek out more penetrating legal concepts and mechanisms to address inequalities. In particular, equal treatment for men and women is insufficient to tackle structural inequalities, and individual litigation is not effective as a sole means for achieving real change. Instead, we need to have in place rights to *substantive* equality. Moreover, this should be accompanied by new mechanisms for achieving change, including positive duties on authorities to achieve equality and corresponding activism on the part of women on the ground.

Although there is growing consensus on the need for substantive equality, its meaning and application remain contested and under-developed. Does substantive equality mean that women should be given equal opportunities with men or does it mean that the outcomes for women and men should be equal? Both equality of opportunity and equality of outcome have been incorporated into law in various jurisdictions, but neither has proved to be a panacea. Alternatively, dignity is increasingly regarded by courts and academics as constituting the core of equality. However, on its own, dignity can be both flimsy and fickle. Instead, it is necessary to develop a multi-dimensional principle of equality, which can address both socio-economic disadvantage and prejudice, as well as aim to achieve equal participation for women in decision-making. In addition, substantive equality should have space for differences between women and be capable of dealing with cumulative discrimination. The Convention on the Elimination of All Forms of Discrimination against Women (CEDAW) is the international instrument which comes closest to taking a substantive view of equality for women. As a point of reference for women in all societies and contexts, it is of great importance that we continue to develop CEDAW in the direction of substantive equality. This paper briefly considers why formal equality on its own has been unable to achieve genuine equality for women, before considering alternative conceptions of equality. It then examines the extent to which CEDAW incorporates a substantive view of equality. I conclude by focusing on the limits of substantive equality in CEDAW and the ways in which it should be further developed.

Formal equality

Formal equality is based on the premise that individuals should be treated as individuals, on the basis of their own merit, rather than their gender. It is usually summed up by the Aristotelian formula that likes should be treated alike. In legal contexts, it finds expression in the principle of direct discrimination or equal treatment, which makes it unlawful to treat a woman less favourably on grounds of her gender than a man; or, conversely, to treat a man less favourably on grounds of his gender than a woman. It has taken many years of political struggle to reach the point of recognition that gender is an irrelevant criterion for key political and civil rights and, in some countries, women have still not achieved formal equality.[1] Its achievements should not be underestimated.

However, even in countries were women have achieved formal equality before the law, experience has quickly demonstrated that inequalities persist, whether in the labour market, political representation or at home. Thus, women predominate in precarious forms of work, such as temporary work, work in the informal sector or other forms of work without job security. In addition, there remains a stubborn wage gap in almost all societies and jurisdictions. Women are significantly under-represented in legislatures and other positions of power in society, and violence against women is a continuing scourge. How can these continuing inequalities be explained despite the introduction of formal equality?

This question can be answered by looking more closely at the limitations of formal equality. At least six limitations can be highlighted. The first is the assumption that the aim of equality is to treat everyone on the basis of merit, rather than gender. This assumes that merit is an objective characteristic which can be scientifically measured. However, merit is itself a function of previous advantage. Treating gender as irrelevant merely ignores the ongoing disadvantage experienced by individuals who have previously been unequal before the law or subject to social prejudice.[2] The result is to entrench disadvantage. Second, formal equality assumes that the aim is identical treatment. In fact, given antecedent inequality, it may be necessary to provide very different sets of resources to achieve genuine equality. As Sen has argued: "Equal consideration for all may demand very unequal treatment in favour of the disadvantaged. The demands of substantive equality can be particularly exacting and complex when there is a good deal of antecedent inequality to counter".[3]

Third, formal equality is premised on an abstract and universal individual. However, the possibility of an individual abstracted from her gender is illusory. In reality, the abstract individual is clothed with male characteristics, which are then asserted as if they were universal. Only those who can conform to this male norm are sufficiently 'alike' to be entitled to 'like treatment'. The result is that formal equality demands conformity as a price for equal treatment. For example, women will only be entitled to equal pay or equal treatment to men if they can do the same jobs and work the same hours as their male counterparts. Women with child-care responsibilities will be excluded from equal treatment unless they are able to find other women to look after their children, and the latter are invariably low paid. Yet the aim should be to change existing structures which exclude women, rather than to require women to conform. Working hours should be reformulated to make it possible for both men and women to engage in child-care as well as to enter the paid workforce. The aim should not be to eliminate difference, but to prohibit the detriment attached to such difference.

Fourth, formal equality is a relative concept. It requires only that two similarly situated individuals be treated alike. This means that there is no difference in principle between treating men and women equally badly and treating them equally well. For example, where men have no land rights, the equality principle holds out no promise for women. Similarly, equal pay laws are of no benefit to a low paid woman if the only similarly situated male comparator is equally badly paid. It is here that equality can be no substitute for substantive rights. Moreover, because formal equality is agnostic as to the substantive outcome, it can be fulfilled by removing benefits from men rather than extending benefits to women or vice versa. This means that the achievement of formal equality can be a hollow victory or even a defeat. For example, in the United Kingdom and France, 'protective legislation' prevented women from engaging in night work, underground work in mines or other hazardous work. This was challenged as breaching the equality principle. However, instead of extending protection to men, the response in the UK was to remove protection from women. The result is that women are worse off and men are not better off.

Fifth, formal equality is also based on a negative conception of liberty, aiming to restrain the State from interfering with individual rights, rather than placing positive obligations on the State to promote equality. Thus, even if the State itself refrains from discriminating against women, it is not required to take positive steps to dismantle structures which give women a marginal position in the labour force or politics or which subject them to violence.

Finally, and perhaps most importantly, little will change given the persistence of a rigid public/private divide, with some women in the world still consigned wholly to the private sphere, and others allowed to enter the public only on condition that they leave their children behind in the private space. It is crucial address the division of labour whereby women still have primary responsibilities towards children, and whatever work women do in the 'private sphere', whether it be agricultural or domestic, continues to be devalued.

Substantive equality

Substantive equality is fashioned to address each of these limitations. First, substantive equality does not aim to abstract the individual from the social context. It takes into account existing power structures and the role of gender within them. Rather than assuming that everyone should be treated as if their gender did not matter, it recognises that women's life chances are heavily influenced by their gender. Substantive equality is therefore asymmetrical: its focus is on redressing women's disadvantage, rather than on rooting out all differential treatment on grounds of sex. For example, given women's substantial antecedent disadvantage, it may require women to be treated better than men in certain circumstances. This may be a breach of formal equality, but, far from breaching substantive equality, would be a means of achieving it. Second, and as a result of this, substantive equality does not simply aim at equal treatment. Where equal treatment leads to disadvantage for women, it may be necessary to treat women differently in order to achieve substantive equality. Third, substantive equality is not neutral as to the outcome. Equality cannot be achieved by treating all equally badly or by removing benefits from the advantaged class. It is substantive in the sense that it advances individuals rather than formal in ensuring only consistency. Fourth, substantive equality moves beyond the need for a male norm. In its transformative form, substantive equality requires social institutions to change, rather than expecting the individual to conform. Finally, substantive equality can go beyond a model which requires a finding of breach of the law before action can be taken, to one which includes positive duties on the State to respect, protect, promote and fulfil.

Framing substantive equality as a response to the limits of formal equality has achieved considerable consensus. However, the specific content of substantive equality remains contested. There is a temptation to reduce substantive equality to a single dimension, such as dignity, or to redefine equality in terms of equal opportunity or equality of results. Each of these is problematic. While dignity can function as a core rationale for substantive equality, it should not be the central component of its definition. Regarding dignity as a legal component of the definition of equality has led courts to reject claims of detrimental treatment on the grounds that this should not be regarded as an affront to dignity. Similarly, equality of opportunity on its own is too vague to function as a legal component of substantive equality. While it is possible to remove barriers at the point of entry, this will not guarantee that women are in a position to make use of these opportunities. Nor will it transform structures which lead to the inequality in the first place. For example, the opportunity to work part-time might make it possible for more women to enter the workforce and equal pay for equal work for part-time workers might improve their conditions, but the predominance of women in part-time work will not change. Indeed, this might increase their burden of combining paid work with family work, unless the division of labour in the home is changed and men taken on equal responsibility for child-care. A further example can be found in the case of education for girl children. Several jurisdictions have increased opportunities for girls to go to school through incentives for parents to send their daughters to school and increasing the availability of schools. However, if social norms continue to regard educated girls as attracting less bride price or, conversely, as requiring a larger dowry, it will remain difficult for girls to make use of these opportunities.[4]

Equality of results is more quantifiable than equality of opportunity and, correspondingly, more effective. However, on their own, policies aiming simply at results are also insufficiently transformative. 'Feminisation of work' is often associated with decreasing pay and status. For example, in the UK, an increase of women in managerial positions in catering coincided with a decrease in pay. A change in the gender composition of a grade or sector, while to some extent positive, might reflect only an increasingly successful assimilationist policy. Thus, women who achieve these positions might have done so by conforming to 'male' working patterns, contracting out their child-care obligations to other women, who remain as underpaid and undervalued as ever. A further example is found in Tomasevski's work on education. Improved enrolments of girls in primary education may seem to be a significant move towards equality of results. However, unless there are also more openings for educated girls in paid work, such education may be of little value in achieving structural change.

Each of these concepts has its strengths and should not be downgraded. But none can function on its own to constitute the substantive core of equality. I argue instead that this has four different dimensions.[5] First, it is an asymmetric principle. Rather than the abstract individual of formal equality, substantive equality focuses on disadvantage. It aims to break the cycle of disadvantage associated with women, rather than to treat gender as irrelevant to decision-making. Second, substantive equality promotes respect for the equal dignity and worth of all, thereby redressing stigma, stereotyping, humiliation and violence directed against women. Sexual harassment, domestic violence and other forms of violence against women are outlawed by the dignity element of equality. Third, substantive equality does not exact conformity as the price of equality. Instead of requiring women to conform to male norms, it insists on transformation of existing male-oriented institutions and social structures. Fourth, it should facilitate full participation of women in politics, society and economics. All of these dimensions entail both positive and negative duties on the State. Thus, the State should itself refrain from discriminating, protect individuals against discrimination by other individuals and take positive steps to promote and fulfil equality.

CEDAW

This section considers the extent to which CEDAW reflects the four-dimensional conception of substantive equality identified above: i.e., (i) asymmetry, focusing on disadvantage; (ii) dignity, addressing stigma, prejudice and violence; (iii) transformation of the male norm in institutions and practices; and (iv) full participation of women in society. In most respects, CEDAW comes close to the goal of substantive equality, reflecting all these dimensions. As a start, it is expressly asymmetric. Instead of outlawing discrimination on the grounds of sex or gender, CEDAW aims at the elimination of discrimination specifically against women. According to the CEDAW Committee, "[t]he Convention goes beyond the concept of discrimination used in many national and international legal standards and norms. While such standards and norms prohibit discrimination on the grounds of sex and protect both men and women from treatment based on arbitrary, unfair and/or unjustifiable distinctions, the Convention focuses on discrimination against women, emphasizing that women have suffered, and continue to suffer from various forms of discrimination because they are women".[6] Nor is it sufficient to provide formal equality or to open up opportunities which women are unable to utilise. The emphasis is on ensuring that women are actually in a position to make use of their rights.[7] Article 1 defines "discrimination against women" in terms of the impairment of women's enjoyment or exercise of human rights and fundamental freedom in the political, economic, social, cultural, civil or any other field. This means that equality is allied with both civil and political rights and socio-economic rights, including rights to equality in education [Article 10], employment [Article 11], social security [Article 11(e)] and health care [Article 12]. Furthermore, CEDAW specifically goes beyond equal treatment, requiring special measures for women where necessary to achieve equality. In particular, special measures for maternity protection are recommended and "shall not be considered discriminatory" [Article 4].

Reflecting the third dimension (transformation of the male norm), CEDAW does not insist on conformity as a price for equality. Instead, it demands structural change. Most importantly, the Convention actively addresses the social and cultural assumptions and prejudices which keep women in the private sphere. Article 5 is particularly transformative in its approach, requiring State Parties to, "take all appropriate measures to modify the social and cultural patterns of conduct of men and women, with a view to achieving the elimination of prejudices and customary and all other practices which are based on the idea of the inferiority or the superiority of either of the sexes or on stereotyped roles for men and women". This is accompanied by a requirement to ensure that, "family education includes a proper understanding of maternity as a social function and the recognition of the common responsibility of men and women in the upbringing and development of their children".[8] Article 16 requires that all discrimination against women in matters relating to marriage and family relations must be eliminated, including rights to property, guardianship of children and inheritance. Notably, CEDAW is the only human rights treaty to mention family planning. States Parties are obliged to include advice on family planning in the education process [Article 10(h)] and to develop family codes that guarantee women's rights "to decide freely and responsibly on the number and spacing of their children and to have access to the information, education and means to enable them to exercise these rights" [Article 16(e)].

Finally, CEDAW reflects the fourth dimension of substantive equality (participation), taking particularly seriously the importance of representation of women in decision-making. This includes not just the bare right to vote in elections, but also the right to participate in the formulation of government policy, hold public office and participate in non-governmental organisation [Article 7].

Nor is CEDAW limited to negative duties or duties of restraint on the State. It requires States Parties to take "all appropriate measures, including legislation, to ensure the full development and advancement of women, for the purpose of guaranteeing them the exercise and enjoyment of human rights and fundamental freedoms on a basis of equality with men" [Article 3]. The State has positive duties to "protect, promote and fulfil this right to non-discrimination for women and to ensure the development and advancement of women in order to improve their position to one of de jure as well as de facto equality with men".[9]

Limitations of CEDAW

While there are many aspects of CEDAW which further substantive equality, a closer look at the Convention reveals that it speaks with more than one voice. In several important respects, it retains a formal equality approach. Nevertheless, there remains important scope for development. Through the CEDAW Committee's reports and, in particular, its General Recommendations, it is possible to infuse new dynamism into the existing text. In two important respects, namely violence and affirmative action, this has already happened. But there remain important parts of the Convention which need continued engagement to ensure that the voice of substantive equality is the dominant one and, more importantly still, that the gendered structure of society can be transformed through its approach.

Perhaps the most startling limitation is the absence of direct reference to a prohibition on violence against women. This is clearly one of the most serious issues that women face in their struggle for equality, but is not expressly dealt with in the Convention. Nevertheless, this again is evidence of its dynamic nature, the CEDAW Committee has made it clear that gender-based violence clearly falls within the definition of discrimination in Article 1, since it inevitably impairs or nullifies the enjoyment by women of human rights and fundamental freedoms.[10] In its General Recommendation 19 regarding violence against women, the Committee shows how violence is implicated in most of the Convention rights, even when not expressly mentioned. Thus States Parties are required by Article 6 to take measures to suppress "all forms of traffic in women and exploitation of the prostitution of women". Consistent with the second dimension of substantive equality identified above (dignity), the Committee stresses that these practices are incompatible with the equal enjoyment of rights by women or respect for their rights and dignity and put women at special risk of violence and abuse.[11] Similarly, gender-specific violence includes sexual harassment at the workplace, which can seriously impair equality for women in the workplace.[12] Violence against women is clearly a breach of the right to equal access to healthcare, which is part of States' duties under Article 12. The duty of the State extends to the protection of women against violence perpetuated by culture and tradition, such as female circumcision, dietary restrictions for pregnant women and preference for male children.[13]

A further limitation was found in the Convention's approach to affirmative action, referred to as "temporary special measures" in Article 4(1). Instead of regarding affirmative action as a means to achieve equality, the reference to "temporary special measures" gave the impression that measures specifically directed at women were an exception to equality, even when they were aimed at redressing previous disadvantage. However, after detailed consultation with women's groups and others,[14] the Committee issued General Recommendation 25 on temporary special measures. In a detailed affirmation of substantive equality over formal equality, the Recommendation makes it clear that affirmative action is by no means a breach of equality, but may be necessary to achieve substantive equality. This reaffirms the asymmetry of substantive equality.

At the same time, there remain important areas in which CEDAW requires further development to have a true impact. Although CEDAW is innovative in combining equality with both civil and political rights and socio-economic rights, it tends to present equality as simply an 'add-on' to socio-economic rights. In other words, socio-economic rights should be made available to women in the same way as they are to men, without the need to transform socio-economic rights themselves. Articles 11 (work), 12 (health) and 13 (credit, benefits and recreation) are all formulated in these terms: that is, extending existing rights to women on the same basis as they apply to men. The formula in each is to require States Parties to "take all appropriate measures to eliminate discrimination against women...in order to ensure on a basis of equality of men and women, the same rights". However, I would argue that merely adding equality on to socio-economic rights is not sufficient. It is necessary to *engender* socio-economic rights, that is, to transform them through the principle of substantive equality. Simply extending existing rights to women in the same way as they apply to men is a reversion to formal equality and will not achieve sufficient change.

The importance of infusing socio-economic rights with gendered equality can be seen particularly with respect to the right to work and the right to education. Article 11(a) refers to "the right to work as an inalienable right of all human beings". On one level, this could be seen as giving women the right to exit the private sphere and thereby to attain economic independence. On the other hand, it is premised on an intensely male model of work: the assumption being that 'work' equates with paid work outside of the home. This negates the fact that women have always worked, albeit unpaid and in the home. Moreover, for women to be in a position truly to exercise the right to paid work outside of the home, the structure of paid work itself must be transformed, so that both men and women participate in parenting and perform unpaid work in the home. Otherwise, women's continuing responsibility for unpaid work in the private sphere will necessarily inhibit their ability to find good quality paid work.

A similar point can be made regarding other parts of Article 11. Article 11(b) gives women the right to the same employment opportunities, including the application of the same criteria for selection in matters of employment. However, substantive equality requires that the criteria for selection be scrutinised and, where necessary, changed so as to make it possible for women to make use of their opportunities. For example, time spent on unpaid work and child-care should be regarded as relevant experience and working hours and conditions of work should be sufficiently flexible to allow women and men to reconcile work and family life. Similarly, Article 11(e) gives women the equal right to social security, "particularly in cases of retirement, unemployment, sickness, invalidity and old age and other incapacity to work, as well as the right to paid leave". Here too, women will not achieve de facto equality unless eligibility criteria and contribution requirements are changed to reflect women's interrupted work patterns. Especially challenging is the application of social security to the numerous women who work in the informal sector.

Pregnancy and maternity rights are particularly challenging for the concept of substantive equality. Although it is of crucial importance for women to be protected against dismissal or detriment on grounds of pregnancy, the question of maternity leave is more complex. The indisputable right of women to paid maternity leave could reinforce the assumption that women have primary responsibility for child-care unless similar rights are also afforded to men. After the short period needed for women to recover from the actual childbirth, the care of children should be regarded as the responsibility of both parents, and paternity and parental leave should be provided. Article 11 on its own does not go far enough to achieve this, providing only paid maternity leave (in addition to protection against dismissal on grounds of pregnancy), without requiring proper paternal and parental leave for fathers. It does make a gesture towards equality, by requiring States to encourage the provision of child-care facilities to enable men and women to combine work and family. But since men are likely to undertake paid work even if there is no child-care, this is not sufficient to fully engender Article 11. Similarly, Article 5(b) of CEDAW makes a gesture towards a substantive approach, requiring States to take all appropriate measures "to ensure that family education includes a proper understanding of maternity as a social function and the recognition of the common responsibility of men and women in the upbringing and development of their children". However, this too does not go far enough in ensuring that men can and do take on their proper share of childcare responsibility.

Similarly, the right to education in Article 10 speaks with two voices. The first is the voice of formal equality. Article 10 gives the right to "(a) The same conditions for career and vocational guidance, for access to studies and for the achievement of diplomas…(b) Access to the same curricula, the same examinations, teaching staff with qualifications of the same standard and school premises and equipment of the same quality… (c) The same opportunities to benefit from scholarships... (d) The same opportunities for access to programmes of continuing education, including adult and functional literacy programmes". However, as Katarina Tomasevski, the previous Special Rapporteur on Education (1998–2004), demonstrates,[15] sustainable change will not be achieved if girls are slotted into existing educational structures without corresponding change in these structures themselves. She argues that societal norms are not automatically changed through the equal right to education for girls: "What girls can do with their education determines the attractiveness of schooling. If women cannot be employed or self-employed, own land, open a bank account, get a bank loan, if they are denied freedom to marry or not to marry, if they are deprived of political representation, education alone will have little effect on their plight". In some societies, "the intrinsic value of education, which is so optimistically assumed, clashes with social norms which confine girls to early marriage, negotiated between their parents and those of the prospective bridegroom. The price which a girl can fetch, for the Karimojong in Uganda, is reduced if the girl has gone through formal schooling. The price which the girls' parents have to pay to the bridegroom's family, as lamented by a Nepali mother, increases with the girl's formal schooling". Particularly important is the insight that primary education is not sufficient to achieve the desired gains of decreasing fertility, increasing health and reducing female poverty. Thus, the interaction between rights is crucial. Even at the level of the primary education delivery, it is necessary to restructure schools to make education meaningful for girls. As Tomasevski argues, the widespread practice of expelling pregnant girls and child mothers must end, and school must adapt to child parents.

The voice of substantive equality, although muted, is nevertheless found in Article 10(c) which requires the "elimination of any stereotyped concept of the roles of men and women...by encouraging coeducation...and, in particular, by the revision of textbooks and school programmes and the adaptation of teaching methods". Curricula which continue to depict girls in stereotypical household roles will perpetuate fixed roles and limit girls' self-expectations. It is this voice which needs to be developed and strengthened.

Conclusion

Moving beyond formal equality to substantive equality holds out much promise for women. Particularly important is its potential, well beyond the court-room, to function as a vehicle for women to continue to shape our own future as agents of change rather than victims. CEDAW already has many features which facilitate such agency and the same agency will help overcome its limits. Ultimately, the process is as important as the result and it is through our participation in the process that change will come about.

Notes

[1] Sandra Fredman, *Women and the Law* (Oxford Monographs in Labour Law), Oxford: Oxford University Press, 1997, Chapter 1.

[2] See further, Sandra Fredman, *Discrimination Law* (Clarendon Law Series), Oxford: Oxford University Press, 2002, Chapters 1 and 5; Christopher McCrudden, "Merit Principles" in *Oxford Journal of Legal Studies*, Volume 18, Number 4, Winter 1998, pp 543–579.

[3] Amartya Sen, *Inequality Re-examined*, Oxford: Oxford University Press, 1992.

[4] Katarina Tomasevski, "Rights-based Education as Pathway to Gender Equality" in I. Boerefijn *et al* (Eds.), *Temporary Special Measures: Accelerating De Facto Equality of Women Under Article 4(1) UN Convention on the Elimination of All Forms of Discrimination Against Women*, Intersentia, 2003. Tomasevski gives as an example of the Arab states, which increased the enrollment of girls up to1995, but then saw enrollment falling off from 1995–2000.

[6] CEDAW General Recommendation Number 25, Paragraph 5 (2004).

[7] CEDAW Article 1.

[8] CEDAW Article 5(b).

[9] CEDAW General Recommendation Number 25, Paragraph 4.

[10] CEDAW General Recommendation Number 19, Paragraph 7 (1992).

[11]CEDAW General Recommendation Number 19, Paragraphs 13–14.
[12]CEDAW General Recommendation Number 19, Paragraphs 17–18.
[13]CEDAW General Recommendation Number 19, Paragraphs 19–20.
[14]See I. Boerefijn *et al* (eds.), *Temporary Special Measures: Accelerating De Facto Equality of Women Under Article 4(1) UN Convention on the Elimination of All Forms of Discrimination Against Women*, Intersentia, 2003.
[15]See Note 4 above.

3 The Concept of Substantive Equality and Gender Justice in South Asia[1]

Savitri W. E. Goonesekere

Introduction

The post independence Constitutions of all South Asian countries – Bangladesh, Bhutan, India, Maldives, Nepal, Pakistan and Sri Lanka – guarantee equality before the law and, in general, the right not to be discriminated on the ground of sex, as a fundamental right. In doing so, they make a link between gender equality and human rights.[2] Yet equality in general, and gender equality in particular, are often misunderstood concepts. Direct and indirect discrimination against women is sometimes justified by reference to a standard of 'equity' or fairness rather than equality, failing to recognise that equality and elimination of discrimination is essential to achieve equity and fairness. Constitutional standards and values are invariably not internalised, recognised or perceived within many countries as the foundation of economic growth and human development. This has made it difficult to move beyond the rhetoric. South Asia is not unique in this regard for, as the CEDAW Committee acknowledged in 2004, at the 25th anniversary of the adoption of the Convention, "in no country in the world has women's full de jure and de facto equality been achieved".[3]

Despite commitments under Constitutions and treaties, adherence to gender equality standards is sometimes perceived as 'alien', 'imposed or 'foreign'. We must remind ourselves that South Asia has been a great melting pot for diverse cultures, traditions, and religions, from across borders, for centuries. Some tend to see the spread of ideas that originate in Western cultures today as a necessary evil associated with the free market and globalisation. However, it is a historical fact that trade routes, including the Silk Route, were established centuries ago and that the fertilisation of South Asian cultures through an exchange of thought and ideas, technology, the arts and even cuisine has a centuries-old history. Similarly our laws and institutions of governance have evolved and changed over centuries of interaction with Western colonial powers. In the 21st century, economic transformation, globalisation and human rights have provided a new connectivity.

Recent work on harmonising various religious and cultural ideologies and international human rights has shown how the core values of respect for human dignity are almost universal, providing space for interpretations that strengthen the linkages.[4] A strong link between human dignity and equality can be found in the Buddhist *Suttas* that interpret nobility and aristocracy in terms of human behaviour rather than an external social and economic hierarchy. For instance, the *Vasala Sutta* declares, "Not by birth is one a Brahmin, but by deed; Not by birth is one an outcast, but by deed". Scholars on Islam and judgements in the courts have referred to texts in Islam that support the rights of women. They interpret the texts in harmony with constitutional concepts of equality rather than a general standard of equity or fairness.[5] In general, however, inequalities have been justified and rationalised in our region in the past and even today on the basis that our cultures are communitarian and duty based, rather than aggressively individualist. It is argued that the reality of difference in the human condition prevents de facto equality and that a just society demands recognition that different human beings must be treated differently by the State as well as in private relations. This perception continues to provide a justification for State policies and private action that distinguish between equality and equity and foster discrimination against women.

It is against this historical reality that we need to understand the concept of substantive equality in South Asia. Developments that have taken place in the West interpreting the concept of equality do not make it 'Western'. They provide us with insights that can help us internalise a core human rights standard, so as to accelerate gender justice in our own region. Substantive equality is an idea that originated in Western jurisprudence and politics, but one that we have made our own through our national Constitutions and treaty obligations under international law. We need to celebrate the creative interpretations of the concept by many people in the West, including Western feminists, recognising them as part of our shared heritage of ideas in accelerating gender justice. The manner in which the concept of substantive equality developed in the West demonstrates how for centuries discrimination was tolerated and rationalised in Western countries according to views that we encounter in our own countries in South Asia today. These developments contributed significantly to challenging the idea that discrimination based on sex was justified.

Understanding and integrating the concept of substantive equality in development is crucial if we are to build on the positive changes that have taken place in South Asia, eliminate the gaps that we have recognised and achieve the goal of gender equality and justice set out in Constitutional and international standards. This paper examines the evolving concept of substantive equality and its implications for South Asian countries that have a foundation of law and policy based on the core norm of equality. The paper argues that substantive equality is closely linked with the human rights based approach to gender equality, and making the connection to this concept is essential to accelerate balanced development and achieve gender justice in our region. It concludes by examining strategies to accelerate the norm of substantive equality, through a rights based approach to achieving gender justice in South Asia.

Substantive equality as an evolving concept

The early history of the concept: formal equality and substantive equality

Aristotle, whose work was one of the earliest contributions to Western jurisprudence and legal thought on equality, made the link between equality and justice. "The just," said Aristotle, "is the lawful and the equal, and the unjust is the unlawful and the unequal".[6] However, as feminists in the West have been quick to point out, Aristotle's was a selective concept of justice and equality: he interpreted equality as sameness of treatment among equals or treating likes alike according to merit. The implication is that injustice does not follow when differences are recognised, and the different are treated in an unlike manner. Aristotle also perceived equality and justice as relevant only to the State and the political and public sphere. His norm of equality and justice did not prevent recognition of the status quo in slavery and the patriarchal domination of a family. Accordingly, "there can be no injustice in an unqualified sense towards things that are one's own".[7] Equality, though equated with justice, did not encompass the idea of impact and circumstances to achieve equality for all. Equality referred merely to a formal concept of sameness of treatment among persons placed in similar circumstances. The idea that "like should be treated as like" legitimised differences in treatment based on ethnicity or sex. Since men and women were biologically different and racial characteristics were different, different treatment was not deemed an infringement of equality. Further, in emphasising sameness of treatment, without regard to impact and circumstances, formal equality also denied the significance of disadvantage that could result in different outcomes when people placed in different circumstances were treated in the same manner. As Anatole France has remarked, this approach reflected "the majestic equality of the law, which forbids rich and poor alike to sleep under bridges, to beg in the streets and to steal their bread".[8] This ideology sometimes continues to be endorsed in South Asia to differentiate between equity and equality, justify discrimination and resist efforts to integrate the concept of equality for all and equality for women and men.

These perceptions of justice and a formal model of equality had a profound impact on the development of Constitutional jurisprudence on equality in the United States. This jurisprudence is particularly relevant for South Asia because it has influenced judicial interpretations and developments in India and Sri Lanka and Indian cases have been followed in other jurisdictions.[9]

The early Constitutional cases in the U.S. Supreme Court interpreted equality in the context of formal law and policy of the State in government action. In *Plessy v Ferguson* (1896),[10] the Supreme Court refused to strike down public transport legislation that provided for segregation between blacks and whites on the grounds that segregation did not imply the inferiority of either group; rather, it provided separate but similar facilities for each group. This formal interpretation of equality was based on the Aristotelian reasoning discussed above.

The formal approach to equality provided an opportunity to perpetuate conservative attitudes and a "protectionist" approach to women as a vulnerable group. These two perspectives combined to justify 19th century American laws preventing women from voting and entering the legal profession. In *Bradwell v Illinois* (1873) for instance, the U.S. Supreme Court rejected the claim of a female attorney, Myra Bradwell, that a refusal to admit her to practice law in the State of Illinois was a denial of equality and discrimination on the basis of her sex. Justice Bradley stated that, "man is or should be woman's protector and defender. The natural and proper timidity and delicacy which belongs to the female sex evidently unfits it for many of the occupations of civil life...The paramount destiny and mission of women are to fulfill the noble and benign office of wife and mother".[11] The public/private dichotomy to which Aristotle referred and the "like must be treated as like" concept justified treating men and women differently and entrenched gender bias and exclusion in what were perceived as gender neutral laws and policies.

It took many decades to challenge this exclusive focus on formal equality. In *Brown v Board of Education* (1955), the U.S. Supreme Court decided that, "separate educational facilities (for blacks and whites) are inherently unequal".[12] This landmark case has been hailed for transforming jurisprudence on equality and discrimination in the U.S. for it introduced the concept that the circumstances in which people are placed must be taken into account and that equality must be interpreted according to impact and the context and reality of disadvantage. The decision paved the way for moving from Aristotle's model of formal equality to equality in substance or substantive equality, with an interpretation of equality that assessed outcome and result. In time, substantive equality was interpreted to legitimise taking special measures on behalf of disadvantaged groups so as to address the inequalities and disadvantages of context and provide a level playing field. Thus, in *Regents of the University of California v Bakke* (1978),[13] it was decided that the disadvantage of race could be taken into account as a factor in determining preferential or special policies based on race in university admissions.

The U.S. Supreme Court developed a jurisprudence that gave limited recognition to substantive equality by developing the idea of equal opportunity to address the context of disadvantage, exclusion and discrimination. Substantive equality was understood within the familiar standard of equal treatment. Introducing special measures (or affirmative action) to prevent discrimination in impact was controversial because this could not easily be reconciled with the concept of equal treatment in a formal sense. Special measures have, therefore, been described as "preferential treatment" or "reverse discrimination" that require strict scrutiny by the Courts and special justification. The traditional constitutional doctrine of reasonable, non-arbitrary classification of the group that is treated differently and connection to a legitimate objective that is to be achieved by the classification has been applied to determine whether the special measures are legal.

However, the movement away from formal equality did not, in general, include interpretations that addressed the broad context or reality of disadvantage, and the inequality in impact, outcome or result because of these circumstances. Affirmative action or special schemes for women in the workplace to give them promotion prospects not available to men have been recognised.[14] Yet a comprehensive approach to the reality of disadvantage that women suffer because of their situation has not been adopted. When, for instance, employment benefits for both men and women require a specified period of service, the reality could be that most women workers would not qualify for these benefits, because they have been employed for that period as casual workers. This type of female specific inequality in result is not generally incorporated into the concept of substantive equality of opportunity.[15] The emphasis continues to be on equality of opportunity for men and women, a position justified by the argument that, "equality of opportunity may not result in equal treatment, but it does respect every persons right to treatment as an equal".[16]

Protectionist legislation

Since inequality was addressed through formal equality of treatment, the early women's rights campaigns in the West also focused exclusively on achieving formal equality of opportunity and identical treatment with men. They challenged direct discrimination that excluded women from specific aspects of public life accessible to men. Thus, there were campaigns for women's right to vote, their entry into the legal profession and legal capacity to contract and own property. These campaigns and court litigations were based on the need to challenge stereotypical notions of protecting women, remove formal discrimination and legal disabilities and give women the same legal rights as men.

The priority given to achieving formal equality by eliminating legal discrimination and barriers was soon followed by an era in which women's rights activists in the West had to address the reality of exploitation of women in the employment sector, where they were denied acceptable wages and decent working hours and exposed to occupational health hazards. One response was to introduce labour legislation that attempted to give women benefits regarding working conditions that were not available to men. When addressed from a formal equality perspective, these labour laws were attacked for violating standards of equal treatment in the workplace. They were justified on the grounds of reasonable classification of women workers and a connected legitimate objective of protecting them from hazardous working conditions. These justifications were presented in terms of the traditional attitude of 'protecting women workers because of their vulnerability'. This labour legislation gave women minimum wages and specified working hours and types of employment as protective measures suited to their sex. The laws excluded women from night work and certain types of employment considered 'hazardous' for women. Inevitably, these labour laws came to be described as "protective legislation".

Feminists as well as judges in the U.S. were divided on the approach to protective labour legislation. Some feminist advocates of protective legislation and trade unionists perceived these as essential measures or 'beneficial' discrimination. Anticipating a later discourse on substantive equality that sought to address the reality and context of gender discrimination, they agreed that de facto equality was more important than formal equality, and that these protective measures for women workers were valuable. They argued that repealing protective legislation would impact negatively on women workers' lives. They saw protective labour legislation that restricted working hours or night work and excluded women from certain occupation because of biological differences as humane measures that addressed imposed disadvantages because of their situation as women. Other feminist activists, however, attacked protective labour legislation for reinforcing stereotypical attitudes on women's vulnerability, perpetuating a sense of their incapacity and inferiority. They thought that regulating working conditions was a move to reinstate protectionist approaches that they had fought to eliminate when they campaigned for equal opportunities. They argued that these were short term measures that legitimised different treatment and limited livelihood opportunities, preventing women from achieving equal economic status with men, even resulting in legislating women out of work.

These criticisms were often validated by the gender bias reflected in judicial decisions that upheld protective legislation by stereotypical references to gender roles. For instance, in *Muller v Oregon*[17], a leading case that recognised the validity of regulating the working hours of women laundry workers, the U.S. Supreme Court said that, "woman had always been dependant on man" and "women's physical structure and the performance of maternal functions place her at a disadvantage in the struggle for subsistence... especially when the burdens of motherhood are upon her. The physical well being of women became an object of public interest and care in order to preserve the strength and vigour of the race". On the other hand, Court decisions that rejected protective legislation on the grounds of women's individual right to autonomy and freedom of contract, also provided employers with a cheap source of labour. In *Adkins v Children's Hospital,*[18] for instance, laws to ensure minimum wages for women workers were struck down on the ground that they were inconsistent with a woman's right to freedom of contract. A feminist writer has pointed out that in some areas, women's wages "fell to one third and one half, after the decision."[19]

Feminist interpretation of substantive equality

Feminist research and scholarship from the 1960s addressed the limitations of the formal equality and equal opportunities concept from the perspective of gender equality.[20] There was a growing understanding that the male standard of sameness used in determining formal equality of treatment and opportunities and discrimination, failed to take account of women's experiences and so perpetuated the disadvantage they suffered because they were women. The new scholarship on stereotypical gender roles and attitudes and their discriminatory impact on women emphasised that women were not vulnerable by nature, but suffered from imposed disadvantage. It was argued that if these disadvantages were eliminated, there would be no further need for 'protection'. The deconstruction of laws and legal concepts that were gender biased, entrenching patriarchy and male perspectives, contributed to challenging a model of (formal and even substantive) equality that made men the reference point for women's equality. It is this initiative that had a profound impact in developing the original limited concept of substantive equality to accommodate a broader concept of eliminating the disadvantages that women have suffered as women. The feminist critique of formal equality drew on the original doctrine of substantive equality and developed it in a manner that enabled it to be absorbed into national and international laws on equality and women's rights.

The gender sensitive concept of substantive equality was strengthened by jurisprudence on equality in the Canadian Supreme Court. In cases originating from a leading case, *Andrews v Law Society of British Columbia* (1989), the Supreme Court, in interpreting the right to equality in the

Canadian Charter of Rights and Freedom, rejected the traditional model of formal equality. A Canadian statute limited entry into the legal profession to Canadian citizens. Andrews was able to show that, though qualified to enter the legal profession, he was disadvantaged because he was not a citizen. The Supreme Court of Canada interpreted equality so as to take into account context, the reality of disadvantage suffered by the victim of discrimination and impact.[21] In adopting this interpretation, the Court moved from the idea of achieving formal equality of treatment and opportunity to focus on equality of result.

The concept of substantive equality determined by outcome and result has now been incorporated in the Bill of Rights of the South African Constitution (1996).[22] This Constitution included the concept of private non-State actors having a duty to conform to the human rights standards set by the document. Article 9 also states that, "equality includes the full and equal enjoyment of rights". The same article authorises legislative and other measures to protect or advance persons or categories of persons disadvantaged by "unfair discrimination". This broad definition interprets equality as going beyond formal legal equality. The reality of disadvantage and context, taking results and impact into account, is addressed in determining whether there is discrimination. Equality is linked to other human rights. The goal is not merely formal equality of treatment, but also extends to eliminating discrimination of outcome or result. The impact of laws, policies and programmes to eliminate discrimination must be evaluated from this perspective. Since gender based discrimination in substance violates the norm of fairness, it becomes difficult to argue that a standard of equity (fairness) is different from equality.

CEDAW and substantive equality

It has been pointed out that the CEDAW also reflected the limitations of the formal equality approach, even though it went beyond the international human rights covenants and incorporated the idea that equality for women must include measures to realise both de jure and de facto equality.[23] While the CEDAW Convention incorporated a male standard in its general approach to equality, it is important to recognise that it contained important specific provisions were in harmony with the new feminist ideology of substantive equality and that have enabled the CEDAW Committee to develop a jurisprudence that goes beyond the traditional limitations of formal equality of opportunity in the public sphere. In Concluding Comments on State Party Reports, the CEDAW Committee has, over the years, used specific articles such as Articles 1 and 3 on women's human rights, Articles 2(e) and 5 on eliminating sexual stereotypes and the State obligation to make private, non-State actors accountable and modify stereotypical attitudes, to move out of the limitations of the male focused equality of opportunity conceptual framework. Violence against women is not covered in a specific provision of the Convention, with the exception of Article 6 on trafficking in women. Yet the Committee was able to use the emerging feminist discourse on violence against women as a denial of substantive equality in its wider meaning of gender based discrimination, and develop General Recommendation Number 19 on the subject.

The Committee has constantly drawn the attention of State Parties to the need to define gender based discrimination in harmony with general Articles 1, 2, 3 and 4 of the Convention. These Articles require States to eliminate both discrimination of effect and purpose (intended and unintended discrimination) and require measures to achieve a standard of both de jure and de facto equality. Further, the Committee's most recent General Recommendation Number 25 on Article 4 interprets equality as including substantive equality and requires countries that adopt gender neutral laws and policies which treat men and women, boys and girls in the same manner, to eliminate discrimination and disadvantage that results from their impact. The Committee expects State Parties not to limit themselves to adopting formal equality approaches to eliminate direct discrimination and emphasises the need to eliminate discrimination in result or outcome.

This interpretation of substantive equality, as in the case of the South African Constitution, reinforces other core human rights such as the right to personal security and access to basic needs in health and education, or socio-economic rights. In linking with the enjoyment of other human rights, equality becomes an expression of the indivisibility of all human rights. The concept of the right to life ceases to be merely a civil and political right not to be denied life without due process of law, and instead becomes a right to live in dignity, with equality and equal access to resources.

The link made between substantive equality and other human rights can help to clarify thinking on and provide a new dimension to the issues of protective measures and affirmative action, both of which have attracted controversy even within women's movements. Equality now becomes a channel to exercise women's human rights, including substantive equality, imposing a duty to achieve results by respecting, protecting and fulfilling these rights. Article 11(3) of CEDAW states that protective legislation, "should be reviewed periodically...and shall be revised, repealed and extended as necessary". Article 4 and General Recommendation Number 25 clarify that special measures of protective legislation adopted to accelerate substantive or de facto equality for women shall not be considered justified differentiation but will be treated as temporary measures that will be "discontinued when the objective of equality of opportunity and treatment have been achieved". (As per General Recommendation Number 25, interventions to realise human rights such as the right to education or health, including reproductive health or personal security, cannot be temporary. However, some traditional protection measures on women's working conditions or preferential promotion schemes or quotas for women will be temporary measures of affirmative action that can be phased out when gender parity is achieved.) General Recommendation Number 25 emphasises that the use of these measures should be in conformity with human rights discourse to achieve the goal of substantive equality in enjoyment of rights and must not be perceived as measures on behalf of a weak and vulnerable sector of the population. This perspective addresses the traditional objection to these measures as initiatives which reinforce sexual stereotypes and women's vulnerability and weakness, without accelerating or ensuring long term gender justice and equality.

Article 4 of the Convention states that, "special measures aimed at protecting maternity shall not be considered discriminatory". This has sometimes created the impression that pregnancy-related measures also come within protection legislation. General Recommendation Number 25, paragraph 16 clarifies that the non-identical treatment of men and women in the context of pregnancy should not be perceived as "temporary special measures or affirmative actions" and that they are of a permanent nature. Implicit is the recognition that pregnancy measures link to Article 12 on health and Article 11 on the right to work, which also include measures on pregnancy as a dimension of a woman's rights in the area of reproductive health and working conditions. This interpretation challenges those legal systems which continue to give limited pregnancy leave on the basis that pregnancy is a woman's disability which should attract employee insurance schemes as a dimension of a woman worker's right to be protected and treated differently because of her vulnerability. General Recommendation Number 25 has clarified Articles 12, 11 and 11(2) which differentiate between pregnancy-related measures and traditional protective legislation to ensure that women enjoy substantive equality and do not suffer disadvantage as workers.

In many ways, General Recommendation Number 25 encapsulates the work of the CEDAW Committee and the jurisprudence that moved beyond the limits of the

Aristotelian concept of equality. The word "substantive" focuses on substance and reality rather than merely form. It does not replace or undervalue the need for laws and policies to eliminate direct discrimination and disability. It only emphasises that accelerating gender equality requires formal equality measures to be combined with others to ensure an effective outcome. It is, therefore, unfortunate that General Recommendation Number 25 has defined the term "substantive equality" as "de facto" equality. To begin with, de facto equality is a much more distant goal than accelerating equality by legal and other measures that take context and circumstance into account to create a level field for the enjoyment of human rights by both men and women. Using the term de facto equality as synonymous with substantive equality also undervalues the significance of law and de jure equality as a necessary support for achieving equality in result. Nevertheless, the acceptance of a clear concept of substantive equality linked to other human rights is an important contribution to the evolving discourse on human rights and development, and can facilitate more consistent action at the national level in achieving gender justice. This link also highlights that substantive equality cannot be accelerated or achieved without adopting a rights based approach in development.

The concept of substantive equality is especially important in South Asia in areas like poverty alleviation, responses to conflict and natural disaster, access to land, violence, taxation, social security and employment, where formal laws and policies that are gender neutral can, in fact, impact to further disadvantage and disentitle women. While eliminating direct discrimination and introducing formal equality laws and policies is necessary, evaluating impact – as required by substantive equality – can help to ensure that these laws are combined with other supportive measures to ensure that they, in fact, accelerate equality. Formal equality must be perceived as an important dimension of equality, rather than its parameter. Too often States and women's groups focus on putting the law in place through formal equality measures without addressing the critical need to assess impact and result. The discussion on South Asia and country examples will demonstrate the importance and relevance of the substantive equality approach.

Internalising substantive equality in South Asia

(i) Norms and realities

CEDAW, the international legal framework on women's rights, binds all countries of the region, with the last ratification of the Convention by Pakistan in 1996. Bhutan, Nepal and Sri Lanka have ratified CEDAW without reservations, while Bangladesh and Maldives have withdrawn some reservations entered at ratification. Several countries have reported regularly under CEDAW, while Bangladesh, Maldives, Nepal and Sri Lanka have ratified the international complaints mechanism established under the Optional Protocol to CEDAW (2000). The only regional Convention of the South Asian Association for Regional Cooperation (SAARC) countries on trafficking for prostitution has been ratified by all countries and has also become a legally binding document. Sri Lanka has enacted domestic legislation in 2006 that incorporates the instrument directly into domestic law.[24] Bangladesh, India, Pakistan, Nepal and Sri Lanka are also bound by the International Labour Organization's (ILO) norms on core labour standards and its instruments on equal remuneration and discrimination in employment. All countries have adopted the Cairo Plan of Action. Several countries have also ratified the international covenants on human rights and other human rights treaties which contain guarantees on gender equality. Consequently, a basic international and national framework of standards of gender equality is in place in all countries and reinforces the Constitutional guarantees on gender equality, the Beijing Platform for Action (BPFA) and Goal 3 of the Millennium Development Goals (MDGs) on women's empowerment. It has become increasingly difficult for governments to argue that a local standard of 'gender equity' or fairness rather than equality must be the determining concept in law and policy reform.

In harmony with Constitutional and CEDAW norms and political commitments, each country in South Asia has developed gender equality action plans, established gender management systems and institutions and engaged in law reform initiatives. The region has vibrant women's groups which have often engaged constructively with governments in formulating legislation and policy and delivering services and programmes to carry forward the agenda on equality for women.

The unfortunate reality of continuing discrimination is in stark contrast to these achievements and has been amply documented.[25] Violence against women because of their sex and circumstances is pervasive. The problem of institutionalised discrimination against women due to discriminatory cultural practices and values, personal laws and politicised fundamentalist religious movements has been recognised. Women's lack of access to decision-making posts in legislative assemblies and public administration has also been highlighted. Poverty programmes do not reflect an understanding of the need to perceive women as a large segment of the population that has basic rights such as health and education that are necessary to move out of poverty and obtain economic empowerment, including a livelihood. With economic transformation, poverty programmes have become more minimalist, focusing on reduction of poverty among the absolute poor. In these programmes, women are perceived as a vulnerable group needing assistance, rather than as people with human capacity and a right to national resources, including land. Access to basic health services, including reproductive health services, and responses to HIV/AIDS remain inadequate, despite the reality of sexual exploitation and trafficking in women. Migrant workers in all countries are generally women from low income families. While welfare programmes and regulating employment agencies have helped somewhat, the critical issues of high rates of female unemployment, unsafe conditions of work and risk of violence and discrimination in host countries have not been addressed in bilateral agreements.

Women's special circumstances as head of households or primary caregivers in the family are not addressed. Yet this affects their capacity to obtain economic opportunities and equal remuneration for work of equal value. Infrastructure projects on roads, water and sanitation sometimes create a situation where women's economic productivity and access to markets is hampered and even facilitates practices such as trafficking. International trade agreements have led to the closure of garment factories, resulting in a loss of jobs and retrenchment. Similarly, privatisation can result in job losses among women in formal areas of employment. There are discrepancies in wage structures and exploitative working conditions continue to be prevalent in industries regulated by law, as well as in unregulated sectors like domestic service or subcontracting linked to home-based work.

Despite law reform and programmatic interventions on violence against women and cross border trafficking in all countries, law enforcement and resources for law enforcement and victim support are weak. Gender bias continues to be reflected in judicial attitudes and among prosecutors and law enforcement agencies. These inadequacies have helped perpetuate stereotypical attitudes and social customs and traditions that legitimise violence and have contributed to the high incidence of domestic and community violence. The gender bias of colonial law in the criminal justice systems of India, Pakistan, Bangladesh and Sri Lanka has not been eliminated. Specific reforms to criminalise trafficking, marital rape and gender based violence sanctioned by law, religion or custom have been ad hoc and rarely comprehensive.[26]

The failure to take account of women's specific needs in internal displacement and their lack of access to general health care and reproductive health facilities as basic rights have compounded the suffering of women affected by conflict. A growing incidence of early marriage of girls in conflict situations in Sri Lanka has been raised as an issue of concern by women's groups. The issue of impunity and lack of women's access to compensation and remedies for violence has not been adequately addressed in conflict situations, despite women's activism.[27] In countries affected by natural disasters there is a common concern about women being marginalised in livelihood programmes, allocation of housing and shelter and access to land and other resources for recovery. The concept of the male head of household is often reinforced in disaster management, so that women do not receive their entitlements in cash, land or housing.[28]

The reality of discrimination and violence perpetrated in the name of religion and culture is rarely denied.[29] Resurgent religious fundamentalism and a lack of voice for women in fashioning cultural and religious norms have continued to hamper government performance on the commitments undertaken under national constitutions and international treaties and standards. The law on family relations reflects the gender bias of received colonial law as well as custom and religion. Maldives has demonstrated that family law reform consistent with equality can be introduced through a sharing of comparative experience and interpretation of Islamic law. However, fundamentalist religious movements and conservative male attitudes have combined to undermine the implementation of the law. Similar movements in other South Asian countries have prevented a review and interpretation of these laws in harmony with human rights law.[30] The politics of identity and religious fundamentalism have made governments reluctant to interfere with personal, custom and religion based laws, which reflect gender discrimination, even though these laws are often derived from a misinterpretation of custom and religion and reflect transformations caused by interaction with colonial law. The introduction of uniformly applicable family laws that can be accepted by exercise of choice remains a distant goal. Fundamentalist lobbies misinterpret efforts to introduce uniform codes as majoritarian initiatives to marginalise minority communities. Women's groups are sometimes divided on the issue, unwilling to take a stand because of the pressures of national identity politics. Similarly, religious and customary local tribunals, with male-biased systems of informal dispute settlement, pronounce judgements that infringe women's human rights under constitutions and CEDAW with impunity, because interventions to hold them accountable are considered politically sensitive and unpopular with powerful fundamentalist lobbies. Jurisprudence in Pakistan and Bangladesh has used CEDAW and the Constitution in efforts to eliminate discrimination and recognise gender equality. The Superior Courts of India have sometimes used Constitutional norms of equality to reject cultural norms. These developments have not been as consistent as in Nepal where the Superior Courts have used the monist legal tradition to incorporate CEDAW norms on equality and non-discrimination and reject negative customary laws and practices.[31]

(ii) Moving from formal equality to substantive equality: the challenges for South Asia

The gap between norms and implementation in South Asia is a reflection of the limitations of focusing exclusively on formal equality and draws attention to the importance of the standard of substantive equality. Constitutional provisions need to be interpreted so as to harmonise with the concept. Constitutional reform processes should be used by women's groups to advocate for a definition of gender based discrimination that harmonises with substantive equality.

However, we should remember that, despite the description of substantive equality as de facto equality in CEDAW General Recommendation Number 25, formal de jure equality through legislative and policy measures continues to be important in South Asia. Gender equality legislation that defines non discrimination as substantive equality is essential to accelerate gender justice. Such legislation can repeal discriminatory legal provisions and undermine discriminatory practices. It can also confer rights, remove disabilities and set normative standards on non discrimination. As has been stated earlier, formal equality must be perceived as a dimension of equality, rather than its parameter.

Affirmative action

South Asia's own reality of inequality and disadvantage led to developments in constitutional law that recognised the need to move from formal to substantive equality even before the transition had been made in the US. The Indian Constitution of 1948, adopted long before *Brown v Board of Education,* emphasised the importance of impact and context in interpreting equality and contained provisions for special measures or affirmative action for caste groups and for women and children. The Indian Constitution derives much of its inspiration from the Irish Constitution. The Irish Constitution provided that equality "shall not be held to mean that the State shall not have due regard to differences of capacity, physical and moral, and of social function". The founding fathers in India, including Ambedkar, were clearly inspired to adopt a model of equality that had room for accelerating equality by taking context and disadvantage into account. Other South Asian Constitutions also recognise the importance of substantive equality for women and authorise governments to take temporary special measures or affirmative action to address disadvantages suffered by women and children.[32] Such measures are not considered a denial of equality, because they simply provide a framework for temporary laws, policies and programmes to accelerate substantive equality and achieve gender justice. They are limited in time and can be phased out when parity and gender balance is achieved.

Pakistan, Bangladesh and India have now introduced affirmative action measures to reserve quotas and seats for women in local government, in a response to the under representation of women in this forum. This has ensured that a critical mass of women have voice in matters that affect them and the community. These interventions have been evaluated as successful in achieving their objective of accelerating equality of result in women's participation in political decision-making at this level.

However, there is a general resistance to reservations for women in national legislative assemblies. Proposals have been discussed in electoral reform initiatives, but changes have not been introduced. Despite the fact that women in South Asia have held the highest political office of Head of State or Prime Minister, there are very few women ministers, high level executives or heads of universities. Women have been bypassed and not appointed without protest. The inadequacy or lack of sex disaggregated data and monitoring indicators suggests that the negative impact on women may be even more significant than is captured in the available information.

A landmark decision of the High Court in *Shamima Sultan v Bangladesh* has reinforced the importance of affirmative action. The Court used the Constitutional guarantees on equality and CEDAW to prevent the administration restricting the powers of women commissioners elected to seats reserved for women in a local authority.[33] Affirmative action policies in Bangladesh on giving girls access to free education up to grade eight and increasing positions for women teachers have increased education participation rates. Scholarships, recruitment of female teachers and other policies such as reservations to encourage girls' education have been introduced in some states in India and in Nepal. India and Nepal also provide for affirmative action measures to appointments to posts in the public service sector.

Affirmative action is controversial because it denies the merit principle and is sometimes perceived even by feminists as reinforcing stereotypical attitudes about women's weakness and incapacity. However, substantive equality concepts require us to proactively address the reality of disadvantage. The very limited use of Constitutional provisions on affirmative action for women[34] has prevented the introduction of gender sensitive laws and policies to give ownership and management rights so women can access important resources such as land and housing in State-sponsored schemes, gain access to secondary and tertiary education, including technical education, and obtain senior management positions in the public and the corporate sectors. We shall observe later in discussions on law and policy that the traditional response to gender equality in South Asia has been to introduce protective legislation and policies, combined with formal equality of opportunity measures that mandate equal treatment of men and women in defined sectors.

Protectionist legislation in South Asia

Protectionist labour laws in South Asia are often derived from colonial legislation that limits or regulates women's working hours in certain sectors and prohibits night work or employment in certain types of physically hazardous work such as mining. The repeal of this legislation can have negative impacts on women workers. For example, Sri Lanka renounced ILO standards that it had earlier accepted and removed the prohibition on night work in the early 1980s in a measure that the government publicised as equal opportunity legislation. Posters and publicity stated that a government committed to economic liberalisation had brought women out of their kitchens to work in nation-building, shoulder to shoulder with men. Very soon, however, research highlighted the rapacious and exploitative conditions of work for women in industry, especially in the Investment and Export Promotion Zones. They were exposed to occupational health hazards, physical violence in the work place and while on their way to night work and gruelling production targets. This research and the activism of women's groups helped to put in place revised factories legislation that imposed mandatory facilities to protect women from occupational health hazards and Penal Code reforms on sexual harassment and rape to safeguard personal security.[35]

In addressing the context of exploitation and disadvantage in employment, protective legislation reaffirms substantive equality in access to employment and other connected human rights regarding personal security and basic health. In South Asia, protective legislation, in regulating working hours, flexi-time and transport at night, thus goes beyond beneficial discrimination that addresses women's vulnerability. It provides a norm of appropriate non-exploitative working conditions that harmonises with women's right to work in an environment conducive to health, personal security and freedom from violence. Laws on sexual harassment against women in the work place have a similar rationale and are justified as a dimension of substantive equality linked to the human right to personal security, rather than as 'protection' which denies and limits gender-neutral equality of opportunity in the work place.

Measures to improve women's access to justice in cases of violence – such as redefined penal offences including rape laws, domestic violence legislation and victim-friendly changes to evidentiary rules in sex crimes – are sometimes regarded as being similar to protective measures. For instance, policy documents often use the language of "protection" to justify violence against women affected by natural disasters or conflict as a matter of priority concern. Since criminal justice is perceived as relevant to the whole community, criminal laws are defined in a gender neutral manner. In this context, there is a tendency to resort to the idea of "reasonable classification" used for taking affirmative action and temporary special measures to justify gender specific amendments to criminal law as "protective legislation".[36]

However, violence against women involves the infringement of distinct human rights in health and personal security. These rights become a dimension of the right to substantive equality, as the denial of access to criminal justice and gender-specific violence are invariably a reflection of denial of all these rights.[37] This is demonstrated in a case like *Vishaka v State of Rajasthan*,[38] where the gang rape of a worker in her place of employment was determined by the Indian Supreme Court as a Constitutional case on the infringement of her right to life, personal security and freedom from sexual harassment, as well as the right to substantive equality in employment. The Supreme Court took note of the fact that the absence of a law on sexual harassment created an environment of gender based discrimination in the work place where there was also a failure to protect bodily security and the right to live and work in dignity.

The idea of protection from the infringement of a range of human rights thus helps to link them to equality rights in South Asia and move beyond the traditional discourse on protective legislation as a response to women's vulnerability. The capacity to link the protection of rights, rather than protection, to the concept of substantive equality also clarifies that some measures are not merely temporary protection measures to accelerate equality for working women. As CEDAW General Recommendation Number 25 points out, social policies and measures responding to the infringement of women's human rights can be measures that impact on equality, but are also related to the right to bodily security and reproductive health. They cannot, therefore, be phased out, unlike other protective measures on working conditions that may be reviewed and phased out if an environment conducive to women's participation in the workplace has been achieved. Thus, protective regulations on night work and exclusion from certain types of work can be periodically reviewed, for example to permit night work in certain areas like the IT sector.

It is in this context that legislation regulating maternity leave must not be perceived as a temporary special measure to provide an appropriate working environment and prevent exploitation or traditional protective legislation to address women's vulnerability or disability. It must be considered as legislation that promotes substantive equality while also protecting women's human rights on reproductive health.

Those who advocate against traditional protectionist approaches argue for protective legislation that is gender neutral and applies to both men and women. However, the above analysis shows that traditional protectionist approaches can become a method for realising the right to substantive equality and accelerating economic empowerment of women on their own terms in South Asia. Initiatives on formal equality and traditional protection approaches in employment can, thus, be absorbed into a single strategy for accelerating substantive equality and women's human rights. The removal of gender bias in the criminal justice system and measures to provide maternity leave also illustrate the connectivity between substantive equality and other human rights of women. All countries must develop national level laws, policies and programmes to realise this integrated standard of substantive equality accepted by the CEDAW Committee in its interpretation of the Convention. Accelerating substantive equality in the comprehensive meaning of the concept should provide the foundation for all development initiatives in South Asia.

The above approach to substantive equality imposes obligations on governments as the duty bearer. When the private and corporate sector is moving into many areas of activity, there can be pressure to follow only a formal and traditional protectionist approach to gender equality. The argument of economic efficiency, in particular, may be used to press for a model of equal treatment, with limited exceptions as "protective" measures for women. This is a challenge that will be discussed in dealing with strategies for implementing substantive equality.

Dualism, monism and treaty incorporation

Under international law and the Vienna Convention on Treaties, a State Party is bound to implement a treaty in good faith and cannot use domestic law as a justification for not fulfilling it. A Treaty Act in Nepal clarifies that, upon ratification, CEDAW and other human rights treaties are directly incorporated into domestic law. Nepal's monist approach to international law differs from the dualist approach followed in other countries. According to the dualist approach, international treaties are applicable only when they are incorporated into domestic law or a law is enacted to give effect to treaty provisions. Direct incorporation of CEDAW in law and policy has not taken place in South Asia, and even the recent domestic violence legislation in India and Sri Lanka does not refer to CEDAW in its preambles or long titles. Yet, these references are important reminders that domestic laws are linked to international treaty standards.

A few judicial decisions in courts in South Asia integrate CEDAW and other treaties into the analysis of Constitutional guarantees on fundamental rights. India's and Nepal's superior courts have a good record in this respect. Incorporation of treaty standards is easier for Nepalese Courts because of the country's monist approach mentioned above.

The Bangalore Principles on Domestic Application of International Human Rights Norms require courts to adopt proactive interpretations of national law so as to integrate human rights treaty norms into domestic jurisprudence. The Bangalore Principles have influenced judicial decisions in many Commonwealth jurisdictions. Case law in South Asia demonstrates that Constitutional standards on equality, as well as other rights such as the right to life and personal security, have provided an opportunity to integrate CEDAW standards and strengthen the domestic response to gender inequality and jurisdiction. Courts in Nepal, Pakistan,

Bangladesh and India have used these Constitutional standards to integrate CEDAW while deciding cases on marital rape, sexual harassment, forced marriage and guardianship, discriminatory and harmful traditional and customary practices, and political participation. This judicial approach must be strengthened to compensate for inadequacies in direct incorporation of treaty standards.[39]

Sri Lanka adopted a Women's Charter in 1993, a policy document that incorporated CEDAW. However, Sri Lanka's record in following up on recommendations of treaty bodies under the Protocol to the Covenant on Civil and Political Rights has been inadequate because international treaties are not enforceable in the courts. Its superior courts have never cited CEDAW although they have cited and used other international treaties in their decisions. A recent judicial decision in the Supreme Court reiterates the monist position and emphasises that specific incorporation of international law is essential.[40] A strict monist approach thus represents a challenge to harmonising CEDAW in South Asia.

Some National Strategies to Realise Substantive Equality through a Rights Based Approach

(i) Integrating substantive equality into development planning

CEDAW contains the most comprehensive set of norms on substantive equality and women's human rights, although it does not specifically cover freedom of association, trade union participation, and freedom of information. Nor does it set out specific standards on refugee women or women affected by armed conflict. However, the general articles of the Convention on protection of human rights can and have been used by the CEDAW Committee in the context of reports submitted by countries from the region, to include concluding comments on women affected by armed conflict. Besides, with the setting up of the office of the High

Commissioner for Human Rights, the practice of treaty bodies having general days of discussion on themes and regular meetings of Chairpersons of treaty bodies, there is a greater effort at promoting complementarity in interpreting human rights treaty standards on substantive equality and monitoring implementation. Current UN treaty body reform is also expected to accelerate this process. However, international commitments on taking women's human rights and substantive equality seriously can be translated into action only if national institutions integrate these rights into national plans, governance and administration. This rights based approach involves setting goals and targets to achieve results in eliminating all aspects of gender based discrimination and enabling women to enjoy their rights.

The lack of understanding of human rights treaty obligations and their relevance in development planning has resulted in a failure to adopt a substantive equality and rights based approach in national development plans. National plans on gender equality, including on violence against women, remain in Women's Ministries and departments, and do not guide the drafting of national planning documents. Nodal gender equality institutions must have a voice in development planning if CEDAW commitments and a rights approach are to influence national plans. Strong, highly placed gender institutions within government can make a difference in integrating a rights based approach into key areas of development. This is why CEDAW Article 1(b) calls upon the State Party to ensure that women have a right to participate with men in formulating government policy and planning implementation.

The lack of gender expertise within government institutions to scrutinise development plans and engage in gender analysis contributes to ad hoc responses rather than rights based planning. Human rights and gender equality are often considered distinct aspects which relate exclusively to protection from violence and law enforcement, reflecting a common misunderstanding that they refer to civil and political rights rather than social and economic ones. Gender expertise and an understanding of CEDAW's integration of civil, political and socio-economic rights as indivisible aspects of gender equality are critical for adopting a rights based approach linked to substantive equality in development planning. Finance and planning ministries usually lack the necessary expertise. It is vital that national plans on gender include the creation of gender expert posts within Finance and Planning Ministries at the highest level or provide for scrutiny of national plans by and consultation with the nodal gender agency. Strengthening data processes and developing quantitative and qualitative gender disaggregated data through the UNIFEM supported SAARC initiative can become a crucial support for integrating a substantive equality and rights based approach in development planning.

The new development agenda on the MDGs must also be harmonised with CEDAW and other treaty obligations. If this is not done, there is a contradiction between the limited scope of MDGs and the more expansive treaty commitments on substantive equality. The CEDAW Committee links the Beijing Platform for Action with CEDAW commitments and, thus, provides guidance on harmonising both in its Concluding Comments on country reports. These Concluding Comments set a framework for a national rights based approach to accelerating substantive equality which governments should follow. UNIFEM's work in analysing the complementarity of these documents[41] is also an important contribution to development planning and should be used to prevent over-prioritising the more limited MDGs.

(ii) Professional and institutional support for implementation

The development of Public Interest Litigation (PIL) in South Asia has become a strategy to scrutinise legislation, its implementation and State action that infringes human rights.

This is clear from litigation on environmental issues, appointments and promotion to public office and land use.[42] The judiciary can, therefore, make its contribution to a successful rights based strategy and help to accelerate substantive equality.

Some cases[43] in the superior courts of the region have developed a positive jurisprudence and advanced substantive equality. They have recognised women's rights to equal inheritance, access to medical education and decision-making in local governance. Equal rights have been mandated for appointments in the public sector and regarding employment opportunities without marital and pregnancy discrimination. There is also jurisprudence on visa applications and guardianship of children that recognises that a standard of formal equality must be maintained. Some of these cases cite CEDAW and other human rights standards. Judicial decisions have used the constitutional guarantees on equality, the right to life and freedom from torture to provide relief to women who have suffered acts of discrimination and gender based sexual violence, including marital rape, forced marriage and sexual harassment. Though education is not guaranteed as a fundamental socio-economic right in the region's Constitutions, cases in India on access to education as a dimension of equality and the right to live in dignity have impacted to confer a right to education that has been incorporated in the Constitution by an amendment (2002). There are examples of PILs in India and Nepal requesting the courts to scrutinise effective implementation of laws restraining early marriage which prejudices both equal access to health and education.

Yet, gender bias in the judiciary in South Asian countries is reflected in many cases of violence against women and in family disputes. Judicial training and training for lawyers on this jurisprudence can contribute positively to jurisprudence on substantive equality in the region. Justice Sujatha Manohar has pointed out[44] that the ratification of the Optional Protocol to CEDAW can become a device for sensitising the judiciary and bureaucracy on the need to integrate a rights based approach. The CEDAW Committee constantly requests State Parties to ratify the Optional Protocol to CEDAW.

While universal ratification of the Protocol in the South Asian region should be advocated, it is important to combine this with mainstreaming human rights education programmes in business, law and medical schools, and continuing human rights programmes for judges, the civil service, armed forces and law enforcement agencies. Human rights education and gender sensitisation programmes usually focus on ad hoc initiatives without confronting the challenge of mainstreaming these issues into school and university courses as part of the regular curriculum. A survey of business, medical and law schools in the region will indicate that these courses are rarely, if ever, integrated into the curricula of these institutions. Optional Women's Studies courses are generally followed by a very small, usually female, student population. Creating a professional understanding on rights and gender sensitivity among this wide category of public servants, the judiciary and professionals is essential for carrying through a rights based agenda in development.

Such initiatives can complement the creation of gender expertise in the planning and development branches of government. This is most important because of the misperception of human rights as an alien discourse or the argument of the foreign office and government lawyers that treaties do not automatically apply in domestic law without incorporation. It is especially important that government economists and planners become aware of CEDAW Concluding Comments, through close interaction with strong national gender machineries, so that restrictive development agendas like MDGs do not undermine the treaty and international policy commitments on gender equality and, especially, on CEDAW.

Several South Asian countries have National Women's Commissions that have impacted to initiate law reform, especially in areas like violence against women. These

Commissions, with NGO-based professional representation, have played an important role in the enactment of domestic violence legislation in India and Sri Lanka and consistently agitated for the repeal of the Hudood Ordinance and legislation on honour crimes in Pakistan. In Sri Lanka, the National Committee on Women has given leadership and contributed to reform of discriminatory citizenship laws and some gender biased provisions in the Penal Code. Sri Lanka's gender institutions, working with women's groups, drafted the Women's Charter in 1993, which incorporates CEDAW in a single policy statement.

The weakness of the national machinery on women has made it difficult to have a sustained voice in policy making and integrate a rights based approach. Sri Lanka's National Committee on Women, with representatives of women's groups, drafted a Women's Rights Bill establishing a strong, independent National Women's Commission and giving legal status to the Women's Charter. This Bill is still with the legal draftsman. This is an important model of intervention to create an environment conducive to sustaining a holistic rights based approach on substantive equality in governance. Specific gender equality legislation as in East Asia with strong institutional mechanisms to monitor and enforce these laws also provides an important model to integrate CEDAW and a rights based approach.[45] National Women's Commissions should work in partnership with National Human Rights Commissions. The independence of these Commissions, their investigation powers and capacity to take on the agenda of civil, political and socio-economic rights can strengthen their capacity to integrate a substantive equality perspective into their work.

(iii) Duty bearers and rights holders: modifying concepts

A rights based approach is premised on the idea that the State is duty-bound to realise rights. Traditionally, human rights law only held States accountable for the negative duty not to violate treaty commitments, since they were the exclusive actors on the international scene. However, over the years it has been recognised that accelerating substantive equality and eliminating discrimination against women requires an active engagement of interest by a range of non-State actors, including the family and community.

International law and constitutional jurisprudence have moved in that direction, breaking down the public/private divide and today international law recognises the indivisibility of civil, political and socio-economic rights reflected in CEDAW. As the Concluding Comments of the CEDAW Committee on country reports indicate, the State has a duty to respect these indivisible rights and must not violate them. There is also a duty to protect these rights by preventing third parties from violating them. A State must take positive measures to fulfill these rights. Inevitably, non-State actors have been brought within the scope of these widely stated obligations on human rights.

Constitutional jurisprudence has developed to recognise State liability in failing to prevent violence by non-State actors. This is sometimes described as the State's obligation of due diligence. The concept of due diligence and the liability of non-State actors for violence against women have been incorporated in CEDAW General Recommendation Number 19 and the UN Declaration on Violence Against Women (1993). It has recently been endorsed in complaint and inquiry proceedings under the Optional Protocol to CEDAW dealing with State inaction in domestic violence and murder cases.[46] Humanitarian law in the Geneva Convention and Protocols places an obligation on private actors in armed conflict to follow human rights norms which are not considered standards that apply exclusively to the State. This has made it possible to subject both the government and non-State actors to international scrutiny for violation of human rights in conflict situations through active involvement or passive inaction. Promoting this scrutiny is a critical aspect of realising substantive equality, preventing impunity and ensuring reparation where women's rights have been violated in community violence or in armed conflict.

CEDAW incorporates the concept that "any person, organization or enterprise" must be held accountable by the State to realise substantive equality [Article 29(e)]. This idea has been developed further in national constitutions. The South African Constitution of 1996, for instance, has a clear provision that makes non State actors responsible for adhering to human rights, including norms of non-discrimination and substantive equality [Article 8(2)]. Current human rights scholarship and analysis has also indicated the manner in which the early Statist approach to human rights can be replaced by bringing non-State and corporate entities within the scope of accountability on human rights.[47]

The idea of corporate social responsibility, which has developed as a self regulatory dimension of good governance, has enabled many multinationals and major corporations to take on projects to realise women's rights, especially in improving working conditions for women and providing opportunities for promotion and career development. Micro credit programmes and livelihood support in the aftermath of natural disasters have attracted the interest of the corporate sector. It has also voluntarily partnered with government in fulfilling socio-economic rights of women in the area of health and education. The corporate sector is a key player in an environment of economic transformation and expanding the concept of duty bearer to include this sector is an essential dimension of a rights based approach to accelerating equality. This aspect of the rights based approach is reinforced in Goal 8 of MDGs, which calls for a global partnership for development. This goal should be interpreted and extended to include the accountability of the private corporate sector by integrating it with commitments under CEDAW Article 29(e). Globalisation, the reduced role of the State and the growth of a de-regulated economy have made it essential that human rights ideologies respond to this challenge. Goal 8, Target 12 of the MDGs on developing a global partnership in development and a non-discriminatory trading and financial system should be linked with commitments under CEDAW and Paragraph 528 of the BPFA to bring international and regional financial institutions within the scope of human rights accountability.

There is also a growing pressure to bring international trade law and Multilateral Lending Institutions (MLIs) within human rights law. They have been created by international regimes to operate closely with States, and it is argued that they are no less obligated than are States to abide by the Universal Declaration of Human Rights. The concept of good governance and corporate social responsibility has helped to create an environment in which self-regulatory private sector entities now recognise that they are partners in respecting, protecting and fulfilling human rights. It is likely that the international legal regime will also respond with clearer principles on the liability of MLIs and the private sector to adhere to human rights standards, including substantive equality.

Reaching men, community leaders and traditional tribunal leaders who have an official role in alternative dispute settlement with the message of gender equality is a challenge for South Asian countries. Some of the worst infringements of human rights have taken place in intra family, domestic and communal violence, and in the abuse of power by traditional tribunals. While the State is accountable for non-State actors, the expanded concept of human rights sees the family and these groups as duty bearers in relation to realising human rights. NGOs and women's groups have, therefore, assumed the responsibility to develop legal literacy programmes and other projects that target these groups.

The right to organise and freedom of association in pursuing gender equality captures the multifaceted dimensions of human rights. Non-State actors – including women's groups and NGOs as members of the community –

are rights holders in relation to the State, but, increasingly, are also recognised in international and national human rights law as duty bearers in promoting accountable governance based on respect for human rights. An environment that is conducive to realising the right of freedom of association, though not covered by CEDAW, is a core dimension of a rights based approach, since NGOs and women's groups must be free to participate as citizens who have an active role in realising a human rights agenda.

Holding private, non-State actors accountable in their own sphere of activity and recognising the right to freedom of association is not to suggest that they should take over the primary responsibilities of accountable governance from the State or local bodies charged with these responsibilities. Regional variations in the situation of women in South Asia has been highlighted by the CEDAW Committee and empowered local bodies and community based women's groups that can articulate women's voice are an essential resource in realising substantive equality. However, women's groups and NGOs cannot take over the task of governance to further equality by assuming that weak governance is a measure of a failed State. This encourages the State – which is a powerful player in accessing resources at the local and international level – to avoid accountability to the people. The major responsibility for realising a rights based approach to equality is the State. Non-State actors must partner with the State in creating a culture conducive to human rights, promote accountability and monitor State performance rather than take over the responsibilities of the State.

(iv) Revisiting state interventions in law and policy in South Asia

Law policy and resource allocation must combine to accelerate substantive equality. Too often putting the law in place and focusing on formal equality through legislative reform has undermined the crucial importance of policy measures and resource allocation for implementation. The synergy of these elements is the essence of a rights based approach. Performance on gender equality has been uneven in South Asian countries because this synergy has not been recognised as the essence of the CEDAW commitments and a rights based approach.

Formal equality laws: their scope and relevance

All countries have a range of discriminatory laws in many areas which deny equal opportunity, create disabilities and deny formal equality. For instance, land rights and personal laws in all South Asian countries invariably infringe Constitutional guarantees on equality. Nepal has legislation which restricts women's access to employment in the armed forces and the police, while job segregation is maintained by Pakistan's Constitutional provision on public sector jobs "suitable for women". A clear example of discrimination in transfer of citizenship is seen in Bangladesh. Pakistan and Nepal have amended their citizenship laws, but discrimination continues against women and children when the husband is a foreigner. The emphasis on formal equality and removal of these legal disabilities continues to be important in South Asia. The repeal of these discriminatory laws and reformist formal legislation and policy set new normative values. They can help prevent direct discrimination and legal disability and create enforceable rights.

In countries like India and Nepal, where courts have the power of judicial review, gender activists have challenged discrimination and an activist judiciary in the apex courts has sometimes given guidance, helping the State to introduce necessary reforms. Nepal's legislative reform process, stimulated by the Supreme Court, has been more consistent in this regard than in other countries. For instance, past legislation cannot be challenged for infringements in Sri Lanka and its courts have limited power of judicial review. In this situation, legislative reforms are ad hoc and not comprehensive. A partnership between women's groups and the government, lobbying and advocacy has helped to initiate a slow pace of reform to eliminate discrimination in specific priority areas like citizenship in India, Sri Lanka, Maldives and Nepal; Hindu Inheritance Law in India and Nepal; and violence against women, including trafficking, in all countries in South Asia. Recent legislation in Pakistan has amended the Hudood Ordinance to distinguish between adultery and rape and reintroduce the concept of statutory rape. Honour crimes can also be prosecuted. These reforms represent years of effort to introduce changes in law and policy. Yet, further advocacy and lobbying are required to change the Islamic law concepts of compensation and blood money and colonial rules of evidence, whose persistence weakens the reforms.[48]

The CEDAW reporting process and UNIFEM's strengthening of State institutions and NGOs have often contributed to these reform efforts. In general, family law has been resistant to legislative reform in all countries, with courts too being ambivalent in their attitude to discrimination in personal laws. However, Sri Lanka reformed its law on family support to eliminate the male breadwinner concept. Maldives has introduced a comprehensive Family Law Code which has attempted to reconcile CEDAW norms using the strategy of interpretation of religious law.[49]

The process of systematic review and reform of discriminatory laws in citizenship, land rights and family law, including family support, to accelerate formal equality has been long delayed and is critical to harmonise Constitutional and CEDAW commitments.

Protectionist Laws and Policies in South Asia

Traditionally, ad hoc reforms in criminal law and criminal justice, including laws on sexual violence and trafficking, are perceived as protectionist responses on behalf of women and have failed to set a clear normative framework of legal values. Bhutan has repealed an earlier Rape Act and introduced a new criminal law on rape, but this is limited in its definition of offences and sanctions. Nepal has recognised marital rape as an offence and an infringement of equality and the right to personal security. Pakistan has recently introduced amendments which undermine the gender biased Hudood laws on sexual violence. Legislative reform has also criminalised honour crimes. India and Sri Lanka have colonial Penal Codes that only recognise marital rape in circumstances of judicial separation or when a child bride below the minimum age of marriage is raped. Judicial separation is a hardly used remedy and there has not been a single prosecution for raping a child bride, though the British probably introduced this law to discourage child marriage and sexual violence against children. Though anti-trafficking legislation has been enacted, some areas like the law on prostitution continue to be embedded in gender discriminatory colonial vagrancy laws that criminalised street prostitution.[50]

Domestic violence legislation was introduced in India and Sri Lanka in 2005 and is under consideration in Pakistan, Nepal and Bangladesh. Bangladesh has already enacted laws that address sexual and domestic violence and the special problem of acid throwing. It is not clear how the existing laws will harmonise with the proposed domestic violence legislation. The Indian Act is confined to domestic violence against women, while the Sri Lankan Act is gender neutral, applicable to men, women and children, and perceives domestic violence as an infringement of bodily security and health that impacts on everyone. When India's women-specific Protection of Women from Domestic Violence Act (PWDVA) is being challenged in pending litigation as a violation of men and children's rights, it is tempting to justify it as protection legislation for women. However, the concept of substantive equality can be used to justify women-specific laws and deny the protectionist rationale which perceives women only as victims and, thus, reinforces the violation of equality and other human rights that occurs in domestic violence.[51]

All countries have included or proposed a procedure in domestic violence legislation to empower the court to issue a restraining order against the abuser. This is a civil remedy to protect a woman and prevent the abuser from having access to her residence or place of work. The civil remedy is a response to the need to move beyond merely criminalising violent conduct in general or special provisions of Penal Codes.[52] Counselling spouses and family members and other supports and preventive measures have been integrated into the legislative response. However, Pakistan's draft law on domestic violence provides for diverting a case through amicable settlement and at the preparatory stage: a provision that fails to recognise that domestic violence is a serious offence that should not be settled by private arrangements before the offender is brought before the courts.

In emphasising the civil aspects of the remedy for domestic violence, South Asian domestic violence legislation has not addressed the specific issue of whether the State should adopt a "no drop" policy as Pacific countries like Fiji have done. This would mean that investigation and prosecution is mandatory and that mediation is not an alternative when grave violence has occurred. A "no drop" policy gives a normative message on domestic violence as criminal conduct in the community, and the possibility of introducing it in South Asia needs to be considered. The drafting and adoption of this legislation in the region can be an occasion for experience sharing among countries, with a view to strengthening the response to this common problem as an infringement of substantive equality.

The criminal justice codes of all South Asian countries are founded on discriminatory colonial laws that have not been reviewed and reformed comprehensively in light of substantive equality standards. For instance, the Penal Code reforms in Sri Lanka have been a limited initiative and have not been accompanied by a comprehensive review of discrimination in criminal investigation, evidentiary rules and trial procedures. This is a gap in all countries.[53]

Similar challenges have not been addressed in the area of protective labour legislation. India has an Equal Remuneration Act (1976) and Pakistan and Sri Lanka have minimum wage laws. Protective legislation that sets hours of work and excludes women from night work or certain occupations has not been reviewed systematically with a view to introducing necessary changes in job opportunities without sacrificing women's right to health and personal security. The tendency has been to eliminate restrictions outright, as in Sri Lanka and India, without addressing the reality of exploitation of women workers that a blanket withdrawal of the restrictions can encourage. If protective legislation reform is addressed in the future with the goal of achieving substantive equality, this exploitation of women will not be reinforced by what is incorrectly perceived as progressive legal reform to eliminate protection.[54]

Maternity leave legislation has become a norm in South Asia but sometimes reflects protectionist approaches to this issue.[55] In Sri Lanka, Pakistan and Nepal, maternity leave is a general right. In Bangladesh, it is restricted to places of work with a specified number of women employees and is considered an employment benefit for women. India has similar limiting legislation that applies only in the private sector. These restrictions undermine the impact of the legislation as a measure which realises substantive equality by taking working women's reproductive health rights into account. Limitations on employer responsibility to provide crèche facilities in some countries reflects the same approach that pregnancy leave and child care is a privilege rather than a right to work and maintain a healthy work and family life balance.

Maternity leave legislation in South Asia needs to be reviewed and combined with supportive social policies on child care or by placing responsibilities on employers to invest in these services as an aspect of good management and social responsibility. Some private and public sector organisations in Sri Lanka already provide these services.

NGOs in all countries provide some child care services. Maternity leave legislation supported by child care measures must be prioritised if the promise of substantive equality in access to work outside the home and economic empowerment is to become a reality for women who value a work/family life balance. As the CEDAW Committee has pointed out, the State has an obligation both to set the norms in this regard and to ensure that the corporate sector conforms. Legislation and judicial decisions in the region have also declared that marital and pregnancy discrimination in the workplace is a violation of women's rights.[56] Advocacy is essential to prevent violations and non-employment of women on grounds of market efficiency.

Gender analysis of law and policy to accelerate substantive equality

Some new developments are not covered by legislation. For instance, HIV/AIDS is generally addressed in gender neutral national policy documents, although women are perceived as a high risk group. These documents do not adopt a rights based approach or recognise the need for legislative intervention to eliminate gender based discrimination. Bangladesh has a National Committee on HIV/AIDS with a women's wing; this is an initiative that can help to generate interest with regard to legislative reform. Legislation, when introduced, should move from gender neutral approaches to address the specific circumstances of disempowerment and discrimination suffered by women affected by HIV/AIDS in access to shelter and safe spaces, property and health care and their right to freedom from violence.

The consistent failure to regulate and set employment standards for female domestic service is a special concern in the context of female domestic service and migration. Even when market forces operate to determine wages, women tend to be paid less for domestic work. The failure to regulate female domestic work within the country, recognise rights and prevent women's exploitation hampers governments from working on bilateral agreements with regard to women migrant workers with host countries that receive these workers from the South Asian region.

Putting the law in place to eliminate direct discrimination and accelerate formal equality of opportunity and treatment has been a challenge in itself. Consequently, countries have not addressed the urgent need to accelerate substantive equality by addressing the discriminatory impact on women of apparently gender neutral laws.[57] Employment laws have not been reviewed for their impact in eliminating disadvantage and gender based discrimination. Equal remuneration laws and employee benefits are not evaluated to address the reality of job segregation and respond to the casualisation of women's labour or the more burdensome work that women in certain occupations undertake for similar wages. Inadequate labour inspection and enforcement can affect more women workers in industry. Public administration regulations on employment in the public service, though apparently gender neutral and "equal", may, in fact, disadvantage women more. Thus, a two child limit for employment as engineers or police officers can impact to prevent achieving a gender balance in services which have traditionally been male dominated.

The criminal law that covers domestic violence is considered gender neutral and free from bias. The police can prosecute for acts of physical violence against men or women. However, gender biased attitudes of law enforcement authorities in fact legitimise domestic violence as an internal family dispute that should be ignored. Although individual laws covering issues such as dowry violence, cruelty, acid throwing and domestic violence have been criminalised, the basic criminal law in the Penal Code, including defences such as grave and sudden provocation, has not been reformed to address the manner in which it impacts differently on women accused of crimes. These defences are perceived as gender neutral and are not interpreted to take account of women's experience of violence or the battered woman syndrome. In Sri Lanka, torture is defined as a crime by public officials, thus excluding acts of torture suffered by women within the family and community.

Extensive review and reform of Penal Codes preceded by gender analysis in line with the norms of substantive equality should be prioritised and considered a necessary support for implementing the new gender sensitive laws on domestic violence in South Asia. The insistence on gender neutrality in Penal Codes has sometimes led to unintended interventions or criminal liability. For instance, a Sri Lankan reform of the Penal Code which modified a provision criminalising homosexuality changed the reference from males to persons, and created a new offence of lesbianism that was not part of the law on sexual offences!

There has also been no effort to review received colonial law on the male breadwinner as head of household which continues to undermine substantive equality for women in receipt of family benefits. Sri Lanka removed this concept from its maintenance law in 1999, but continues to recognise it in other areas of family law. This concept reinforces patriarchal attitudes among bureaucrats who are required to administer service delivery programmes, even when there are no legal provisions that require preference for males. Public administrators use the concept of male breadwinner in poverty alleviation, State land and shelter allocation and in relief programmes in disaster and conflict situations. Women who are de facto heads of household or caregivers thus become a marginalised sector with no access to important services and benefits. Sometimes, in Sri Lanka, women's entitlement to equal wages in sectors like plantations regulated by labour law is undermined by the practice of paying wages to the male head of household. Laws and policies that adopt a gender neutral approach and place a ceiling on ownership of land for a joint spousal unit of husband and wife without specifying shares, can impact to force the woman to forfeit her land. When tax relief is given only to registered businesses, women who conduct small scale businesses will be denied these benefits. Gender neutral tax provisions or laws on allocation of State lands and the rights of "surviving spouses" impact negatively on women because they are not perceived as breadwinners or persons who contribute significantly to family income. Accelerating substantive equality requires a wholesale review of the application of the breadwinner and head of household concept in law and policy.

Implementation gaps

Exploitation of girls and violence perpetrated in early marriage and child labour demonstrate the importance of moving beyond formal equality. The same minimum age for boys and girls for compulsory education and in prohibiting child labour and child marriage can be set by laws and regulations. However, these laws often fail to impact and accelerate substantive equality because their different impact on girls is not considered and necessary social policies and services are not introduced and supported with sufficient budgetary resources. The failure to provide girls with access to schooling up to secondary school (except in Maldives and Sri Lanka and, to some extent, in Bangladesh) has contributed to undermining South Asian laws on child labour and minimum age of marriage. The prevalence of these problems in conflict areas in Sri Lanka and the failure to eliminate them in the plantation sector to date are related to Sri Lanka's failures in monitoring girls' school participation in this sector and the disruption of girls' schooling due to conflict. Similarly, lack of access to facilities for birth registration and difficulties in proving age have reinforced the exploitation of girls in domestic service and in early marriage. The recent priority given to birth registration through combined government inter-agency and NGO programmes is an important initiative. The failure of the government to implement laws prohibiting early marriage has been recently challenged in PILs in India and Nepal.[58]

In 2002, following Supreme Court decisions, India introduced the 86th Amendment to its Constitution making access to compulsory education a fundamental right and a dimension of the right to life. However, compulsory education has not yet been introduced or resourced consistently as State policy.[59] The MDGs incorporate the goal of achieving access to primary education. The experience of Sri Lanka, Maldives and Bangladesh suggests that South Asian countries must introduce policies on access to compulsory education up to secondary school to effectively implement laws on child labour and minimum age of marriage and any Constitutional provisions that guarantee the right to education.

Criminal laws on violence against women are not effectively enforced due to the failure to introduce policy measures supported with resource allocation. For instance, domestic violence legislation requires the establishment of shelters and one-stop crisis centres that deliver integrated services to victims and the provision of adequate resources for the police units investigating and handling these cases. Yet, these resources are not made available in all areas and when facilities are provided, coverage is limited. The Equal Remuneration Act in India has recognised that women's groups can assist in monitoring compliance. This dimension of involvement of these groups needs to be developed in all countries by building partnerships with women's groups so as to strengthen the State's capacity to enforce domestic violence legislation, prosecute where necessary and offer services to victims. Improving resources for investigation, including access to forensic medical technologies such as DNA testing, capacity building and gender sensitisation of law enforcement personnel and prosecutors has been identified in all countries as a critical need for effective law enforcement in cases of violence against women.[60]

The lack of commitment and political will in implementing laws or engaging in holistic law and policy measures to realise substantive equality in South Asia is often traced to the issues which are common to many other regions. Women's human rights receive lower priority because of the need to realise other rights or because of completing claims for budgetary resources. This has made it difficult to sustain gender equality initiatives, including gender budget responses. Yet, addressing the issue of competing rights and resources is critical if substantive equality is to be realised and a rights based approach integrated into national efforts to accelerate gender equality.

(v) Competing rights and resource allocation

(a) Religion, culture and equality rights

South Asia is home to a diverse population and its countries have different forms of government. A common historical trend in governance is the politicisation of issues that are perceived as connected with religious, ethnic or group identity. Constitutions guarantee universal norms on human rights, including gender equality. However, other rights including the right to freedom of conscience and religion and the right to enjoy one's culture are also guaranteed. The political and judicial spheres are often the site for addressing, resolving or ignoring the tensions that surface in accommodating these different rights. Religious fundamentalism, as well as armed conflict centred on respect for identity, access to resources and power sharing with minorities have made the balancing of conflicting interests in governance a special challenge. Fundamentalist movements sometimes perceive the application of universal human rights norms as majoritism. The concept of gender equity is often suggested as an alternative to the norm of gender equality.

In this environment governments have lacked the political will to initiate significant legal and policy reforms to address gender discrimination and equality. This is reflected especially in the reluctance to introduce necessary reforms to eliminate direct discrimination and legal disabilities in personal laws based on ethnicity, custom or religion that apply to different groups. The courts have been equally cautious, sometimes refusing to review personal law or striving to adopt interpretations that seek to reconcile women's right to equality with the need to respect culture and religion and harmonise the conflicting legal norms.[61]

On occasion, however, the superior courts have addressed the conflict and ensured that the norms of equality prevail. This is clear in a decision in India, followed in Sri Lanka, that prohibited unilateral male conversion from one religion to another which resulted in a diminution of the wife's rights to divorce under her marriage contract. Similarly, uniformly applicable legislation on obligations of family support has been interpreted by the Indian Supreme Court so as to enable a woman to receive family benefits not available under her personal religious law. In recent decisions, the Nepal Supreme Court has refused to recognise customary laws that deny women equal inheritance rights and a custom that involved inhuman and degrading treatment after menstruation or pregnancy. A Bangladesh High Court has reinforced Constitutional guarantees by reference to religious texts in Islam in the recent case on equal rights of elected women members to reserve seats in a local authority. A Pakistan High Court has interpreted Islamic law and harmonised it with Constitutional guarantees and CEDAW in refusing to recognise a forced marriage.[62]

However, when a proposal for reform creates tension with a minority group, governments have been swift to address religious sensitivities by either backtracking on proposed law reform or actively introducing legislation to reverse a court decision. For instance, legislation in 1986 in India denying Muslim women the right to claim maintenance under the generally applicable colonial statute on family support was enacted as the Muslim Women (Protection of Rights on Divorce) Act. Similarly, when Penal Code reforms were introduced in Sri Lanka in 1995, the Minister of Justice withdrew legislation that attempted to rationalise the existing regulatory framework on termination of pregnancy to include rape and incest and also modified a draft law raising the age of statutory rape, supposedly to accommodate concerns of a Muslim and Catholic religious lobby. Though other countries in the region with Islamic jurisdictions have introduced laws to restrain early marriage, such marriages are legal for the Muslim community in Sri Lanka. Setting a minimum age for marriage has been difficult in a context where Muslims are a minority religious group. The Sri Lankan government's failure to introduce a common standard has impacted negatively on the rights of women to be governed by generally applicable human rights norms on personal security and equality. In Nepal, on the other hand, the Supreme Court, in the exercise of judicial power to scrutinise legislation, declared void reformist legislation that conferred upon unmarried daughters equal rights of inheritance to property and yet imposed a forfeiture of these inheritance rights after marriage.[63] Such a power of judicial review is not available under the Sri Lankan Constitution.

The controversy around applying either relativist approaches to rights or universal norms is one that is common to many countries. The CEDAW Committee has, in its Concluding Comments on reports from South Asian countries, used the general articles as well as Articles 5 and 16 to challenge relativism and reservations entered on these Articles. Article 5 requires the State to take measures to undermine and eventually eliminate stereotypical attitudes to women that result in discrimination. Article 16 clarifies that traditional cultural values do not justify the perpetuation of gender based discrimination against women in marriage and the family. The CEDAW Committee has urged countries to extend the application of uniformly applicable laws that eliminate direct discrimination. It has also encouraged using comparative experiences on reform in Islamic law to enact changes that recognise women's human rights and gender equality.[64] However, governments have not yet satisfactorily confronted this challenge with proactive measures. A rights based approach to accelerate substantive equality requires this area to be revisited and made the centre of reform initiatives.

There are practical strategies to develop a common approach that accelerates substantive equality and undermines inequality and discrimination. Custom and tradition are never static and have evolved over a period of time. Article 17(i) of the African Protocol on Women's Rights (2003) of the African Charter on Human and People's Rights recognises culture and tradition as positive forces in accelerating equality, if women can have a voice in formulating culture and tradition so as to link with universal standards. Muslim women's groups in many countries have studied Islamic jurisprudence and deconstructed the male biased interpretations, highlighting areas that can be harmonised with equality norms.[65]

Women's groups can also link across ethnicity, caste and religion to support legislation and policy measures in common areas of concern and advocate for a standard of substantive equality. It is important to create a broad based understanding that equity and fairness demand recognition of gender equality. This approach has already been adopted in lobbying for legislation on domestic and sexual violence and trafficking in Nepal, India, Bangladesh and Sri Lanka. Pakistan's changes to the Hudood laws and honour crimes laws represent efforts to use human rights norms to challenge repressive religion-based laws. New areas for common approaches include allocation of State housing and shelter and access to land, livelihood opportunities and credit, which have become priority concerns for women, particularly in post conflict and disaster reconstruction, rehabilitation and resettlement. Political participation also represents an area in which women of all communities can come together and lobby for quotas or reservations for women in both legislative assemblies and local bodies. If women can organise themselves to present a common front on these issues, they will set an example to male groups, including caste groups, that compete with each other in lobbying for affirmative action to address disadvantage.

Cause lawyering networks in the region can strengthen capacity to use a national litigation strategy and challenge discriminatory laws and practices, sharing comparative experience where there are similar Constitutional or statutory provisions. Such networks can also help to build capacity to bring complaints under the Optional Protocol to CEDAW, where it has been ratified.

The concepts of "reasonable" and "purposive" limitation of rights have been used creatively by courts in South Africa to balance conflicting interests. South Asia's superior courts interpreting fundamental rights have also used these concepts and sometimes broadened jurisprudence on the concept of equality. Judicial training and sharing of case law in the region can help stimulate interest in balancing conflicting rights with regard to culture and equality. This technique of interpretation becomes more difficult in the case of religion since freedom of religion is an absolute right. However, the concept of limiting manifestation of religion can be interpreted with the same insight of reasonableness and purpose to strengthen equality rights.

(b) Women's rights and children's rights

Conflicting concern with realising children's rights can undermine an agenda of achieving substantive equality for women. All countries in South Asia have social and legal traditions that identify children (particularly girls) and women as disempowered groups that have limited rights. Consequently, women's rights and child rights groups have not experienced the difficulties that feminist activists in the West have encountered in developing common initiatives. South Asian activists have recognised the complementarity of goals in their work on issues such as violence, including sexual violence, child marriage, trafficking and exploitative working conditions. The institutionalised discrimination against girl children in South Asia has encouraged a sensitivity to the need to address discrimination against women in a life cycle approach. Women's groups have collaborated with child rights groups to obtain legal and policy changes in areas like child marriage, child labour and sexual violence and abuse. These areas of complementarity should not, however, mask the need to address tensions.

South Asian realities may require giving families additional incentives to send girls to school. Scholarships for girls, transport and facilities for sibling care have been introduced in some countries. These policies are sometimes criticised for reinforcing the idea that women and girls need protection rather than equality rights. Similarly, statutory rape laws that make men and boys criminally liable for sex with girls under a specified age, irrespective of the issue of consent, are critiqued for undermining equality and being overly protective of girls. As long as education for girls is made compulsory by formal law, there should be no objection to providing supports that facilitate access. Similarly, it can be argued that the issue of consent must be determined according to an age threshold, in the best interests of the child. Statutory rape laws, thus, aim to prevent sexual exploitation and abuse.

Laws and policies that focus only on children's rights can ignore or undermine women's rights with regard to work outside the home. The recognition of socio-economic rights in areas such as basic health and education often provides an incentive to introduce laws and policies that impact positively on women and both boys and girls. In Sri Lanka, for instance, education has been a catalyst for improving social indicators for women and children. However, family responsibilities and child care policies sometimes tend to be prioritised over women's economic rights. Bangladesh and Nepal have reviewed their policies on restricting women's rights to migrate for employment. The Ministry of Women's Affairs in Sri Lanka was reconstituted recently as the Ministry of Child Development and Women's Empowerment, and one of its recent initiatives proposed restricting the overseas migrant work of women with children under five years of age. Such restrictions fail to recognise women's contribution to family income and the need to provide women with child care support so that they can to maintain a work/family life balance. Maternity legislation that extends leave beyond a reasonable period in the interests of children without the necessary sensitisation and advocacy in the private sector can also legislate women out of the formal work force.

Unless the complementary and conflicting concerns of women's and children's rights are balanced with sensitivity in legal regulation and policy planning following CEDAW standards on substantive equality, women will find it increasingly difficult to benefit from the positive economic opportunities created by globalisation. Balancing these interests in careful law and policy formulation is essential to accelerate substantive equality.

(c) Some other areas of conflict

Arguments on economic efficiency and rights of the private and corporate sectors in investment and business in a global economy can come into conflict with women's right to substantive equality, unless these rights are understood and integrated into poverty alleviation, development and investment programmes. Harmonisation can be achieved through the partnership and legal strategies discussed earlier in dealing with private, non-State actors.

The group right to personal security in times of armed conflict can also be used to justify extensive powers being given to the armed forces and the police. In this area, too, the jurisprudence of the Courts recognising the command responsibility for violence by persons who exercise State authority can be a limitation on State power and promote access to justice for custodial rape and violence against women.[66] Impunity of these agencies in situations of armed conflict can be addressed through human rights norms and substantive equality in relation to gender based violence.

Legislation (such as anti terrorism laws) and public security ordinances (such as the Armed Forces Special Provisions Act in India) need to be reviewed. The CEDAW Committee and women's groups have referred to the urgency of reviewing such legislation in order to ensure that concerns for public security do not legitimise gender based violence in conflict situations or civil unrest.[67]

An understanding of gender based violence as a phenomenon that infringes on women's substantive equality and right to life must be created in the community and among professionals to resist challenges by men to domestic violence legislation which is women-specific. When formal rather than substantive equality is emphasised, male resistance to women-specific law and policy initiatives in the areas of employment and violence encourages a non-interventionist attitude by the State. Traditional arguments on reasonable classifications and protectionist approaches may also be challenged by referring to the emphasis in State law and policy on achieving on women's empowerment.

(d) Competition in resource allocation

The issue of resources is perhaps the most important area in which a women's equality rights agenda competes with other interests. CEDAW is one of the earliest international human rights instruments to recognise the equal importance, indivisibility and interdependence of civil, political and socio-economic rights. CEDAW does not contain a provision familiar to other constitutional documents and international instruments that refer to the allocation of maximum available resources for implementing rights. When Articles 2 and 3 require State's Parties to take "all appropriate measures" to realise women's human rights, it assumes women's right of equal access to national resources for law enforcement and basic needs in areas such as health and education. Consequently, the poor record of South Asian countries, except Sri Lanka and Maldives, in providing services in key areas such as birth registration, health and education, has been referred to in Concluding Comments of the CEDAW Committee.[68] The high expenditure of South Asian countries on defence in contrast to social expenditure has been commented upon in development reports over many decades. South Asian countries distinguish between enforceable fundamental rights and non-enforceable Directive Principles of State Policy, which refer to socio-economic rights in basic needs. However, the Indian Supreme Court's interpretation of the right to life has led to the recognition of an enforceable right to education, and this requires resource allocation.[69]

It is within this scenario that the claims of women – who constitute over 51% of the population – to national resources to accelerate substantive equality has assumed special importance. NGOs and think tanks in the region have engaged in budget analysis to demonstrate irregularities in resource distribution and low expenditure in the vital social sector. They have sometimes helped women in local bodies to understand budgeting processes.[70] These analyses are not, however, usually linked to government budgetary processes so as to impact and facilitate budget reviews. Government budgetary processes and discussions are not usually transparent or accessible to people outside the government.

Therefore, Gender Responsive Budgeting (GRB) initiatives have added value for accelerating substantive equality in South Asia. GRB (sometimes referred to as gender sensitive budgeting) can become a strategy to avoid the gender neutrality that reinforces women's marginalisation and give priority instead to implementing rights issues of concern for women. The failures of implementation discussed earlier – even in areas such as domestic violence – demonstrate that budget resources are essential to ensure productive results of law and policy measures. GRB also becomes a strategy for ensuring transparency in budgetary procedures so that the outcome and result of a government's legal and policy measures can be evaluated in terms of the actual resources committed for effective implementation.

UNIFEM and the Commonwealth Secretariat have helped to build technical expertise in this area and have developed a knowledge base for accelerating substantive equality. A recent UNIFEM publication[71] analyses and provides suggestions for monitoring budgets in compliance with CEDAW. This is an effective tool for both budget analysis and monitoring decision-making and resource allocation. The publication also records best practices in countries such as the Philippines, Brazil and South Africa where, in addition to the annual Appropriation Acts of Parliament, specific provisions on budgeting are combined with the enactment of laws. In the Philippines, from 1996, the Appropriation Act and the Women in National Budgeting Act require all government agencies to allocate a minimum of five percent of their budgets to projects on gender issues. The Philippines National Commission on Women monitors compliance. When women's nodal agencies have an important role in monitoring, there is a greater likelihood that they will be consulted by Finance Ministries in making budget decisions and negotiating development assistance, reinforcing CEDAW Article 7 on giving voice to women in policy formulation and resource allocation.

Conclusion

The meaning of equality has evolved over a period of time. It was originally interpreted in Western Constitutional jurisprudence as Aristotelian formal equality or sameness of treatment: the idea that like should be treated as like. However, this encouraged discrimination against women due to biological differences between the sexes. The first challenges to this view by women in the West, therefore, focused on eliminating disabilities or adopting protectionist labour laws that would address women's vulnerability in the workplace.

An exclusive reliance on the formal model of equality was eventually rejected in favour of a model that would take into account context and the reality of disadvantage experienced by some sectors of the community, so as to achieve equality of outcome. This meaning of equality in substance, or substantive equality, was further challenged by Western feminists who rejected the concept of using a male comparison in determining substantive equality for women. The broader feminist interpretation of substantive equality that addresses the reality of disadvantage suffered by women and focuses on equality in outcome and result has been recognised as the standard of equality in the General Recommendations which interpret CEDAW. The CEDAW Committee has emphasised that substantive equality also connects with the enjoyment of other human rights such as personal security and socio-economic rights. Traditional protectionist laws and policies can, therefore, be reinterpreted with a new focus on eliminating imposed disadvantage and protecting human rights rather than the stereotypical 'vulnerability' of women. Substantive equality also undermines arguments that equity (fairness) can be achieved without equality. Formal equality laws and policies are sometimes challenged in South Asia on the grounds that achieving fairness and equity is more important than formal equality. By demonstrating that the failure to take into account outcome and result disadvantages women, substantive equality focuses on the fact that equity cannot be achieved without equality.

All South Asian countries have ratified CEDAW and some have ratified the Optional Protocol. Though all countries except Nepal adopt a dualist approach to international law, the international and Western interpretation of substantive equality has influenced equality jurisprudence and Constitutional interpretation in the region. Formal equality and legislation and policies to eliminate direct discrimination continue to be important for all countries in the region. However, Constitutional provisions, including those on special measures for women, can and should be used to incorporate and develop the standard of substantive equality and accelerate gender justice in South Asia.

The concept of substantive equality has special relevance for South Asia where, despite some achievements, the reality of discrimination against women is all pervasive. It provides a framework for moving away from an overemphasis on achieving formal equality through law reform and the inadequate attention given to implementation. A focus on substantive equality encourages incorporating a human rights based holistic approach to all aspects of development. A standard of substantive equality requires moving beyond formal equality and legislation and policies to eliminate direct discrimination. This will involve broader use of affirmative action or temporary special measures provisions already provided for in South Asian Constitutions. Substantive equality also facilitates a review of the traditional protectionist approaches to law and policy formulation in South Asia and expands the scope of accountability of non-State actors.

The link made to other human rights can help to undermine a protectionist approach in labour regulation and issues such as violence against women. It can be used creatively in judicial interpretations and policy measures to resolve conflicts between competing rights, including those rights connected with custom and religion. Women's voices in transforming custom and interpreting religion are inherent in the idea of accelerating substantive equality and the concept can be used to foster an inter community and interfaith agenda on gender justice in conformity with CEDAW standards. This norm also helps to analyse and balance conflicting interests claimed on behalf of children and men. It encourages governments to adopt rational and gender responsive policies on budgeting and resource allocation, which are critical for effective implementation.

A Canadian judge once remarked that, "equality is a process, a process of constant and flexible examination, of vigilant introspection, and of aggressive open-mindedness…it is evolutionary contextual and persistent."[72] The concept of substantive equality has evolved from formal equality and developed creatively in this manner mostly out of the experience of women. It is part of women's universal history. South Asian countries too must make their own contribution to fashioning this concept, so that it provides a meaningful foundation for achieving gender justice and equality for women.

Notes

[1] This is an edited version of a paper originally commissioned by UNIFEM South Asia Sub Regional Office for the Sixth South Asia Regional Ministerial Conference, "Commemorating Beijing," co-hosted by the Ministry of Women and Child Development (Government of India) and UNIFEM (New Delhi, January 2008). The paper in its original, extended version is available at: http://www.unifem.org.in/PDF/e%20Concept%20of%20Substantive%20Equality%20-final%20-%2031-12-07.pdf [*Editor's Note*: Please note that because this paper was written in 2008, some of its information about recent legal developments – such as the drafting of the Constitution of Nepal, the passing of the Right of Children to Free and Compulsory Education Act, 2009 in India, etc., – might be dated. Readers are encouraged to consult other sources for the most current information on these ongoing developments. For Nepal, in particular, Sapana Malla's essay in this volume, "Nepal: From Equality to Gender Justice", is helpful in providing current information on some laws relating to women.]

[2] Bangladesh: Article 27; Bhutan: Article 7; India: Articles 14 and 15; Pakistan: Article 25; Maldives: Article 13 (no specific reference to sex discrimination); Sri Lanka: Article 12.

[3] http://www.un.org/womenwatch/daw/cedaw25anniversary/cedaw25-CEDAW.pdf.

[4] Abdullahi Ahmed An-Na'im (Ed), *Human Rights in Cross-Cultural Perspectives: A Quest for Consensus*, Philadelphia: University of Pennsylvania Press (1992); Shaheen Sardar Ali, *Conceptualizing Islamic Law, CEDAW and Women's Human Rights in Plural Legal Settings: A Comparative Analysis of Application of CEDAW in Bangladesh, India and Pakistan*, UNIFEM South Asia Regional Office, New Delhi (2006); Martha C. Nussbaum, *Women and Human Development*, New Delhi: Kali for Women (2000).

5 Shaheen Sardar Ali, op.cit. and "A Comparative Perspective of the Convention on the Rights of the Child and the Principles of Islamic Law: Law Reform and Children's Rights in Muslim Jurisdictions" in *Protecting the World's Children: Impact of the Convention on the Rights of the Child in Diverse Legal Systems*, UNICEF/Cambridge University Press (2007); *Shamima Sultana v Bangladesh* [57 DLR 2005 p 201].

6 Aristotle, *The Nichomachean Ethics* and Otto A. Bird, *The Idea of Justice*, New York: Frederick A. Praeger Inc. (1968).

7 Aristotle, ibid.

8 As quoted in William M. Wiecek, *Liberty Under Law: The Supreme Court in American Life*, Maryland: Johns Hopkins University Press (1988).

9 H. M. Seervai, *Constitutional Law of India*, New Delhi: Universal Book Traders (1996); S. Sharvanand, *Fundamental Rights in Sri Lanka*, Colombo: Arnold Pvt. Ltd. (1993); R K W. Goonesekere, *Fundamental Rights and the Constitution: A Case Book*, Colombo: Law and Society Trust (2003); *Shirin Munir v Government of Punjab* [PLD 1990 SC 295 (Pakistan)].

10 163 U.S. 537 (1896).

11 83 U.S. 150 (1873), as quoted in Wieckek, op.cit.

12 349 U.S. 294 (1955), as quoted in Wiecek, op.cit.

13 438 U.S. 265 (1978).

14 *Johnson v Transportation Agency Santa Clara County* [480 U.S. 616 (1987)]

15 Michael Rosenfeld, *Affirmative Action and Justice: A Philosophical and Constitutional Inquiry*, Yale University Press (1991); Kathleen E. Mahoney, "Canadian Approaches to Equality Rights" in Rebecca Cook (Ed.), *Human Rights of Women: National and International Perspectives*, Philadelphia: University of Pennsylvania Press (1994).

16 Michael Rosenfeld, Ibid.

17 208 U.S. 412 (1908).

18 261 U.S. 525 (1923).

19 Deborah L. Rhode, *Justice and Gender: Sex Discrimination and the Law*, Harvard University Press (1989).

20 Deborah L. Rhode, ibid.; Catherine A. MacKinnon, *Towards a Feminist Theory of the State*, Harvard University Press (1989); Hilaire Bennett, *Introduction to Feminist Jurisprudence*, London: Cavendish Publishing Ltd. (1998); Rebecca Cook (Ed.). op.cit.; Catharine A. MacKinnon, "Reflections on Sex Equality under Law" in *The Yale Law Journal*, Volume 100, Number 5 (March 1991); Kathleen E. Mahoney, "Canadian Approaches to Equality Rights" in Rebecca Cook (Ed.), op.cit. and "Gender and the Judiciary: Confronting Gender Bias" in Kirstine Adams and Andrew Byrnes (Eds.), *Gender Equality and the Judiciary: Using International Human Rights Standards to Promote the*

Human Rights of Women and the Girl-Child at the National Level, London: Commonwealth Secretariat (2000).

[21] *Andrews v Law Society of British Columbia* [1989 I.S.C.R. 143] and other cases discussed by Kathleen E. Mahoney, "Canadian Approaches to Equality Rights" in Rebecca Cook (Ed.), op.cit.

[22] Iain Currie and Johan de Waal, *The New Constitutional and Administrative Law* (Volume I), Cape Town: Juta Legal and Academic Publishers (2001).

[23] Hilary Charlesworth, "What are Women's International Human Rights" in Rebecca Cook (Ed.), op.cit.

[24] Convention on Preventing and Combating Trafficking in Women and Children for Prostitution Act No 3 of 2005. The SAARC Social Charter 2004 is a policy document and not a legal instrument.

[25] Mahbub Ul Haq Human Development Centre, *Human Development in South Asia 2000: The Gender Question*, Oxford University Press [Pakistan?] (2000); *Pursuing Gender Equality Through the Millennium Development Goals in Asia and the Pacific*, Asian Development Bank (2006); *Progress of South Asian Women 2005: A Series for the Fifth South Asian Regional Ministerial Conference Celebrating Beijing Plus Ten*, UNIFEM South Asia Sub Regional Office (2005); *Women, War, Peace The Independent Experts' Assessment on the Impact of Armed Conflict on Women and Women's Role in Peace-Building (Progress of the World's Women 2002, Volume 1)*, UNIFEM (2002).

[26] Savitri W.E. Goonesekere (Ed.), *Violence, Law and Women's Rights in South Asia*, UNIFEM South Asia Sub Regional Office (2004); *Report on the Regional Thematic Meeting on Violence Against Women*, IWRAW Asia Pacific (2005); *Not a Minute More: Ending Violence Against Women*, UNIFEM (2003); see Notes 43 and 51 below; recent amendments to criminal law in Pakistan's Criminal Law Amendment Act 2006 amending Hudood Ordinance, and Human Trafficking Ordinance 2004.

[27] *Pursuing Gender Equality Through the Millennium Development Goals in Asia and the Pacific*, op.cit.; *Progress of South Asian Women 2005: A Series for the Fifth South Asian Regional Ministerial Conference Celebrating Beijing Plus Ten*, op.cit.

[28] Savitri W.E. Goonesekere, *A Gender Analysis of Tsunami Impact: Relief, Recovery, and Reconstruction in Some Districts in Sri Lanka*, UNIFEM South Asia Sub Regional Office and Centre for Women's Research, Colombo (2006); *Pursuing Gender Equality Through the Millennium Development Goals in Asia and the Pacific*, op.cit.

[29] See Notes 25 and 26 above; Ruth F. Hayward, *Breaking the Earthenware Jar: Lessons from South Asia to End Violence Against Women and Girls*, UNICEF Regional Office for South Asia (2000); *Asian and Pacific*

Women's Resource and Action Series: Law, Kuala Lumpur: Asian and Pacific Development Centre (1993).

[30]Savitri W.E. Goonesekere, *Children, Law and Justice: A South Asian Perspective*, Sage Publications (India) and UNICEF (1998); *LAWASIA Family Law Series*, Volumes I (1979) and II (1981), Singapore: Singapore University Press; *Asian and Pacific Women's Resource and Action Series: Law*, op.cit.; Savitri W.E. Goonesekere (Ed.), *Violence, Law and Women's Rights in South Asia*, op.cit.; *NGO Shadow Report on CEDAW, Maldives: A Commentary on the Combined Second and Third Periodic Report of the Government of Maldives to the CEDAW Committee*, November 2006 [http://www.iwraw-ap.org/resources/pdf/Maldives%20Shadow%20Report%20-%20final.pdf].

[31]See Note 43 below.

[32]Irish Constitution: Article 40; Indian Constitution: Article 15(3) on women and children and Article 15(4) on other specific categories of disadvantaged persons; Nepali Constitution: Article 11(3); Pakistani Constitution: Article 25(3); Bangladeshi Constitution: Article 28(4); Sri Lankan Constitution: Article 12(4).

[33]*More v State of Bombay* [AIR 1953 Bombay 311]; *Shamima Sultan v Bangladesh* [57 DLR 2005]; *Progress of South Asian Women 2005: A Series for the Fifth South Asian Regional Ministerial Conference Celebrating Beijing Plus Ten*, op.cit.; *Women of the World: Laws and Policies Affecting their Reproductive Rights South Asia*, New York: Center for Reproductive Rights (2004).

[34]Christine Chorine, Mihir Desai and Colin Gonsalves (Eds.) *Women and the Law (Volume I)*, Bombay: Socio-Legal Information Centre (1999); *Government of Andhra Pradesh v Vijayakumar* [1995 11 CLR 128]; *Women of the World: Laws and Policies Affecting their Reproductive Rights South Asia*, op.cit.

[35]*Women of the World: Laws and Policies Affecting their Reproductive Rights South Asia*, op.cit.; Penal Code Amendment (1995) in Sri Lanka.

[36]See discussion on domestic violence in notes below. Legal challenges to women-specific domestic violence legislation in India: Karnik Petition 2005 and Andhra Writ Petition 2005, as per information provided by Lawyer's Collective (Women's Rights Initiative), New Delhi; and challenges in the Philippines: *Rosalie Garcia v Drilon*, Court of Appeals Philippines, 2006 [pending], as per information provided by Attorney Rowena Guanzon.

[37]Savitri W.E. Goonesekere (Ed.), *Violence, Law and Women's Rights in South Asia*, op.cit.

[38]1997 6 SCC 241.

[39]India: Re. sexual harassment: CEDAW cited in *Vishaka v State of Rajasthan* [1997 6 SCC 241]; *Apparel Export Promotion Council v A. K.*

Chopra [1999 1 SC 759]; Re. guardianship: *Githa Hariharan v Reserve Bank of India* [1999 2 SCC 238]. Nepal: Re. rape: *FWLD v HMG Nepal* [Writ No 56/058 2 May 2002]; Re. marital rape and CEDAW: *FWLD v HMG Nepal* [Writ No 55/048 2 May 2002]; re. employment: *Reena Bajracharya v HM Govt. of Nepal* [Writ No 2812/054 1997–1998]; for other Nepali cases, see *Discriminatory Laws in Nepal and their Impact on Women: A Review of the Current Situation and Proposals for Change,* Forum for Women, Law and Development, Kathmandu, Nepal (2006). Also see the Bangalore Principles on Domestic Application of International Human Rights Norms (1988); Commonwealth cases from Australia and the Pacific are considered in *Pacific Human Rights Law Digest (Volume 1)*, Pacific Regional Rights Resource Team, Fiji (2005); Sujatha Manohar in *Bringing International Human Rights Law Home: Judicial Colloquium on the Domestic Application of the Convention on the Elimination of All Forms of Discrimination Against Women and the Convention on the Rights of the Child,* UN Publications (2000); c.f. Pakistan's pending domestic violence bill whose preamble refers to CEDAW; Kirstine Adams and Andrew Byrnes (Eds.), op.cit.; Robyn Emerton, Kirstine Adams *et al* (Eds.), *International Women's Human Rights Cases,* London: Cavendish Publishing (2005).

[40] *Nallaratnam Singarasa v Attorney General* [SC Spl (LA) 182/99 15.9.2006].

[41] Lee Waldorf, *Pathway to Gender Equality: CEDAW, Beijing and the MDGs,* UNIFEM (2004).

[42] See references in Note 9 above.

[43] Inheritance rights (India): *Madhu Kishwar v State of Bihar* [1996 5 SCC 125], Hindu Succession Act 2005; Inheritance rights (Nepal): *Meera Dhungana v Ministry of Law and Justice* [NKP 2052 (1995) Vol 37 462], followed by legislative reform in the 10th Amendment to Muluki Ain (Country Code) 2002; Medical education (Pakistan): *Shirin Munir v Govt of Punjab* [PLD 1990 SC 295]; Public sector appointments (India): *Govt of Andhra Pradesh v Vijayakumar* [1995 11 CLR 128]; Equal powers of women members in reserved seats to a Municipal Authority (Bangladesh): *Shamima Sultan v Bangladesh* [57 DLR 2005 p. 201]; Access to medical colleges (India): *P Sagar v State of Andhra Pradesh* [AIR 1968 AP 165] and other cases on reported in C. Chorine *et al,* op.cit; Pregnancy discrimination (India): *Air India v Nergesh Meezra* [1981 4 SCC 335]; Marital discrimination in foreign service (India): *Muthamma v Union of India and Others* [1979 4 SCC 260]; Retirement age (Nepal): *Reena Bajracharya and Others v HM Govt. Nepal* [Writ No 2812/054 (1997–98)]; Marital discrimination in inheritance (Nepal): *FWLD v Office of Prime Minister Nepal* [Writ No 110/059 July 29, 2004]; Sexual harassment (India): *Vishaka v State of Rajasthan* [1997 6 SCC 241]; Rape (Nepal): *FWLD v HMG Nepal* [Writ No 56/058 2 May

2002]; Marital rape (Nepal): *FWLD v HMG Nepal* [Writ No 55/048 2 May 2002]; *Chhaupadi* pollution custom considered cruel and degrading treatment of women (Nepal): *DNF v HMG Nepal* [Writ 3303/061/2.5.2005]; Government order by the Supreme Court to criminalise torture and ill-treatment of women accused of being witches (Nepal): *Reshma Thapa v HMG Nepal* [SCB 2004/05 volume 12, 24]; Forced marriage (Pakistan): *Humaira Mehmood v The State and Others* [PLD 1999 Lah 494]; Violent sexual abuse in custody (Sri Lanka): *Yogalingam Vijitha v Wijesekere* [SC Appl FR 186/2001]; Gang rape in custody (Sri Lanka): *Volu Arasa Devi v Premathileka and Others* [SC FR 401/2001]; Access to education (India): *Unni Krishnan v State of Andhra Pradesh* [1993 ISC 645], *Mohini Jain v State of Karnataka* [1992 4 SC 292], followed by the 86th Constitution Amendment in 2002 introducing Article 21(A) to recognise access to education from ages 6–14 as a fundamental right and aspect of the right to life; Public Interest Litigation on early marriage (Nepal): *Meera Dhunghana v HMG Nepal* [2006]; Public Interest Litigation on early marriage (India): India case 2002 as reported at the Conference organised by UNICEF and Wellesley Centre for Women, Bangkok, December 2007; Savitri W.E. Goonesekere (Ed.), *Violence, Law and Women's Rights in South Asia*, op.cit.; c.f. Kathleen E. Mahoney, "Gender and the Judiciary: Confronting Gender Bias" in Kirstine Adams and Andrew Byrnes (Eds.), op.cit.

[44]Sujatha Manohar, op.cit.

[45]Hong Kong: Anti Discrimination Law 1995 and Women's Commission; Japan: Equal Employment Opportunity Law 1985; Vietnam: Law on Gender Equity 2006.

[46]Non-State actors in India not covered in *University of Madras v Shantha Bhai* [1954 Mad. 67], but liability is now recognised in cases of inaction on violence against women: *Saheli Women's Resource Centre v Commissioner of Police Delhi* [AIR 1990 SC 513], *Padmini v State of Tamil Nadu* [1993 Cr LJ 2964 (Mad)], *Apparel Export Promotion Council v A.K. Chopra* [1999 1 SC 759], *Bodhisattwa Gautam v Subhra Chakraborty* [AIR 1996 SC 923]; In Sri Lanka, regarding assault of a man by a private person: *Faiz Mohomed v Attorney General* [1995 I Sri LR 372]; For countries outside the region, leading cases are: *Velasquez Rodriguez v State of Honduras* [Inter American Court of Human Rights, July 29, 1988] and *Fernandes v Brazil* [Inter American Commission on Human Rights, April 16, 2001; Cases under the Optional Protocol to CEDAW are: *A.T. v Hungary* [CEDAW Communication No 2/2003, adopted January 26, 2005] and Finding Recommendations in Mexico Inquiry Report [CEDAW/C/2005/OP.8/Mexico, January 27, 2005], regarding the abduction and murder of 300 women in Ciudad Juarez, Mexico.

[47]Savitri W.E. Goonesekere (Ed.), *Violence, Law and Women's Rights in South Asia*, op.cit.; Indira Jaising (Ed.), *Men's Laws, Women's Lives: A*

Constitutional Perspective on Religion, Common Law and Culture in South Asia, New Delhi: Women Unlimited (2005); *Bringing International Human Rights Law Home,* op.cit; Jan Bauer and Anissa Hélie, *Documenting Women's Rights Violations by Non-State Actors*, International Centre For Human Rights and Democratic Development and Women Living Under Muslim Laws, Canada (2006); J. Olaka-Onyango and Deepika Udagama, *Globalization and its Impact on the Full Enjoyment of Human Rights*, Progress report submitted in accordance with Sub-Commission resolution 1999/8 and Commission on Human Rights decision 2000/102, E/CN.4/Sub.2/2001/10, July 2, 2001; *Business and Human Rights*, Harvard Law School (1999).

[48]Savitri Goonesekere (Ed.), *Violence, Law and Women's Rights in South Asia*, op.cit.; *Discriminatory Laws in Nepal and Their Impact on Women: A Review of the Current Situation and Proposals for Change,* op.cit.; Indira Jaising (Ed.), op.cit; Presentations on law reform at the Expert Group Meeting on CEDAW for National Machineries and Senior Law-Making Officials on How to Effectively Integrate and Implement CEDAW at the National Level to Promote the Human Rights of Women, Bangkok (July 2007): (i) Justice Majida Razvi (Pakistan), "Violence against Women: Overcoming the Traditional Resistance to Change and Amending the Hudood Ordinances in Pakistan" [http://www.unescap.org/esid/GAD/Events/EGM-CEDAW2007/Country%20presentation-Pakistan.pdf] and (ii) P. Wangdi (Bhutan), "Gender Justice and Parallel Justice Institutions in Bhutan: The Legal Framework at the National Level for the Implementation of CEDAW" [http://www.unescap.org/esid/GAD/Events/EGM-CEDAW2007/Gender justice-Bhutan.pdf]; Pakistan: Protection of Women Criminal Law Amendment Act 2006 amending the Hudood Ordinance, Human Trafficking Ordinance 2004, Criminal Law Amendment Act 2006 permitting prosecution of honour crimes; Nepal: Citizenship Act 2006; Sri Lanka: Citizenship Amendment Act 2003.

[49]See Note 48 above; Maintenance Act Sri Lanka 1999; Maldives Family Law Code 2003; See the section on Maldives in Part One of the *Report of the Committee on the Elimination of Discrimination against Women*; 24th (January 15–February 2, 2001) and 25th (July 2–20, 2001) Sessions, presented at the UN General Assembly's 56th Session; Supplement No. 38 (A/56/38); United Nations (2001) [http://daccess-dds-ny.un.org/doc/UNDOC/GEN/N01/534/56/PDF/N0153456.pdf?OpenElement].

[50]See Note 48 above; *Bodhisattva Ghautam v Subhra Chakraborthy* [AIR 1996 SC 923] considers rape in cohabitation an infringement of a woman's fundamental right to personal security (India); Citizenship Amendment Act Sri Lanka 2003; Bangladesh Citizenship Act 1951; Pakistan Citizenship Act 1951, amended 2000; Convention on Preventing and Combating Trafficking in Women and Children For

Prostitution Act 2005 (Sri Lanka): a legislation incorporating commitments under the SAARC Convention on Trafficking 2002; Penal Code Act Bhutan 2001.

[51]India's Protection of Women from Domestic Violence Act (2005) is women-specific; Sri Lanka's Prevention of Domestic Violence Act (2005) covers women, children and men; Bangladesh's pending Domestic Violence Bill covers women, children and men; the Preamble to Pakistan's Prevention of Domestic Violence Bill (2005) refers to women, children, the family and CEDAW commitments, but the Act's provisions can cover complaints by men as family members. On challenges to the Indian Act and in the Philippines, see Note 36 above.

[52]General provisions discussed in Savitri W.E. Goonesekere (Ed.), *Violence, Law and Women's Rights in South Asia*, op.cit.; India has a specific offence of cruelty that covers domestic violence: Section 498A of the Indian Penal Code; Sri Lankan law is discussed in Savitri W.E. Goonesekere and Camena Guneratne, *Women, Sexual Violence and the Legal Process in Sri Lanka: A Study on Rape*, Colombo: Centre for Women's Research (1998).

[53]See Note 52 above; *Discriminatory Laws in Nepal and Their Impact on Women: A Review of the Current Situation and Proposals for Change*, op.cit.

[54]*Women of the World: Laws and Policies Affecting their Reproductive Rights South Asia*, op.cit.

[55]Ibid.

[56]CEDAW General Recommendation Number 24 on Article 12 (Health); India: *Air India v Nergesh Meezra* [1981 4 SCC 335] and *Muthamma v Union of India and Others* [1979 4 SCC 260]; *Reena Bajracharya and Others v HM Govt. Nepal* [Writ No 2812/054 (1997–98].

[57]Sri Lanka: Land Development Ordinance (1935), Torture Act (1994), Land Reform Law (1992); Diane Elson, *Budgeting for Women's Rights: Monitoring Government Budgets for Compliance with CEDAW*, UNIFEM (2006); the Indian State of Chattisgarh has a two-child policy for government jobs in engineering and police (Indian Express, June 30, 2007); *Women of the World: Laws and Policies Affecting their Reproductive Rights South Asia*, op.cit.; Savitri W.E. Goonesekere (Ed.), *Violence, Law and Women's Rights in South Asia*, op.cit.

[58]Nepal: *Meera Dhunghana v HMG Nepal* [2006]; India: India case 2002 as reported at the Conference organised by UNICEF and Wellesley Centre for Women, Bangkok, December 2007.

[59]See Note 43 above; *Women of the World: Laws and Policies Affecting their Reproductive Rights South Asia*, op.cit.; The Government of India's Ministry of Human Resource Development (MHRD) is working on the cost of fulfilling the Constitutional guarantee. It is reported that the cost is not as high as estimated as the child population has declined and that the Prime Minister has requested a high level MHRD Committee to

resolve the issue, giving hope that the Constitutional promise will be achieved; Times of India, June 30, 2007 [http://timesofindia.indiatimes.com/India/HRD-scales-down-cost-of-education-to-all/articleshow/2162921.cms] [Editor's Note: In April 2010, India passed the Right of Children to Free and Compulsory Education Act (2009). The Act gives effect to Article 21A of the Indian Constitution, which recognises the right to education as a fundamental right. Under the Act, all children in the age group of 6–14 years shall have the right to free and compulsory education.]

[60]Savitri W.E. Goonesekere (Ed.), *Violence, Law and Women's Rights in South Asia*, op.cit.; *Women of the World: Laws and Policies Affecting their Reproductive Rights South Asia*, op.cit.; *Report on the Regional Thematic Meeting on Violence Against Women*, op.cit.

[61]Contradictory positions have been taken in India: *State of Bombay v Navasu Appa Malli* [AIR 52 Bom 84] and *Nalini Ranjan Singh v State of Bihar* [AIR 77 PAT 171], regarding personal laws not subject to scrutiny; *Ahmedebad Action Group v Union of India* [1997 3 SC 171], regarding Muslim personal law not subject to review, though contrary obiter dicta in *Masilamani Mudaliyar v Idol of Sri SS Thirukovil* [1996 8 SCC 525]; *Madhu Kishwar v State of Bihar* [1996 5 SCC 125] and *Daniel Latifi v Union of India* [2001 7 SCC 740], regarding efforts to balance conflicting rights to accommodate women's right to equality and right to life; Sri Lanka: *Ghouse v Ghouse* [1988 1 Sri L 25], regarding adoption and Sri Lankan Muslim's inheritance rights accommodated by interpretation; For efforts to accommodate equality and tradition in Nepal, see: *Meera Dhunghana v Ministry of Law and Justice* [NKP 2052 (1995) Vol 37 462]; For cases striking down customary law, see: *FWLD v Office of Prime Minister Nepal* 2004 [Writ No 110/059 July 29, 2004], striking down a new provision in the reformed Country Code requiring forfeiture of share inherited by a daughter after marriage and *DNF v HMG Nepal* [Writ No 3303/061 May 2, 2005], holding the *chhaupadi* custom as inhuman and degrading treatment in violation of Constitutional rights.

[62]*FWLD v Office of Prime Minister Nepal* [Writ No 110/059 July 29, 2004]; *DNF v HMG Nepal* [Writ No 3303/061 May 2, 2005]; *Shamima Sultan v Bangladesh* [57 DLR 2005 p. 201]; *Mudgal v Union of India* [1995 3 SCC 635], followed in Sri Lanka by *Abeysundera v Abeysundera* [1998 1 Sri L 185], which overruled the Privy Council decision in 1964 67 NLR 25 by holding that unilateral conversion does not give a married man the right to practice polygamy; *Mohamed Ahamed Khan v Shah Bano Begum* [AIR 1985 SC 945], regarding Muslim women's right to maintenance under applicable legislation; *Humaira Mehmood v The State and Others* [PLD 1999 Lah 494].

[63]Savitri W.E. Goonesekere and Camena Guneratne, op.cit.; *FWLD v Office of Prime Minister Nepal* [Writ No 110/059 July 29, 2004].

[64]See the section on Maldives, specifically paragraphs 140 and 141, in Part One of the *Report of the Committee on the Elimination of Discrimination against Women*; 24th (January 15–February 2, 2001) and 25th (July 2–20, 2001) Sessions, presented at the UN General Assembly's 56th Session; op.cit.; See the section on India, specifically paragraphs 60 and 61, in Part One of the *Report of the Committee on the Elimination of Discrimination against Women*; 22nd (January 17–February 4, 2000) and 23rd (June 12–30, 2000) Sessions; presented at the UN General Assembly's 55th Session; Supplement No. 38 (A/55/38); United Nations (2000) [http://daccess-dds-ny.un.org/doc/UNDOC/GEN/N00/611/52/PDF/N0061152.pdf?OpenElement].

[65]Shaheen Sardar Ali, op.cit.; Emna Aouij, "Marriage and Family Relations" in *Bringing International Human Rights Law Home*, op.cit.

[66]*Deshapriya v Captain Weerakoon, Commanding Officer, Sri Lanka Navy Ship "Gemunu" and Others* [2003 2 Sri LR 99]; *Lal (Deceased) and Ranee Fernando and Others v OIC Seeduwa Police* [2005 1 Sri LR 40].

[67]See the section on India, specifically paragraph 72, in Part One of the *Report of the Committee on the Elimination of Discrimination against Women*; 22nd (January 17–February 4, 2000) and 23rd (June 12–30, 2000) Sessions; presented at the UN General Assembly's 55th Session; op.cit.; NGO Shadow Report to CEDAW Committee (January 2000).

[68]See the section on India, specifically paragraphs 62–65, in Part One of the *Report of the Committee on the Elimination of Discrimination against Women*; 22nd (January 17–February 4, 2000) and 23rd (June 12–30, 2000) Sessions; presented at the UN General Assembly's 55th Session; op.cit.; See the section on Nepal, specifically paragraphs 140–141 and 147, in Part Two of the *Report of the Committee on the Elimination of Discrimination against Women*; 20th (January 19–February 5, 1999) and 21st (June 7–25, 1999) Sessions; presented at the UN General Assembly's 54th Session; Supplement No. 38 (A/54/38/Rev. 1); United Nations (1999) [http://daccess-dds-ny.un.org/doc/UNDOC/GEN/N99/240/61/PDF/N9924061.pdf?OpenElement].

[69]See Notes 43 and 59 above.

[70]Dianne Elson, op.cit., refers to initiatives of the Karnataka Women's Information and Resource Centre in India.

[71]Dianne Elson, op.cit.

[72]Justice Rosalie Abella of the Ontario Court of Appeal, as cited by Kathleen E. Mahoney, "Canadian Approaches to Equality Rights" in Rebecca Cook (Ed.), op.cit.

4 Gender Equality, Religion and the State[1]

Zarizana Abdul Aziz

Background

Malaysia was formed in 1963 consisting of 13 states and three federal territories. A Federal Constitution was adopted in 1957. In Article 4, the Constitution declares itself to be "the supreme law of the Federation and any law passed after [Independence] Day which is inconsistent with this Constitution shall, to the extent of the inconsistency, be void". In Article 3, it also stipulates that, "Islam is the religion of the Federation; but other religions may be practised in peace and harmony in any part of the Federation". Part II defines the fundamental liberties enjoyed by the citizens of the Federation which include equality, freedom of speech, assembly and association, freedom of religion and rights to education and property and liberty of a person. It also prohibits slavery and forced labour.

In September 2001, the Malaysian Federal Constitution was amended to prohibit discrimination on the ground of gender. Gender now joined other prohibited grounds of discrimination, namely, religion, race, descent or place of birth. The amended Article 8(2) now reads, "Except as expressly authorised by this Constitution, there shall be no discrimination against citizens on the ground only of religion, race, descent, place of birth or gender in any law or in the appointment of any office or employment under a public authority or in the administration of any law relating to the acquisition, holding or disposition of property or the establishing or carrying on of any trade, business, profession, vocation or employment".

In conjunction with the Fourth World Conference on Women, Malaysia ratified the Convention on the Elimination of All Forms of Discrimination against Women (CEDAW) with reservations[2] in 1995.

The original reservations read:

> The Government of Malaysia declares that Malaysia's accession is subject to the understanding that the provisions of the Convention do not conflict with the provisions of the Islamic Sharia' law and the Federal Constitution of Malaysia. With regards thereto, further, the Government of Malaysia does not consider itself bound by the provisions of Articles 2(f), 5(a), 7(b), 9 and 16 of the aforesaid Convention. In relation to Article 11, Malaysia interprets the provisions of this Article as a reference to the prohibition of discrimination on the basis of equality between men and women only.

On February 6, 1998, the Government of Malaysia withdrew its reservations with respect to Articles 2(f), 9(1), 16(1)(b), 16(1)(d), 16(1)(e) and 16(1)(h). Malaysia also made a commitment to review its other reservations. As of the date of publication, however, the remaining reservations have not been withdrawn.

This chapter addresses the following issues:

- Whether a constitutional provision on fundamental liberties is effective in delivering equality and the adequacy of Article 8(2) in prohibiting gender discrimination and promoting equality;
- The effect of Article 4 read together with Article 3 of the Malaysian Constitution;
- Judicial interpretation of equality and discrimination;
- The need to legislate on gender equality; and
- Non-discrimination and Muslim personal laws.

Constitutionality and the prohibition against discrimination

Constitutions by and large seek to set out the limits of governmental powers and the responsibility to protect citizens' rights. They constitute the framework for official action affecting the individual and collective fundamental rights and liberties within the state.[3] In this regard, the state's action is clearly regulated and its powers circumscribed by the constitution. Courts interpret the legality and validity of state actions with reference to the written word of the constitution.

In a democracy, a constitution serves to soften the demarcation between the rulers and the ruled by removing arbitrariness and providing guarantees to the people. In this regard, the constitution is oriented to a certain fixed objective of public good according to which society has agreed to be governed. This objective of public good, however, can vary over time and place. The constitution, under all circumstances, must be a living document which reflects the will of the governed rather than that of the government and imposes obligations on the government to guarantee the rights of its citizens.

The Malaysian Constitution sets out to guarantee fundamental liberties in Part II. Equality before the law is set out in Article 8(1). Article 8(2) prohibits discrimination of citizens in specifically enumerated areas.

Still, the prohibition of discrimination is inherently narrow. First, the prohibition states that, "[T]here shall be no discrimination against citizens on the ground only of religion, race, descent, place of birth or gender". In cases of multiple discrimination – for example, if a person is discriminated against on the basis of her gender and hearing impairment – then, arguably, Article 8(2) does not apply.

Second, it prohibits discrimination only "in any law or in the appointment of any office or employment under a public authority or in the administration of any law relating to the acquisition, holding or disposition of property or the establishing or carrying on of any trade, business, profession, vocation or employment". It appears that the defining criterion under Article 8(2) is state control, i.e., discrimination is prohibited only in areas that are within the state's control. Article 8(2), therefore, imposes effective limits on state power. Defining the areas of prohibited discrimination in this manner is indicative of the reluctance of the Constitution in expressly prohibiting discrimination by non-state actors.

The protection afforded by a constitution exclusively against the vagaries of the state is known as the "vertical effect" of the constitution. Whilst debates rage in other jurisdictions as to whether rights regulate only the conduct of state actors in their dealings with the individual or whether they also regulate relationships between private individuals, Article 8(2) of the Malaysian Constitution is so narrowly set out that Malaysian courts have declined to expand the applicability of this Article to non-state actors and, instead, strictly limit its applicability to state actors.[4]

Third, therefore, the Constitution implicitly or expressly allows for discrimination in several instances. Article 8(2) limits itself to employment under a public authority and does not expressly include employment in the private sector. Article 12(1) prohibits discrimination in education, but was not amended to include gender as a prohibited ground. Provisions on citizenship, namely Articles 14, 15, 24(4) and 26(2), continue to discriminate against women in relation to women's rights to confer citizenship and permanent residence status on their children and husband respectively.

Fourth, Article 8(5) expressly provides that the prohibition of discrimination clauses do not invalidate or prohibit any provision regulating personal law. Muslim personal laws are regulated by the syariah courts administered by the individual States and Federal Territories (there are 14 separate jurisdictions). Thus, Article 8(5) effectively leaves Muslim personal laws unaffected by the prohibition against discrimination and Muslim women particularly vulnerable to legal interpretations that discriminate on the basis of gender.

Finally, Article 8(2) does not impose any positive obligation on the state to promote, protect and fulfill rights, but merely imposes a negative obligation on it not to discriminate on specific grounds. Under the circumstances, the Constitution is wholly inadequate as a charter where citizens may claim their rights. A new law is needed.

The Malaysian Constitution: secular, theocratic or hybrid

Whilst the Constitution, in Article 4, declares itself as the supreme law, it does not exist nor was it created without appeal or reference to other laws, norms, values and instruments. Rather, the Constitution, in proclaiming itself the supreme law, distinguishes between the values, norms and morals that are religious, ethical or cultural on the one hand, and legal principles on the other. Only the latter are recognised by law and are legally enforceable.

Article 3 provides that Islam is the religion of the Federation. Does this provision have any adverse effect on gender equality given that discrimination against women was quite common before the advent of Islam, and the syariah, while restricting the incidence and reducing the scope of gender discrimination, did not eliminate such discrimination in principle? Of course the historical and social landscape at that time was different. What was reasonable and acceptable then may not necessarily be reasonable and acceptable today and vice versa.[5] As reasoned by An-Na'im, people may differ in their view of the historical sufficiency of any justification that may be offered for any particular instance of discrimination.[6]

Still, whether Article 3 affects the status of and discrimination against women is dependant on the relative status of Articles 3 and 4 as the religion and law of the

Federation respectively, i.e., is the Constitution or Article 3 the supreme law of the Federation? In order to interrogate this, it is crucial that we locate the reasons proffered for the inclusion of Article 3 as well as the expectation that Malaysians invest in the Constitution today.

Article 3 was the result of negotiations following proposals submitted by the Alliance [a coalition consisting of the major political parties in Malaysia: United Malay National Organisation (UMNO), Malaysian Chinese Association (MCA) and Malaysian Indian Congress (MIC) each representing Malaysians of the Malay, Chinese and Indian ethnic origins respectively] to the Reid Commission which was charged with drafting the Constitution.

In proposing that Islam be made the religion of the Federation, the Alliance clarified that, "the religion of Malaya shall be Islam. The observance of this principle shall not impose any disability on non-Muslim nationals professing and practising their own religion and shall not imply that the State is not a secular State".

The first Malaysian Prime Minister, Tunku Abdul Rahman, stated in Parliament that, "I would like to make it clear that this country is not an Islamic State as it is generally understood, we merely provided that Islam shall be the official religion of the State." [7]

Subsequent court rulings have supported this view. In the case of *Che Omar bin Che Soh* v *Public Prosecutor*,[8] the court said,

> The question here [whether the mandatory death sentence imposed on the accused was against the injunctions of Islam and therefore unconstitutional] is this: Was this the meaning intended by the framers of the Constitution? For this purpose it is necessary to trace the history of Islam in this country after the British intervention …
>
> When the British came, through a series of treaties with the sultans…the religion of Islam became separated into two aspects, viz, the public aspect and the private aspect. The development of the public aspect had left Islam as a mere adjunct to the ruler's

> power and sovereignty...Thus it can be seen that during the British colonial period, through their system of indirect rule and establishment of secular institutions, Islamic law was rendered isolated in a narrow confinement of the law of marriage, divorce and inheritance only. ...
>
> In our view, it is in this sense of dichotomy that the framers of the Constitution understood the meaning of the word "Islam" in the context of Article 3. If it had been otherwise, there would have been another provision in the Constitution which would have the effect that any law contrary to the injunction of Islam will be void. Far from making such provision, Article 162, on the other hand, purposely preserves the continuity of secular law prior to the Constitution, unless such law is contrary to the latter.

In other words, the court held that to constitute an Islamic state it is insufficient for a constitution to merely provide that the religion of the Federation shall be Islam. The constitution would have to go further to subordinate itself to the injunctions of Islam and declare that any provision contrary to the injunctions of Islam is void.

Such provisions can be seen in the constitutions of Iraq[9] and Afghanistan.[10] The constitution of Pakistan imposes a duty of the State to enable Muslims to live the Islamic way of life.[11] Such provisions are conspicuously absent in the Malaysian Federal Constitution.

The court's decision was echoed by Tun Mohamed Suffian Hashim, Lord President of Malaysia (1974–1982), in his article "The Relationship between Islam and the State in Malaysia" in 1962. Tun Suffian was of the view that Islam in Malaysia "is primarily for ceremonial purposes, for instance, to enable prayers to be offered in the Islamic way on official public occasions such as the installation of the birthday of the Yang di-Pertuan Agong [King], Independence Day and similar occasions".

According to former Chief Justice, Tan Sri Hashim Yeop Sani, "The words 'Islam is the religion of the Federation' appearing in Clause 1 of that Article has no legal effect and that the intention was probably to impose conditions on federal ceremonies to be conducted according to Muslim rites".[12]

Whether Malaysia is a theocratic state or otherwise has a profound impact on the understanding of constitutionalism in Malaysia and the universal applicability of Article 8 of the Constitution. The interpretation given by the court in *Che Som* was by and large unquestioningly accepted until Tun Mahathir Mohamad, then Prime Minister of Malaysia, declared, in June 2002, Malaysia to be not only an Islamic state, but also a model Islamic state.[13]

While many believe that Mahathir's declaration was a political manoeuvre to counter his detractors' claims – in particular, those of the conservative Islamic Party of Malaysia that Mahathir's UMNO had failed the Malay Muslim – predictably, such a sweeping statement did not go unnoticed, especially by other opposition political parties and Malaysian Muslims, as well as citizens of other faiths.

Five years later, the Deputy Prime Minister, Dato' Sri Mohd. Najib Abdul Razak, echoed Mahathir and described Malaysia as an Islamic state.[14] Almost immediately, the government issued a directive to all mainstream media not to publish any news on or debate the issue of whether Malaysia was an Islamic state. "Reaction from political parties and the public cannot be published especially the negative reactions," said a spokesman from the Internal Security Ministry.[15]

In August 2007, almost on the eve of the 50th anniversary of Independence, the Prime Minister Abdullah Ahmad Badawi said, in what appears to be a 'politically safe' reply to a parliamentary question, that Malaysia is neither a secular nor a theocratic state, but an Islamic[16] state administered on Islamic principles and at the same time adheres to the principles of parliamentary democracy and is guided by the supreme law of the land, the Federal Constitution.[17]

The question here is not only whether Malaysia is a non-secular, non-theocratic, hybrid state, but also who should determine the status of Malaysia. Should a politician, even if he is the Prime Minister, be able to make the determination and should such a determination be elevated to the status of a decree?

In any event, despite exhortations that Malaysia is an Islamic state, what appears to be the consensus is that Malaysia is not a theocratic state by virtue of the fact that the Federal Constitution is the supreme law of the country. Consequently, whatever other status is accorded to Malaysia – whether that of a secular state as held by the court in *Che Som* or a hybrid and undetermined form of non-theocratic Islamic state as maintained by three successive Prime Ministers[18] – should not affect the constitutional arguments about equality and discrimination pursuant to Articles 8(1) or 8(2). Neither does it alter the effect of Article 8(5) which excludes the applicability of Article 8 in relation to (Muslim) personal laws, which are administered by the syariah courts pursuant to Article 121(1A) of the Constitution.

Marriage, divorce and Article 121(1A)

In recent years and particularly after tireless lobbying by women's groups in Malaysia, many of the Constitution's legal provisions which were detrimental towards or discriminatory against women were amended. The effect of these amendments was to recognise women's equal rights in marriage and divorce, guardianship of children, equal entitlement to social security and inheritance as well as protection of insurance policies.[19] The amendments also acknowledged a putative father's obligation to maintain children born out of wedlock. In a subsequent amendment, the provision limiting the amount a putative father could be ordered to pay was repealed.

The benefit of many of these amendments has, however, been denied to Muslim women.

Under the Ninth Schedule of the Constitution, Islamic law and personal and family law of persons professing the religion of Islam, including the Islamic law relating to succession, testate and intestate, betrothal, marriage, divorce, dower, maintenance, adoption, legitimacy and guardianship are within the legislative jurisdiction of the respective states of the Federation and are administered by syariah courts. Thus, the equal rights of men and women which were brought about through the series of legislative amendments to civil (common) law mentioned above are not available to Muslim women.

Thus, a Muslim man may marry up to four wives at the same time but a Muslim woman may marry only one man at a time. A Muslim man may divorce his wife by pronouncing *talaq* (repudiation of marriage) without having to give any reasons or justify his actions, while a Muslim woman can obtain divorce only by consent of her husband or by judicial decree on limited grounds or a pre-negotiated contractual condition of the marriage upon the occurrence of certain events. Regarding the maintenance of children born out of wedlock, Muslim fathers are exempt from Constitutional provisions and to date there is no provision to either compel a Muslim putative father to provide for his child or for the State-administered religious fund (*Baitulmal*) to do so. Guardianship of a Muslim child is vested with his or her father and, upon the father's death, with the father's relatives. A Muslim mother, though she may have custody, is not the guardian of her child. By amendments passed in 1996, the proceeds of any insurance policy maintained by a Muslim man for the benefit of his wife or children shall not vest in the named beneficiaries but be subject to distribution in accordance with Muslim distribution rules.[20] Muslim distribution rules provide for unequal distribution in favour of male heirs, contrary to the equal rights to inheritance provided under civil laws.

In relation to matrimonial assets, however, the rights of Muslim women are modified by the cultural practice[21] of jointly acquired property (*harta sepencarian*) which allows women to claim a share of all property jointly acquired by the parties during the marriage. In assessing each party's contribution to the acquisition of the property, the syariah courts recognise both economic and financial contribution as well as non-economic and non-financial contribution.

The gap between the rights of Muslim women and those of women of other faiths is further exacerbated by different rules set up for Muslims. These rules are issued either as policies by the religious authorities or *fatwas* by the various *fatwa* councils and committees. *Fatwas* may be adopted by the respective State legislatures and, if adopted, may be gazetted to become legally binding.

For example, in 2003, a *fatwa* was issued that it was lawful for a husband to pronounce divorce by email or mobile phone text messaging (SMS).[22] There was general dissatisfaction amongst women's groups who felt that divorce, like marriage, should be undertaken with due dignity and solemnity and SMS or email have no place in this process. The *fatwa* on SMS divorce is yet another example of the easing of divorce requirements – compare this to the civil law requirement that compels couples to obtain a court decree for divorce where all ancillary matters like maintenance and arrangement for the children are simultaneously dealt with.

The question of equality for Muslim women within the family must be initiated from within the State's syariah system of laws. A separate and parallel initiative must, therefore, be commenced to address the issue of equality within the Muslim family.[23]

Judicial interpretation of equality and discrimination

The Constitution, while upholding equality and prohibiting discrimination, does not define the meaning of "equality" or "discrimination". In the absence of any other legislative instrument defining discrimination, it is left to the courts to define discrimination and particularise the instances in which discrimination can be held to have occurred.

As mentioned earlier, Malaysia ratified CEDAW, with reservations, in 1995. While CEDAW provides a comprehensive understanding of equality and discrimination, under the dualist legal system adopted by Malaysia, a ratified treaty is not part of domestic Malaysian law unless and until it is passed as legislation by parliament. Although small windows have opened where Malaysian courts have referred to international human rights treaty obligations,[24] this is still a far cry from the courts actually enforcing these obligations.

The adoption of a dualist legal system is shared by many common law countries. While the principle is admirable in that it protects the people and the parliament from executive action – in matters of human rights, the non-incorporation of international human rights norms into domestic law means that human rights treaties are not self-executing and cannot operate as an independent source of individual rights and liberties.

Until Malaysia passes legislation to adopt CEDAW and make it enforceable in domestic courts, courts are not bound to enforce CEDAW or even apply the principles of substantive equality described in the treaty. The Malaysian courts have, instead, adopted their own interpretation of equality and discrimination as can be discerned in the case of *Beatrice Fernandez v Sistem Penerbangan Malaysia*.[25] The case traversed the Malaysian courts, ending in the apex Federal Court of Malaysia in 2005, 11 years after its commencement.

Briefly, the facts of the case are as follows. Beatrice was employed as a flight stewardess by Malaysian Airlines. According to a collective agreement between the airlines and its union in 1988 which applied to Beatrice's employment, Beatrice was required to resign if she became pregnant, failing which she could be dismissed. When Beatrice became pregnant, Malaysian Airlines asked her to resign. Beatrice refused. In 1991, the airline terminated Beatrice's services.

Beatrice applied to the court to have her dismissal declared wrongful and to have the collective agreement provisions requiring her to resign upon becoming pregnant declared invalid. By the time Beatrice's case was argued before the courts, the Constitutional amendments prohibiting discrimination on the grounds of gender had been passed. Beatrice argued that the collective agreement discriminated against her as a woman and that the relevant provision requiring her to resign was unconstitutional.

Was Beatrice discriminated against?

The Court of Appeal answered this in the negative saying, "we do not think that it can be argued that Article 2(3) of the First Schedule of the collective agreement is discriminatory just as it cannot reasonably be argued that the provision of the law giving maternity leave only to women is discriminatory as against men".[26]

The Federal Court upheld this finding saying:

> [T]he job requirements of flight stewardesses are quite different from that of women in other occupations...We take judicial notice that the nature of the job requires flight stewardesses to work long hours and often flying across different time zones. They have to do much walking on board flying aircrafts. It is certainly not a conducive place for pregnant women to be in.
>
> The applicant cannot compare herself with the ground staff or with the senior chief stewardesses or chief stewardesses as they were not employed in the same category of work.
>
> ...our hands are tied. The equal protection in Clause (1) of Article 8 thereof extends only to persons in the same class. It recognizes that all persons by nature, attainment, circumstances and the varying needs of different classes of persons often require separate treatment. Regardless of how we try to interpret Article 8 of the Federal Constitution, we could only come to the conclusion that there was obviously no contravention.

The comparator

It is interesting that the comparison argued before the Court and ultimately adopted by it to determine whether discrimination had occurred was not between a man and woman but between a stewardess and a chief stewardess. This choice may well find its reasoning in the difficulty of framing a male comparator in a pregnancy situation. Pregnancy is a social function which can only be discharged by women. There is no similarly situated male equivalent/comparator, thus perhaps prompting the lawyers as well as judges to compare Beatrice not to a male flight steward, but to a female chief stewardess. The absence of a male comparator may also have compelled the Court to conclude that female flight stewardesses are a separate class of workers who require separate treatment.

With due respect, courts in other jurisdictions have argued discrimination on the grounds of pregnancy differently. Compare the Malaysian dicta to that in *Brooks* v *Canada Safeway Ltd,*[27] where the Supreme Court, in finding that unequal treatment due to pregnancy offends the principle of equality, said:

> I venture to think that the response to that question by a non-legal person would be immediate and affirmative. In retrospect, one can only ask – how could pregnancy discrimination be anything other than sex discrimination?...It is only women who bear children; no man can become pregnant. As I argued earlier, it is unfair to impose all of the costs of pregnancy upon one half of the population. It is difficult to conceive that distinctions or discriminations based upon pregnancy could ever be regarded as other than discrimination based upon sex, or that restrictive statutory conditions applicable only to pregnant women did not discriminate against them as women...Thus, mere equality of application to similarly situated groups or individuals does not afford a realistic test for a violation of equality rights...The denial of benefits was the result of her pregnancy. Since pregnancy is a condition to which only women are vulnerable, the denial should have been characterized as sexual discrimination...discrimination against some women should not be treated any differently than discrimination against all women...It may be unduly restrictive and somewhat artificial to argue that a distinction based on a characteristic such as pregnancy, which is shared only by some members of a group, is not discrimination against the whole group...for discrimination which is aimed at or has its effect upon

> some people in a particular group as opposed to the whole of that group is not any the less discriminatory. This point was made by a board of inquiry...in the case of *Zarankin* v *Johnstone* (1984)... wherein the board stated: "an employer who selects only some of his female employees for sexual harassment and leaves other female employees alone is discriminating by reason of sex because the harassment affects only one group adversely".

Adopting the reasoning in *Brooks*, it can be argued that whilst both men and women can become parents, the manner in which each becomes a parent is different. In this instance we have a contractual document that looks at the differences between people and penalises one group of people because of that difference. Thus, under the test laid out in *Brooks*, what Malaysian Airlines did constituted gender discrimination.

In dismissing another employer's argument that the dismissal of a pregnant employee was not due to her pregnancy but due to her inability to work, the European Court of Justice said, "In circumstances such as those of Mrs Webb, termination of a contract for an indefinite period on grounds of the woman's pregnancy cannot be justified by the fact that she is prevented, on a purely temporary basis, from performing the work for which she has been engaged".[28]

As the theory of equality requires that nobody be discriminated against because of his/her difference, it similarly recognises that unless provisions are made for pregnancy – such as childbirth benefits – women would suffer loss of income and extra expenditure. The fact that these benefits are not made available to men is not discriminatory as equality ensures that nobody should be prejudiced because of his/her differences.

Vertical effect of the Constitution

What is the effect of a constitutional guarantee of equality under the law and prohibition of discrimination on the basis of gender? Quoting with approval from an Indian text book on constitutional law, the Court of Appeal in *Beatrice Fernandez* held that, "[t]he very concept of a 'fundamental right' involves State action. It is a right guaranteed by the State for the protection of an individual against arbitrary invasion of such right by the State. Where the invasion is by another private individual, the aggrieved individual may have his remedies under private law, but the constitutional remedy would not be available".[29]

This was confirmed by the Federal Court, the apex court in Malaysia: "We found that it is simply not possible to expand the scope of Article 8 of the Federal Constitution to cover collective agreements such as the one in question. To invoke Article 8 of the Federal Constitution, the applicant must show that some law or action of the Executive discriminates against her so as to controvert her rights under the said Article. Constitutional law, as a branch of public law, deals with the contravention of individual rights by the Legislature or the Executive or its agencies. Constitutional law does not extend its substantive or procedural provisions to infringements of an individual's legal right by another individual".[30]

The interpretation accorded by the Malaysian courts on the constitutional effect is called the "vertical effect" which essentially stipulates that constitutional law, as a branch of public law, only addresses the contravention of an individual's rights by a public authority. Where the rights of a private individual are infringed by another private individual, constitutional law (substantive or procedural) will take no cognisance of it. The opposite interpretation – i.e., that the constitution affects private dealings between individuals – is known as the "horizontal effect" and has been adopted to varying degrees in other common law and civil law jurisdictions.[31] It was, for instance, adopted in the landmark Indian case of *Vishaka & Ors* v *State of Rajashtan & Ors.*[32]

This case was initiated after an alleged brutal gang rape of a social worker in a village in the Indian state of Rajasthan. *Vishaka* was a class action by social activists and NGOs which sought to focus attention on gender equality. The alleged rape exposed the urgency of curtailing the hazards to which a working woman was subjected. The aim of the legal action was to prevent sexual harassment of working women in all work places – to use the judicial process to fill the vacuum in existing legislation.

In its ruling, the Indian Supreme Court gave a broad meaning to constitutional guarantees:

> Each incident of sexual harassment of woman at workplace results in violation of the fundamental rights...Gender equality includes protection from sexual harassment and the right to work with dignity, which is a universally recognised basic human right. The common minimum requirement of this right has received global acceptance. The international conventions and norms, are therefore, of great significance in the formulation of the guidelines to achieve this purpose...*The meaning and content of the fundamental rights guaranteed in the Constitution of India are of sufficient amplitude to encompass all the facets of gender equality including prevention of sexual harassment or abuse.* [emphasis added]

In contrast, the case of *Beatrice Fernandez* raised concerns regarding the narrow application of a Constitutional prohibition against gender discrimination. *Beatrice Fernandez* set a precedent which not only entrenched the vertical effect of constitutional guarantees in Malaysian law, but also a narrow and literal understanding of equality and discrimination.

The common law tradition

A common law country is defined by the ability of judges not only to interpret legislation but also to make law. Reviewing jurisprudence from common law countries (a tradition shared by Malaysia), it is clear that many countries (such as India, Australia, United Kingdom and Hong Kong) are developing their jurisprudence towards a strong respect for human rights and international human rights norms, using the common law itself, rather than their constitutions, as the source.[33]

In some of these countries, the courts have developed and proclaimed fundamental human rights to be inherent in the common law, without reference to parliamentary instruments: "some rights are inherent and fundamental to democratic civilised society. Conventions, constitutions, bills of rights and the like respond by recognising rather than creating them".[34]

For this reason, there have been efforts in other jurisdictions to temper the effects of the dualist legal system theory particularly where human rights are concerned. Reference to this can be found, for example, in the *Vishaka* judgement:[35]

> Independence of the judiciary forms a part of our constitutional scheme. The international conventions and norms are to be read into them in the absence of enacted domestic law occupying the field when there is no inconsistency between them and there is a void in the domestic law. The High Court of Australia in *Minister for Immigration and Ethnic Affairs* v *Teoh*[36] has recognised the concept of legitimate expectation of its observance in the absence of a contrary legislative provision, even in the absence of a Bill of Rights in the Constitution of Australia. In view of the above, and the absence of enacted law to provide for the effective enforcement of the basic human right of gender equality and guarantee against sexual harassment at workplaces, we lay down the guidelines and norms specified hereinafter for due observance at all workplaces or other institutions, until a legislation is enacted for the purpose.

Taking the *Vishaka* and *Teoh* judgements as persuasive precedents,[37] it is possible to argue that upon Malaysia's ratification of CEDAW, a legitimate expectation was created that the government would observe and enforce the basic human right of gender equality, with or without domestic legislation. The courts can then declare the rights articulated in CEDAW as applicable in the domestic Malaysian context.

Not only was the *Beatrice Fernandez* judgement a lost opportunity for the Malaysian courts to adopt a more contemporary understanding of gender equality and constitutional effect, it was also a lost opportunity for the courts to explore the extent to which common law itself could be used as a source of fundamental rights.

The proposed Malaysian gender equality legislation

Despite its dualist system, Malaysia is not excused from implementing CEDAW as it is a well established principle of international law that once a State ratifies an international treaty, it is bound to implement the treaty provisions in good faith.[38] Whether or not the treaty has been incorporated into domestic law does not alter the State's obligation internationally[39] and Malaysia continues to be interrogated internationally on its failure to implement CEDAW.

In considering the Malaysian Government's report at the 35th session of the CEDAW Committee in 2006, the Committee stressed that Malaysia needed new laws directed specifically at eliminating sex and gender discrimination and recommended that a nationwide mechanism be created to fully guarantee the rights of Malaysian women.

Gender equality legislation is imperative as Malaysian courts have yet to take cognisance of legal judicial developments in other States such as the horizontal effect of the Constitution, substantive equality, legitimate expectation of accessibility by citizens to human rights guarantees under ratified international treaties as well as the centrality of human rights including equality and non-discrimination in national jurisprudence. While it is important to refer to the Constitution as a source of protection of individual rights and freedom, as shown in the *Beatrice Fernandez* case, the Constitution in itself does not afford sufficient protection of women against discrimination. Thus far, neither the Courts nor the government of Malaysia have accorded women comprehensive legal protection from or redress for discrimination on the basis of gender.

Gender equality in both the public and private spheres should be implemented through comprehensive laws with effective remedies if violated. The proposed gender equality legislation must make unequivocally clear that the objective of gender equality shall be applicable in all circumstances.

Chief amongst the concerns to be addressed is the definition and understanding of gender equality, both formal and substantive (equality of opportunity, access and results). Special attention must also be given to the definition of discrimination, both direct and indirect. Discrimination itself must be defined in broad terms and must exclude special protection of women due to pregnancy, childbirth and breastfeeding from the definition of unlawful discrimination.

The legislation must categorically make unlawful discrimination on the basis of gender, irrespective of whether gender forms the sole ground for discrimination or otherwise, and irrespective of whether the discrimination is direct or indirect. This protection must apply regardless of who the perpetrator of such discrimination may be.

The legislation must also adopt CEDAW and grant it the force of law in Malaysia and, for that purpose the legislation must be construed in accordance with the provisions of CEDAW. The gender equality legislation cannot merely refer to CEDAW,[40] but it must categorically state that the purpose of the legislation is to adopt and implement the provisions articulated in CEDAW.

In its promulgation, the legislation must pay special attention to address the legal issues raised in *Beatrice Fernandez* as well as pre-empt any attempt to refer to extraneous sources to whittle away the effect and purpose of the legislation.

The implementation of the gender equality law cannot be restricted by societal beliefs, even if religion is cited as the reason for such beliefs. The rejection of religion as a ground for denying gender equality is supported by many traditional and contemporary religious intellectuals and scholars. In deciding between conflicting opinions, it is important to keep in mind that most religious philosophies uphold justice, equality and equity. Furthermore, many countries of different religious persuasions have found ways to reconcile custom and religion with gender equality.

The legislation must also provide for temporary special measures to facilitate the objective of gender equality where systemic biases exist.

Past or existing mechanisms have been unable to deliver gender equality. A dynamic, independent and effective national mechanism like a Gender Equality Commission must be set up to guarantee women's rights. This mechanism must be transparent and free from political influences. The mechanism must be vested with sufficient authority and power to enforce the provisions of the legislation and be accountable to Parliament with its reports and recommendations tabled, considered and debated by Parliament.[41]

The gender equality legislation must also provide that the legislation shall prevail in the event of conflict with any other law. This will avoid the necessity of auditing and amending all laws and regulations. However, as a legislation cannot prevail where it conflicts with the Federal Constitution, which is the supreme law of the federation, simultaneously with the tabling of the gender equality legislation, amendments to the Federal Constitution must be tabled to remove all discriminatory provisions in the Constitution.

In fact, women's groups in Malaysia have prepared a draft of the proposed Gender Equality Act, but the government has declined to consider tabling such an Act. A brief overview of the proposed Act is as follows.

The Act is divided into nine parts.

Part I contains the preliminaries which incorporate government policy on gender equality and gender discrimination, the basic objectives of the Act, the applicability of international human rights treaties, in particular CEDAW, and the relationship between the proposed Act and other laws (in the event of conflict the provisions of the Act shall prevail).

A broad definition of equality and discrimination is also included, taking into account legal theories and jurisprudence in this area.

Part II establishes the Gender Equality Commission with emphasis on the independence of the Commission. The objective of the Commission is to promote gender equality and eliminate gender discrimination. The Gender Equality Commission shall consist of independent members and the Commission itself shall have access to statutory funds. The Commission has advisory, monitoring, and investigative functions. The Commission may also intervene in cases involving gender discrimination. The Commission is answerable to Parliament and shall submit a report listing its activities and recommendations to Parliament annually for debate. The report shall be made available to the public.

Part III regulates the executive staff of the Commission.

Part IV defines discrimination and equality to include direct and indirect discrimination and formal and substantive equality. Motive and knowledge is irrelevant.

This Part also discusses sexual harassment and provides for exemptions and exceptions whereby protection of women because of pregnancy, childbirth or breastfeeding and special temporary measures do not constitute unlawful discrimination.

Part V prohibits the victimisation of complainants and witnesses. It also prohibits authorisation of discrimination and establishes the vicarious liability of employers and principals for discrimination committed by their employees and agents unless reasonable precautions have been taken by the employers and principals.

Part VI sets out the inquiry procedure and Part VII provides for conciliation for those who favour such procedure provided that such conciliation is undertaken freely and without coercion by any party.

Part VIII sets up the Gender Equality Tribunal. Noting that the court process is formal, cumbersome and unfriendly, and following from the successful industrial court process as well as other newly formed adjudicative boards, the Act sets up a tribunal as an alternative mechanism to expedite adjudication of discrimination cases in a less formal setting. A specialised tribunal will also help develop jurisprudence on gender discrimination.

Part IX contains general provisions such as power to make regulations and prevention of anomalies.

Islam and gender equality

Any gender equality legislation, which is within the Federal legislative powers, shall necessarily not be applicable in those areas where the Federal government has no jurisdiction, unless jurisdiction is specifically conferred on it by the States. This includes Muslim personal laws as well as the "creation and punishment of offences by persons professing the religion of Islam against precepts of that religion, except in regard to matters included in the Federal List; the constitution, organisation and procedure of Syariah courts, which shall have jurisdiction only over persons professing the religion of Islam and in respect only of any of the matters included in this paragraph, but shall not have jurisdiction in respect of offences except in so far as conferred by federal law, the control of propagating doctrines and beliefs among persons professing the religion of Islam; the determination of matters of Islamic law and doctrine and Malay custom".[42]

This separation of legislative powers means that any change in the interpretation of Muslim personal laws towards accommodating gender equality must be undertaken by the States. Theoretically, this should not be difficult as few Muslims deny that Islam upholds justice as well as promotes and protects the rights of women.

Retired Chief Judge of Malaya, the Honourable Tan Sri Siti Norma Yaakob, underlined the relationship between Islam, justice and equality saying, "It is my belief that Islam accords women equal rights with men...Like many Muslims, I do not believe that Islam, which abhors injustices, treats women any less that it treats men. Women, like men, are vice-regents on earth; equal in the eyes of Allah and it is our collective responsibility to ensure that principles of justice and equality are reflected in our laws".[43]

In October 2003, when Dato' Seri Abdullah Badawi became Prime Minister, he espoused an approach to Islam focusing on 10 fundamental principles,[44] one of which is the protection of the rights of minority groups and women "which is authentic and rooted within the tradition, yet human, just and compassionate" and "where women will not feel that statements describing Islam as a religion of justice and mercy in reality only speak to women with exceptions – inadvertently or otherwise".[45]

Explained Abdullah, "Women receive a specific mention because I believe that despite the fact that women in many parts of the world have become more emancipated, women in many Muslim countries continue to be marginalised and discriminated. I find it most lamentable...that [women have not] gained the status that they are entitled to, in terms of rights, equality and justice".[46]

In 2005, Abdullah gave an inspiring and forward looking speech, calling on all Non-Aligned Movement nations to take firm and unequivocal steps to achieve humanity's vision for equality, peace and development and reminding them that "it takes a great deal of moral courage and fortitude to be able to challenge long-held and deeply ingrained societal beliefs about the role of women in society, particularly if religion is cited as the main reason for their subjugation."[47]

While Abdullah appears to advocate a progressive interpretation of Islam, there has been little change in the implementation of age-old Muslim laws to the daily lives of contemporary Muslim women.

Moreover, in recent cases challenging the constitutionality of certain provisions within Muslim laws as implemented by the different States of Malaysia, the courts have stated that the test of whether a matter is to be adjudicated in the common law courts or the syariah courts was to be determined firstly, by the subject matter of the dispute and secondly, by the personal jurisdiction approach.[48]

In the case of *Lina Joy* v *Majlis Agama Islam Wilayah Persekutuan & Ors*[49] the civil courts held that in matters pertaining to conversion into and out of Islam, the syariah courts have exclusive jurisdiction. Therefore, only the syariah court can determine whether a person is a Muslim or otherwise. The fact that a Muslim would not be officially recognised as having converted out of Islam without an order from the syariah court that she has apostasised was held not to contradict Article 11 of the Constitution which guarantees freedom of religion.

In that case Azlina Jamaluddin, a born Muslim, declared herself a Christian at the age of 26. She began practising the Christian faith and was baptised in 1998. While the National Registration Department agreed to record her change of name, they rejected her application to remove the particulars of her religious affiliation – which was noted as Islam – in her national registration identity card.

Her application was dismissed and the dismissal upheld by the Federal Court. In the majority decision, the Court held that the actions of the National Registration Department in requiring an order from the syariah court was reasonable and further that if a Muslim intended to renounce Islam, he would be deemed to be exercising his rights under syariah law which had its own jurisprudence relating to apostasy. Therefore the syariah court, and not the civil court, should decide on Lina Joy's apostasy. Freedom of religion under the Federal Constitution, added the Court, required that Lina Joy comply with the rituals or law of the Islamic religion regarding renunciation of the religion. Once the decision of the religion of Islam had been complied with and the religious authority admitted her apostasy, only then could she profess another religion, namely Christianity.[50]

Conclusion

Equality and equal opportunity are central in a democracy. Gender equality is but a small step towards strengthening our democracy and engendering respect for human rights that is universal, inalienable and indivisible. Unsurprisingly, the jurisprudence of rights has overwhelmingly dominated the discourse of constitutional law. Yet, the ability of the Constitution to initiate change in the promotion of gender equality and prohibit gender discrimination is constrained by many other factors, ranging from restrictions built into the very fabric of the Constitution, political will and structures and the availability of resources to support democratic processes that support gender equality.

What is abhorrent today is different from what was considered abhorrent yesterday. A living Constitution promises unlimited potential in shaping public sentiments as well as legal acceptance of social, legal and cultural practices. For this reason, fundamental rights enshrined in the Constitution should be interpreted expansively.

Still, the Constitution need not be the only site for promotion of fundamental rights. In concluding, I would also like to refer to the decision by Hartmann J in the Hong Kong case of *Equal Opportunities Commission* v *Director of Education*[51] as a reminder of the importance and pivotal status of protection of human rights in a legal system:

> In my judgement, if there is a central pillar around which the edifice of Hong Kong's legal system is built, it is respect for the rights and freedoms of the individual. That is manifest in our instruments of constitution, in our adherence to various international conventions and in our domestic law... These guarantees of equality – the antithesis of discrimination – call for a generous and purposive interpretation by our courts... It is not disputed that the right to equal treatment free of sex discrimination is in our society a fundamental right; as Lord Lester expressed it, a right of high constitutional importance.

Malaysia has proclaimed its commitment to gender equality to the international community as well as its citizenry. It is now time to implement and realise that ideal.

Notes

[1] Parts of this paper were first published as "Mechanisms to Promote Gender Equality in Malaysia: The Need for Legislation" in *Dossier 29: Mechanisms and Structures to Promote and Protect Women's Human Rights and Gender Equality,* Women Living Under Muslim Laws, July 2008.

[2] When a State party ratifies a treaty, it can declare reservations on those provisions by which it does not wish to be bound. Reservations are allowed so long as they are not incompatible with the object and purpose of the treaty. Incompatible reservations may be challenged by other State parties.

[3] Abdullahi Ahmed An-Na'im, *Toward an Islamic Reformation: Civil Liberties, Human Rights and International Law,* Syracuse: Syracuse University Press, 1990.

[4] We return to this issue later in this essay in the analysis of *Beatrice Fernandez v Sistem Penerbangan Malaysia.*

[5] An example is slavery. Islam, while exhorting its adherents to be kind to slaves and to free them, did not expressly abolish slavery. Yet no Muslim country today would support the re-establishment of the institution of slavery.

[6] An-Nai'm, *op cit,* pp 175–176.

[7] Hansard, 1.05.1958.

[8] [1988] 2 MLJ 55 at 56.

[9] Article 2 of the Iraqi Constitution provides that, "Islam is the official religion of the State and is the foundation source of legislation. A. No law may be enacted that contradicts the established provision of Islam". [http://www.uniraq.org/documents/iraqi_constitution.pdf].

[10] Article 2 of the Afghan Constitution states, "The religion of Afghanistan is the sacred religion of Islam. Followers of other religions are free to perform their rites within the limits of the provisions of law". Article 3 provides, "In Afghanistan, no law can be contrary to the sacred religion of Islam and the values of this Constitution". [http://unpan1.un.org/intradoc/groups/public/documents/APCITY/UNPAN015879.pdf].

[11] "Article 31(1) Steps shall be taken to enable the Muslims of Pakistan, individually and collectively, to order their lives in accordance with the fundamental principles and basic concepts of Islam and to provide facilities whereby they may be enabled to understand the meaning of life according to the Holy Quran and Sunnah.

(2) The State shall endeavour, as respects the Muslims of Pakistan:
(a) to make the teaching of the Holy Quran and Islamiat compulsory, to encourage and facilitate the learning of Arabic language and to secure correct and exact printing and publishing of the Holy Quran;
(b) to promote unity and the observance of the Islamic moral standards; and
(c) to secure the proper organisation of Zakat, [ushr,] auqaf and mosques.
[http://www.pakistanconstitution-law.com/const_results.asp?artid=31&title=Islamic%20way%20of%20life]

[12]Tan Sri Hashim Yeop Sani, *Our Constitution*, Law Publishers (M), 1980

[13][http://edition.cnn.com/2002/WORLD/asiapcf/southeast/06/18/malaysia. mahathir/index.html]

[14]Officiating an international conference in July 2007, Najib Abdul Razak said, "Islam is the official religion and we are an Islamic state". [http://www.bernama. com/bernama/v3/news_lite.php?id=273699].

[15][http://www.malaysiakini.com/news/70148].

[16]It is possible that what the Prime Minister meant was that Malaysia was a Muslim State as the Malay language term used by the Prime Minister could mean either an Islamic State or a Muslim State.

[17]August 27, 2007, at 10.00 am. No. 43 Questions for Oral Answers 24. PR-1143-L9923 and [http://www.malaysiakini.com/news/71676].

[18]Mahathir Mohamed, Abdullah Ahmad Badawi and Najib Abdul Razak (when he was Deputy Prime Minister).

[19]Law Reform (Marriage and Divorce) Act 1976 (Act 164); Guardianship of Infants Act 1960 (Revised 1988) (Act 351); Distribution Act 1958 (Revised 1983) (Act 300); Insurance Act 1996 (Act 553).

[20]In 2000, the National *Fatwa* Council issued a *fatwa* that payouts from a deceased's employee provident fund as well as social security should be deemed to be part of the estate to be distributed to the deceased's heirs instead of the deceased's dependants as is the case presently. The *fatwa* was not enforced. [http://www.e-fatwa.gov.my/jakim/keputusan_view.asp?keyID=161].

[21]Islam allows for the adoption and continuation of cultural practices. This practice is prevalent in some Malay communities and was officially incorporated into the respective State Family Law Enactments during the codification exercise in the mid-1980s.

[22]*Fatwa* dated August 27, 2003 [http://www.e-fatwa.gov.my/jakim/keputusan_view.asp?keyID=146].

[23]Malaysian women's groups have advocated for amendments to the Muslim Family Law Enactments to provide for equality. Following from, amongst others, the successful revision to the Moroccan Muslim Family Laws, the international initiative Musawwah was launched in

Kuala Lumpur. Musawwah's objectives include strengthening women's voices demanding equality and justice in the family at the national, regional and international levels and building analysis and strategies that bring together scholarship and experience regarding Muslim jurisprudence, human rights principles, fundamental rights and constitutional guarantees and the lived realities of families in Muslim countries and communities.

[24]See *Abdul Malek Hussin v Borhan Hj Daud* [2007] 1 LNS 460 where the Judge held, "I am mindful of the fact that I am presently dealing with the fundamental liberty of the citizens. The preservation of the personal liberty of the individual is a sacred universal value of all civilized nations and is enshrined in the Universal Declaration of Human Rights and Fundamental Freedoms of 1948". In March 2010, this decision was overturned on appeal by the Court of Appeal, Malaysia. See also *Jakob Renner v Scott King, Chairman of Board of Directors of Kuala Lumpur International School* [2000] 3 CLJ 569.

[25][2004] 4 CLJ 403 (Court of Appeal) and [2005] 2 CLJ 173 at 719 (Federal Court).

[26][2004] 4 CLJ 403 at 408.

[27][1989] 1 SCR 1219.

[28]Carole Louise Webb v EMO Air Cargo (UK); Ltd. (Social policy) [1994] EUECJ C-32/93 (July 14, 1994) [http://www.bailii.org/eu/cases/EUECJ/1994/C3293.html].

[29][2004] 4 CLJ 403.

[30]*Beatrice AT Fernandez v Sistem Penerbangan Malaysia* [2005] 2 CLJ 173 at 719

[31]See also Stephen Gardbaum, "The 'Horizontal Effect' of Constitutional Rights" in *Michigan Law Review*, Volume 102, Number 3, 2003.

[32][1997] 6 SCC 241.

[33]At the same time, common law judges are mindful not to 'usurp' the lawmaking functions of parliament, creating for themselves areas in which judicial law making is acceptable.

[34]*R* v *Secretary of State for the Home Department, ex parte Daly* [2001] per Lord Cooke.

[35]*op. cit.*

[36]128 ALR 353.

[37]See also *R v The Secretary of State for the Home Department ex parte Mohamed Hussain Ahmad* [http://www.bailii.org/ew/cases/EWCA/Civ/1998/1345.html] on the "legitimate expectation" principle in *Teoh* and Gopal Sri Ram, "Human Rights: Incorporating International Law into the Present System"; paper presented at a conference on "Constitutionalism, Human Rights and Good Governance"; September 30–October 1, 2003, Kuala Lumpur.

[38]Article 26 of the Vienna Convention on the Law of Treaties, 1969 states, "Every treaty in force is binding upon the parties to it and must be performed by them in good faith".

[39]Article 27 of the Vienna Convention on the Law of Treaties, 1969 states, inter alia, "A party may not invoke the provisions of its internal law as justification for its failure to perform a treaty".

[40]*Mohd Ezam v Inspector General of Police* [2002] 4 CLJ 309. The Court held that the provision under the *Human Rights Commission Act* which provided that "regard shall be had to the Universal Declaration of Human Rights" was merely an invitation to consider and be persuaded by the Declaration, if need be.

[41]Compare this to the Human Rights Commission. The Commission's reports have yet to be debated by Parliament as there is no provision for the reports to be debated in Parliament.

[42]List II: State List in the Ninth Schedule of the Federal Constitution.

[43]Opening speech at the international conference on "Legislations and Mechanisms to Promote Gender Equality"; August 28, 2006, Kuala Lumpur.

[44]The 10 principles are: faith and piety in Allah, just and trustworthy government, independent citizenry, mastery of knowledge, economic development, quality of life, protection of the rights of minorities and women, cultural moral integrity, restoration of the environment and strength in defence.

[45]Espoused as *Islam Hadhari*. Inaugural lecture by the Prime Minister at the annual Abdullah Ahmad Badawi Women's Institute of Management annual lecture series; January 15, 2005, Kuala Lumpur.

[46]Speech given at the Non-Aligned Movement ministerial meeting on the advancement of women at Putrajaya on May 9, 2005. *Islam Hadhari* has been criticized by the Pan-Malaysian Islamic Party (PAS) for being insufficiently Islamic. For all intents and purposes, *Islam Hadhari* appears to have fallen out of favour after Abdullah's resignation as Prime Minister of Malaysia in 2009.

[47]Speech given at the Non-Aligned Movement ministerial meeting on the advancement of women at Putrajaya on May 9, 2005.

[48]*Subashini Rajasingam v Saravanan Thangathoray* [2008] 2 CLJ 1. Even if the subject matter is within the jurisdiction of the syariah court, if one of the parties to the dispute is not a Muslim, the syariah court cannot be seized with jurisdiction. This is a case involving the conversion of the husband, who then converted his elder son, to Islam. Both parties filed for divorce, the husband in the syariah court and the wife in the civil court.

[49][2005] 4 CLJ 666. For the Federal Court decision, see [2007] 4 MLJ 585.

[50]The minority decision of Richard Malanjum CJ (Sabah & Sarawak) considered apostasy as involving complex questions of constitutional importance especially when some States in Malaysia had enacted legislations to criminalise it and emphasised that the civil courts cannot abdicate their constitutional functions when jurisdictional issues arise.

[51]Hon Hartmann J in the Hong Kong case of *Equal Opportunities Commission* v *Director of Education* [2001] 2 HKLRD 690 (HCAL15555/2000) at paragraphs 80, 97 and 98.

5 Constitutional Validity of Personal Laws in India

Poonam Pradhan Saxena

Introduction

Amongst the multiplicity of personal laws governing diverse communities in India, the commonality of subjugation of women remains a glaring reality. Aware of this fact, the framers of the Indian Constitution incorporated the concept of gender justice as one of the Constitution's primary goals. To give teeth to this concept, the framers provided that no law inconsistent with the basic provisions of the Constitution would have the capability of continuing on the statute books, as the courts can declare such provisions void or *ultra vires* the provisions of the Constitution.[1]

This concept of gender justice, well enshrined in the Constitution, ensures equality before law and equal protection of laws to all Indian citizens [Article 14] and prohibits the State from discriminating only on grounds of religion, race, caste, sex or place of birth [Article 15]. At the same time, it permits the State to positively discriminate in favour of women and children by way of making special provisions to ameliorate their social, political and economic status and to accord them justice [Article 15(3)]. Article 38 enjoins the State to promote the welfare of the people by securing a social order in which justice – social, economic and political – shall inform all the institutions of national life. Article 39(a) and (b) enjoins that State policy should be to secure that men and women equally have the right to an adequate means of livelihood and that the ownership and control of material assets are so distributed as best to subserve the common good. Article 38(2) enjoins the State to minimise the inequalities in status, facilities and opportunities amongst people. Article 46 accords special protection and enjoins the State to promote with special care the economic and educational interests of Scheduled Castes and Scheduled Tribes and other weaker sections of society and to protect them from social injustice and all forms of exploitation. The Preamble to the Constitution specifies a duty on the State to secure social, economic and political justice and equality of opportunity, status and dignity of person to everyone.

Domestic relations and gender parity

India's patriarchal society, thriving on the subjugation of women, stands in sharp contrast to the Constitutional principles of gender parity. The raw deal that women have always received at the hands of their own family members and society cuts across religious barriers and is amply reflected in legislation. The persistence of legislation-sponsored discrimination has proved to be a major obstacle in the path of women's emancipation as its influence on family attitudes and social values is immense. Half-hearted correctional legislations with lax implementation have had little success in eradicating social evils.[2] The fresh taste of Independence and a promise of justice and equality inculcated in the basic law of the land raised the hopes of millions of Indian women whose dreams of attainment of dignity, justice and a discrimination-free world could now be realised by the judicial removal of the very legislative provisions that had worked against them in the past. Soon after the promulgation of the Constitution, therefore, the testing of family laws on the threshold of the basic provisions of the Constitution started. The challenge covered a variety of family law provisions and was initiated by both men and women alleging discrimination predominantly on grounds of religion and sex. It is interesting to note that, while the initiation of challenges at the instance of women was targeted at the removal of gender based discriminatory provisions in then existing legislations or subsequent statutes, men's grievances primarily related to the pre- and post-Independence legislative deprival of unhealthy, unequal and generous facilities that were till then available to them and which perpetuated their superiority and control over women in the private sphere of the patriarchal setup.

Abolition of Bigamy for Hindu Men

The first level of challenge was by men whose liberty of practicing polygamy was taken away by post-Independence legislations[3] providing for compulsory monogamy. Four cases came to the forefront in which Hindu men challenged these legislations, claiming discrimination on grounds of religion, i.e., contending that while the legislature chose to ignore Muslim Personal Law and permitted Muslim men to practice polygamy, it abolished the same for Hindus and provided a penalty for contravention.

A notable judicial pronouncement came in *State of Bombay v Narasuappamali*,[4] where the Constitutional validity of the Bombay Prevention of Hindu Bigamous Marriages Act, 1946 was challenged as infringing Article 25 of the Constitution. The challenge came owing to the conviction of two men guilty of committing polygamy, with a sentence of one day's rigorous imprisonment and a fine of Rs 50 for each of them. The accused had three primary contentions: first, that among Hindus, marriage was an essential *sanskar* and a part of religion, as the basic reason for getting married was not merely the union of the mates, but to beget a son for the spiritual salvation of the father. Their emphasis, therefore, was that the permission of polygamy was an inherent part of Hindu religion. Second, by imposing monogamy selectively on Hindu men and leaving Muslim Personal Law untouched, the State had discriminated on grounds of religion and, therefore, the Act was *ultra vires* the provisions of the Constitution and void. Third, both classical Hindu law and Muslim Personal Law provided for polygamy but not polyandry and, hence, again violated the equality provisions of the Constitution.[5]

Although the Court refused to declare the impugned Act as *ultra vires* the provisions of the Constitution, its reasoning for so doing was difficult to comprehend. The Court held that family laws are not "laws" within the meaning of Article 13 of the Constitution; therefore, not only can the courts not declare or adjudicate upon their Constitutional validity, but also these provisions need not undergo tests of Constitutional validity at all. The Court said:

> It is well known that personal laws do not derive their validity on the ground that they have been passed or made by a legislature or other competent authority in the territory of India. The foundation sources of both the Hindu and Mahomedan laws are their respective scriptural texts[6]...therefore there can be no doubt that both the personal laws cannot be said to have been passed or made by a legislature or other competent authority and do not fall within the preview of the expression "laws in force".[7]

Faced with the argument that, as per Article 13, the expression "laws in force" included any ordinance, order, bye law, rule, regulation, notification, custom or usage having the force of law and also that the State is further prohibited from enacting any law which takes away or abridges the rights conferred by Part III of the Constitution, the Court said that Article 13(2) is prospective and its effect is that if any law is made hereafter by the State, the law would not be valid if it takes away or abridges the Fundamental Rights.

The Court also dismissed the argument that personal laws must be deemed to be included in the expression "laws in force" on the grounds that whatever is included in the word "law" in Article 13(3)(a) must automatically be held to be included in the expression "laws in force" in Article 13(3)(b) and said:

> I feel considerable difficulty in accepting this argument. The Constitution of India itself recognises the existence of these personal laws in terms when it deals with the topics falling under personal laws in item 5 in concurrent List-List-III. This item deals with the topics of marriage and divorce; infants and minors; adoption; wills, intestacy and succession; joint family and partition; all matters in respect of which parties in judicial proceedings were immediately before the commencement of the Constitution subject to their personal law. Thus it is competent either to the state or the Union Legislature to legislate on topics falling within the purview of the personal laws and yet the expression "personal law" is not used in Article 13 because in my opinion the framers of the Constitution wanted to leave the personal laws outside the ambit of Part III of the Constitution. They must have been aware that these personal laws needed to be reformed in many material particulars and in fact they wanted to abolish these different personal laws and to evolve one common code. Yet they did not wish that the provisions of the personal laws should be challenged by reason of the fundamental rights guaranteed in Part III of the Constitution and so they did not intend to include these personal laws within the definition of the expression "laws in force" Therefore I agree...that the personal laws do not fall within Article 13(1) at all.[8]

In other words, the Court held that:

(i) "The social and economic conditions which may once have justified the polygamous provisions were not existing in the present times and a reform in that direction was overdue. The impugned Act attempted to make such a reform and in substance it sought to remove the hardships and disabilities from which Hindu women were suffering so long."[9] "A Hindu Marriage is a sacrament and not a contract and the sentimental love and devotion of a Hindu wife for her husband a well known phenomenon, hence it was for the legislature to take into account the social customs and beliefs and if the legislature thought that it was necessary to provide for special provisions in dealing with bigamous marriages, the penal provisions of the impugned Act cannot and do not constitute discrimination against the Hindus only on the ground of religion."[10]

(ii) The Court dismissed as a political argument not worth consideration the claim that, if the impugned Act constituted a measure of social reform, it should also be made applicable to Muslim citizens of Bombay, so that they too may enjoy its benefits, and that the Union of India, being a secular state, should have refrained from making such a distinction between its citizens on religious grounds. Article 25 of the Constitution guarantees freedom of consciousness and free profession, practice and propagation of religion to all citizens of the Union of India, but the Article itself makes it perfectly clear that the freedom guaranteed by it is subject to some exceptions, such as public order, morality, health and also social welfare and reform. If the State makes a law for social welfare and reform, it would not be a proper argument against the validity of such a legislation to urge that the measure of social welfare and reform impinges upon the religious freedom of any section of the citizens of India. Religious matters are purely of one's belief and if they contravene with social measures, the former have to make way for the latter and, thus, it cannot be said that the legislation, in imposing monogamy, infringes the religious belief of Hindus.

The suit was accordingly dismissed by the Court.

In the second case, *Haisnam Baruniton Singh v Thokchom Ningol Haisnam*,[11] which came from Manipur, a Hindu married man remarried during the subsistence of his first marriage and, upon the criminal complaint filed by the first wife for his prosecution, he prayed for the quashing of the criminal proceedings and challenged the Constitutional validity of Section 5 of the Hindu Marriage Act, 1955 (HMA) on the grounds that:

(i) The Act discriminated between Hindus and Muslims – the latter still being free to take more than one wife according to their personal law – and thus offends the provisions of Article 15(1) of the Constitution.

(ii) According to the Census of 1951, the population of the Union Territory of Manipur consisted of 2,83,685 males and 2,93,950 females, i.e., women outnumbered men. If a man was restricted to only one wife, the excess number of women could not hope to get married and satisfy their biological needs in lawful wedlock. Such a situation was bound to lead to immorality and traffic in human beings, which clearly violated the Constitution.

The Court rejected the contention of the husband on the grounds that:

(i) The difference in the number of males and females may not be constant at all times.
(ii) This difference in number may include children as well.
(iii) Not in all cases would a woman wish to enter into a polygamous union to satisfy her physical needs.
(iv) There is no guarantee that with permission of polygamy all the excess women would be absorbed.

With reference to the Constitutional validity of provisions imposing compulsory monogamy only on Hindus and not Muslims, the Court held that under Article 14, the guarantee of equality is subject to reasonable classification which means that no person of a particular religion, caste, etc., shall be treated unfavourably in comparison to persons of other religions and castes simply on the grounds that he belongs to a particular religion, caste, etc. In other words, other qualifications being equal, the race, religion, etc., of a citizen shall not be a ground of preference or disability. The guarantee of equal protection extended by Article 14, while prohibiting class legislation, does not forbid classification on reasonable grounds of distinction. It only lays down that all persons subjected to such legislation shall be treated alike under like circumstances as regards the privileges conferred and liabilities imposed upon them and that no person or class of persons shall be singled out as a special subject for discrimination and hostile legislation. Therefore, if the classification is arbitrary and without any basis, only then will it attract the provisions under Article 14; otherwise, it shall be valid. The Court held that the right of the State to legislate on questions relating to marriage cannot be disputed and if the legislature, in its wisdom, concluded that monogamy tends to the welfare of the State, then it is not for the courts of law to sit in judgement upon that decision. Therefore, they held that the legislation does not contravene either Article 15 or 25 of the Constitution[12] and upheld the Constitutional validity of Section 5 of the HMA.

The third case in this category was *Srinivasa Aiyer v Saraswati Ammal*,[13] in which the Madras Hindu Bigamy Prevention and Divorce Act, 1949 was held not to offend Articles 15 and 25 of the Constitution. The challenge here was on identical grounds to the two cases discussed above. Taking the same line of argument, the Court said that an Act which amends, alters or repeals parts or whole of the personal law of Hindus which is different from the personal law of Muslims cannot be said to be discriminatory between Hindus and Muslims on the grounds of religion and dismissed the suit.[14]

In the fourth case, *Gogireddy Sambireddy v Gogireddy Jayamma*,[15] the husband's commission of bigamy was, once again, the primary issue. Upon the wife filing a complaint against her husband for commission of bigamy, he challenged the Constitutional validity of Sections 5, 11 and 17 of the HMA on the grounds that they violate Article 15(1) of the Constitution. He contended that the personal laws of Hindus and Muslims had always permitted polygamy and that while the law for Muslims had remained unchanged, the law for Hindus was altered and monogamy introduced only for them. This case met the same fate as the previous ones and by now faced with the stark reality that legal permission for the luxury of polygamy would no longer be available to them, Hindu men accepted the inevitable.

Divorce under the Hindu Marriage Act, 1955

Hindu couples can seek dissolution of their marriage on the establishment of any of the stipulated grounds under the Hindu Marriage Act, 1955 (HMA). It is noteworthy that, while providing for the grounds of divorce, Hindu wives have more options with the availability of four special grounds of divorce that are unavailable to a Hindu man placed in similar situations. Section 13(2)(iv), HMA provides that when a girl under the age of fifteen years is married, she can present a petition for divorce after attainment of fifteen years of age. The remedy is available to her for a period of three years. This ground is unavailable to a boy married under similar situations. The Constitutional validity of this provision was challenged in *Roop Narayan Verma v Union of India*[16] as violative of the gender parity clause in the Constitution as it discriminated against Hindu men. The Court upheld the provision's Constitutional validity in light of Article 15(3) which permits the State to make special provisions for women and children and dismissed the petition.

Adoption by a Hindu married woman under the Hindu Adoptions and Maintenance Act, 1956

Under the Hindu Adoptions and Maintenance Act, 1956 (HAMA), a Hindu woman can adopt a child only when she is unmarried, widowed or divorced. A married woman cannot adopt a child unless her husband is judicially disqualified to do so, i.e., either he ceases to be a Hindu or renounces the world completely and finally or is declared by a court of competent jurisdiction to be of unsound mind. If the husband is alive and is not judicially disqualified, then the wife cannot adopt a child even if she is deserted by the husband or has not lived with him for a single day or even if he has remarried and has children from the second marriage.[17] The patent unreasonableness of this provision can be gauged from the fact that the judiciary has invalidated adoptions where a couple adopts a child with the consent of both spouses, but with the lead role being performed by the married woman.[18]

The Constitutional validity of these provisions was challenged in *Lalitha Ubhayakar v Union of India*[19] by a social worker who wanted to adopt a girl from an orphanage but was denied the permission to do so on the grounds that, as a married Hindu woman, she was in law incompetent to adopt. Ubhayakar claimed that Section 8 of HAMA, which specifically deals with the power of women to adopt, excludes a wife from making an adoption, but permits a single woman to do so. Therefore, the wife is discriminated against in comparison to a divorcee, unmarried adult woman and a widow.

Rejecting her contention and holding that the provisions are within the ambit of the Constitution, the Court held that these provisions are based on reason and there is no discrimination:

> Section 8 confers the right to adopt on women who are single in status. A married woman stands outside this class. Section 8 contemplates the right of women to adopt who are single but who have attained the age of majority, a widow and a woman who has divorced her husband. Therefore compared with those woman [*sic.*], a woman in married status falls into a different class. She cannot complain of discrimination of violation of Article 14 on the ground that a wife needs consent of her husband before adoption while a woman of single status does not need it.[20]

The Court further opined that under Section 7, HAMA, not only the wife but also the husband needs the consent of his spouse before adopting a child and said:

> ...the adoption is to the family and not to individual spouses. The law is made in such a way that the harmony of the family is not destroyed by permitting the wife to adopt separately without the consent of the husband and vice versa. Therefore there is no violation of Article 14. If the right is given to the wife under

> Section 7 of the Act to give consent to her husband's decision to make an adoption that right includes right not to give consent from which it necessarily follows, her right to make an adoption can easily be exercised according to her wishes by giving or withholding the consent in the married status. The same can be said of the husband as well. In other words, the legislature was clear in its concept of adoption by parents desirous of a child in adoption as such an adoption was for both of them and not for each of them separately and distinctly.
>
> This is the practice obtaining in all civilized societies which recognize the family as a unit in such societies. A child is adopted as a child adopted to the family and not the father and mother separately. One cannot think of a situation in any civilized society that a wife may have a separate right to adopt without the consent of her husband and the husband may likewise do so. The complications are one to [*sic.*] many to exhaustively enumerate the disasters that may be fall [*sic.*] such a family. Therefore with all the wisdom the legislature possessed, the parliament has made law in such a way that the harmony of the family is not destroyed by permitting the wife to adopt separately without the consent of the husband or vice versa.[21]

The Court also said that the Constitution does not guarantee to anyone the right to adopt and held that Section 8, HAMA is based on reason and, therefore, does not violate the equality provisions of the Constitution.

Conjugal rights under the Hindu Marriage Act, 1955

Under Section 9 of the Hindu Marriage Act, 1955 (HMA), if either spouse withdraws from the society of the other without a reasonable excuse, the aggrieved party can approach the court and pray for a decree of restitution of conjugal rights and the court, upon consideration of the facts, could order the guilty party to return and give conjugal company to the aggrieved party. This remedy – called restitution of conjugal rights – is gender neutral in its language, but has been challenged on the grounds that as husband and wife are inherently unequal, their treatment as equals violates Article 14 of the Constitution.

In *T Sareetha v T Venkata Subaiah*,[22] the husband filed a suit praying for a decree of restitution of conjugal rights that was granted by the trial court. The wife challenged the Constitutional validity of Section 9 of the HMA, on the grounds that it violates Articles 14 and 21 of the Constitution, in that it treats unequals as equals, violates the wife's rights of privacy and enforces coerced sex on an unwilling wife.

The Court accepted her contentions and pronounced that conjugal rights connote both the right which the husband and wife have to each other's society and marital intercourse and, thus, sexual cohabitation is an inseparable ingredient of a decree for restitution of conjugal rights. Holding that Section 9 of the HMA is *ultra vires* the provisions of the Constitution and, therefore, void, the Court said:

> The remedy of restitution of conjugal rights provided for by Section 9 is a savage and barbarous remedy violating the right of privacy and human dignity guaranteed under Article 21 of the Constitution and constitutes the grossest form of violation of any individual's right of privacy. Hence Section 9 is constitutionally void. Any statutory provision that abridges any of the rights guaranteed by Part III of the Constitution will have to be declared void in terms of Article 13.[23]

On the violation of a woman's right of privacy, the Court said that Article 21 guarantees the right to life and personal liberty against the State's action. It protects the right of privacy and promotes the individual dignity mentioned in the Preamble of the Constitution. Coming down very heavily on the decree of restitution of conjugal rights, the Court said:

> ...it constitutes the grossest form of violation of an individual's right to privacy. It denies a woman her free choice whether, when and how her body is to become the vehicle for the procreation of

another human being. It deprives a woman of control over her choice as to when and by whom the various parts of her body should be allowed to be sensed. She loses her control over her most intimate decisions. Clearly, therefore the right to privacy guaranteed by Article 21 is flagrantly violated.

A wife who is keeping away from her husband, because of permanent or even temporary estrangement cannot be forced, without violating her right of privacy to bear a child by her husband. During a time when she is probably contemplating an action for divorce, the use and enforcement of restitution of conjugal rights against the estranged wife can irretrievably alter her position by bringing about forcible conception permanently ruining her mind, body and life and everything connected with it. During a moment's duration the entire lifestyle would be altered and would even be destroyed without her consent. If that situation made possible by this matrimonial remedy is not to be a violation of individual dignity and right to privacy guaranteed by the Constitution and more particularly Article 21, it is not conceivable what else could be a violation of Article 21 of our Constitution. A court decree enforcing restitution constitutes starkest form of governmental invasion of personal identity and individual's zone of intimate decisions. The victim is stripped of its control over the various parts of her body subjected to the humiliating sexual molestation accompanied by a forcible loss of the precious right to decide when if at all her body should be allowed to be used to give birth to another human being. Clearly the victim loses its autonomy of control over intimacies of personal identity. Above all, the decree for restitution of conjugal rights makes the unwilling victim's body a soulless and a joyless vehicle for bringing into existence another human being. In other words, pregnancy would be foisted on her by the State and against her will. There can therefore be little doubt that such a law violates the right to privacy and human dignity guaranteed by and contained in Article 21 of our Constitution. State coercion of this nature can neither prolong nor preserve the voluntary union of the husband and wife in matrimony. Neither state coercion can soften the ruffled feelings nor clear the misunderstanding between the parties.[24]

The Court also noted that,[25] following the Scarman Commission's recommendation, the British Government abolished the remedy of restitution of conjugal rights in England.[26] This decree of restitution, the Court said, serves neither any legitimate purpose nor any social good. It also did not satisfy the traditional classification test and failed to pass the minimum rationality requirement of any state law and must, therefore, be held to be arbitrary and violative of Article 14 of the Constitution. The Court also noted that, although in theory the gender neutral language of Section 9 does not offend Article 14, bare equality regardless of the inequality of realities is neither justice nor homage to Constitutional principles. In practice, Section 9 is used almost exclusively by husbands and rarely resorted to by wives. By enforcing this decree, the life pattern of the wife is likely to be altered irretrievably, whereas the husband's can remain almost as it was before. This is so because it is the wife who has to beget and bear a child. The practical but inevitable consequence of the enforcement of this remedy cripples the wife's future plans and, thus, prevents her from using this self destructive remedy. Therefore, its use in reality becomes partial, one-sided and available only for the husband's benefit. By treating the husband and wife, who are inherently unequal, as equals, Section 9, HMA offends the Constitutional pledge of equal protection of laws and, for this reason, the formal equality that it ensures cannot be accepted as Constitutional and it should be struck down as violative of Article 14 of the Constitution.[27]

A similar challenge of the same provision (Section 9, HMA) came before the Delhi High Court the following year: in *Harvinder Kaur v Harminder Singh*[28], the husband filed a petition praying for a decree of restitution of conjugal rights against his wife that was granted in his favour by the trial court. The wife appealed to the High Court, challenging the

Constitutional validity of Section 9 on the grounds that it violates Articles 14 and 21 of the Constitution by imposing forced or coerced sex. In support of her challenge, she cited the Andhra Pradesh High Court's judgement in *T Sareetha v T Venkata Subaiah*.

The Delhi High Court disagreed with the views of the Andhra Pradesh High Court and held that Section 9, HMA did not violate Articles 14 or 21 of the Constitution. According to the Delhi High Court, the objective of the restitution decree was to bring about cohabitation between the estranged parties, i.e., so that they can live together in the matrimonial home in amity, the leading idea of Section 9 being to preserve the marriage. The Court said that, from the definition of cohabitation and consortium, it appeared that sexual intercourse is one of the elements that make up a marriage, but it is not the *summum bonum*. The court does not and cannot enforce sexual intercourse. Though sexual relations constitute a most important attribute of the conception of marriage, they do not constitute its whole content nor can the remaining aspects of matrimonial consortium be said to be of unsubstantial or trivial character. The remedy of restitution aimed at cohabitation and consortium and not merely at sexual intercourse. To say that the restitution decree subjects a person, via the long arm of law, to a positive sex act is to take the grossest view of the institution of marriage. Rejecting the contention that the restitution of conjugal rights constitutes the starkest form of governmental invasion of marital privacy, the Court opined that the Indian legislature is firmly convinced that there should not be a sudden break of marriage ties as it believes in reconciliation and that the cooling period is not only desirable, but also essential.[29] Section 9, HMA is a provision designed to encourage reconciliation and, in fact, combines the fault and the breakdown theory in one go.

The Court held that, as either party can apply for this remedy, there is a complete equality of the sexes here and also the equal protection of laws. Thus, restitution of conjugal rights under Section 9 is valid and not violative of Articles 14 and 21 of the Constitution. It is worth noting the comments of the Court on the constitutionality of the family law provision. Justice Avadh Bihari Rohatgi said:

> Introduction of constitutional law in home is most inappropriate. It is like introduction of a bull in a china shop. It will prove to be a ruthless destroyer of the marriage institution and all that it stands for. In the privacy of the home and the married life neither Article 21 nor Article 14 have any place. In a sensitive sphere which is at once most intimate and delicate the *introduction of the cold principles of constitutional law will have the effect of weakening the marriage bond.* The fact that it was abolished in 1980 in England is no ground to hold that it is unconstitutional in the Indian setup. In the home the consideration that really obtains is the natural love and affection which counts for so little in these cold courts. Constitutional law principles find no place in the domestic code. The house of everyone is to him his castle and fortress. The spouses can claim a kind of sacred protection behind the door of the family home which generally speaking the civil authority may not penetrate. The introduction of constitutional law into ordinary domestic relationship of husband and wife will strike at the root of that relationship and will be a fruitful source of dissension and quarrelling. It will open door to unlimited litigation in a relationship which should be obviously as far as possible protected from possibilities of that kind. The "domestic community" does not rest on contracts sealed with seals and sealing wax nor on constitutional law. It rests on that kind of moral cement which unites and produces "two in one ship". [Emphasis added] [30]

The Court also disagreed with the view that this remedy is sought only by men and not women. The Court concluded that there is absolute equality as far as its availability and utility are concerned and that, therefore, Section 9, HMA cannot be struck down as an unconstitutional violation of Article 14. Criticising the Andhra Pradesh judgment, the Court said:

> One great defect of the Andhra judgment...is that it regards marriage as a legalised means of sexual self satisfaction and not primarily as a partnership for life. Marriage does not exist only for sexual congress. Marriage is not gratification of animal appetite. Nor a sheer indulgence into the lusts of the flesh. It creates mutual rights and obligations as all contracts do and beyond that it confers a status.[31]

Once again, in *Saroj Rani v Sudarshan Kumar Chadha*[32] – a case involving a petition for the restitution of conjugal rights – the Supreme Court upheld the view taken by the Delhi High Court, overruled the Andhra Pradesh High Court's judgment in *T Sareetha* and noted that, in India, conjugal rights – i.e., the right of the husband or the wife to the society of the other spouse – are not merely a creature of statute, but such rights are inherent in the institution of marriage itself and there are sufficient safeguards in Section 9, HMA itself to prevent it from being a tyranny. The Court said:

> The essence of marriage is a sharing of common life, a sharing of all the happiness that life has to offer and all the misery that has to be faced in life; an experience of joy that comes from enjoying, in common things of the matter and of the spirit and from showering love and affection on one's offspring. Living together is a symbol of such sharing in all its aspects. Living apart is a symbol of negation of such sharing. It is indicative of a disruption of the essence of marriage-breakdown and if it continues for a fairly long period it would indicate destruction of the essence of marriage-irretrievable. The remedy thus serves a social purpose and as the enforcement of it is only through financial sanction it cannot be called tyrannical at all.[33]

It is difficult to agree with the comments of Justice Rohatgi. The judicial perpetuation of the divide between the public and the private spheres of an individual's life is extremely unfortunate. Indian women, who have borne the brunt of patriarchal inequality since time immemorial, would lose the streak of hope contained in Constitutional provisions of equality on being told that these provisions have no place within the four walls of the home, as their introduction – and, by implication, women's desire for equality – leads to endless litigation and unpleasantness. There appears to be an implied acceptance by the judiciary that unpleasantness and litigations can best be avoided if inequalities and unconstitutional practices are observed in the private sphere. Second, if the "cold principles" of the Constitution (i.e., equality provisions) are presumed to have the effect of weakening the marriage bond, it means that the absence of these principles will strengthen it. This judicial pronouncement cautioning against the implementation of Constitutional principles of equality in the family law zone goes against the very spirit of the Constitution itself. The courts are under a duty to implement Constitutional values – even in the home – and not to advocate their non-implementation. This stand of the Court creates a rift between Constitutional principles and family values and sends a strong message that the protection of the institution of marriage is possible only if gender inequality is practiced and perpetuated in the home. Denouncing Constitutional principles as "cold" shows an unwarranted disrespect and condemnation of the basic law of the land. It is indeed extremely unfortunate that the judicial mechanism, that owes its very existence to the Constitution of India, chooses to describe the law in unconstitutional terms.

Divorce under the Indian Divorce Act, 1869

Under the un-amended Indian Divorce Act, 1869 (IDA),[34] the grounds available to the wife and husband for obtaining divorce differed. The solitary ground available to the husband was the commission of adultery by the wife, but the wife had several – albeit practically tedious – options available to her.[35] Her husband's adultery alone was not grounds for divorce and the wife was required to prove, along with his adultery, desertion, remarriage, cruelty or incestuous adultery, etc. The constitutionality of this sex-based inequality was challenged several times before the courts, leading to conflicting judicial pronouncements, with very interesting observations.

In *Dwarka Bai v Nainan Matthews*[36], the wife filed a petition praying for a decree of divorce on grounds of her husband's adultery. She also challenged the Constitutional validity of Section 10, IDA on the grounds that, while the husband can claim divorce merely on grounds of his wife's adultery, the wife cannot do so and must prove another independent ground along with her husband's adultery to seek dissolution of marriage. This differing requirement amounted to sex-based discrimination, which could not be sustained in light of Articles 14 and 15 of the Constitution.

The Court disagreed with the wife's contention and held that equality under Article 14 can be only amongst equals and as men and women are basically unequal, it is competent for the legislature to come up with different grounds or unequal treatment for them without violating Article 14. The Court held that Section 10 was not *prima facie* repugnant to Articles 13–15 of the Indian Constitution as it appeared to be based on a sensible classification and after taking into consideration the abilities of men and women and the results of their acts rather than being based merely on sex (in which case alone it would be repugnant to the Constitution). The Court said:

> ...adultery committed by a wife is different from adultery committed by the husband. A husband commits adultery somewhere, but he does not bear a child as a result of such adultery, and make it a legitimate child of his wife's to be maintained by the wife. He cannot bear a child, nor is the wife bound to maintain the child. But if the wife commits adultery, she may bear a child as a result of such adultery, and the husband will have to treat it as his legitimate child and will be liable to maintain that child. It is obvious that this very difference in the result of adultery, may form some ground for requiring a wife, in a petition for divorce not only to prove adultery by the husband but also

> desertion and cruelty whereas the husband need prove only adultery by the wife.[37]

Therefore, the challenged was dismissed.

The reasoning that the wife's commission of adultery is different from adultery committed by the husband, with different consequences, and that this is the basis of a reasonable classification, appears not only totally unreasonable, but illogical as well. The wife's ability to give birth to a child as the result of an adulterous connection and the husband fathering a child elsewhere are clearly sex-based consequences. Adultery is primarily the commission of grave matrimonial misconduct and the severity of mental trauma would be the same for either spouse irrespective of the sex. Granting a divorce to the husband on the wife's adultery *simpliciter* and providing an effective getaway to him, but not to the wife in a similar situation, displays the legislative expectations from the wife not only to tolerate her husband's adultery, but also to live in this matrimony with the same husband without any remedy at all. It implies that fidelity and faithfulness can legitimately be expected from the wife, but not from the husband.

The Constitutional validity of Section 10, IDA was challenged once again in *Anil Kumar Mahsi v Union of India*.[38] The aggrieved husband contended that the fact that this Section gives the husband only one ground on which he can present a petition for divorce, while the wife has several options amounts to sex-based discrimination, which violates Article 14 of the Constitution.

Holding that the husband and the wife are primarily unequal and that there is a reasonable classification on which this Section is based, the Court held:

> Taking into account the general muscularly weaker physique of the woman, her general vulnerable physical and social condition and her defensive and non aggressive nature and role particularly in this country, the legislature can hardly be faulted if the said two grounds are made available to the wife and not to the husband for

> seeking dissolution of the marriage. For the same reasons, it can hardly be said that on that account the provisions of Section 10 of the Act are discriminatory as against the husband.[39]

The Court dismissed the petition.

The Constitutional validity of Section 10, IDA was also challenged by a Christian man in *Henry Fernandes v Succorinha Fernandes*.[40] As usual, the Court displayed extreme reluctance to declare the impugned provisions void. In this case, the husband had filed a petition seeking divorce on grounds of his wife's cruelty. The Court dismissed his prayer, holding that since this ground is not available under the Act, the husband cannot seek divorce on the same. The husband challenged the Constitutionality of Section 10 in light of Articles 14, 15 and 21 of the Constitution, pleading that as the husband has only one ground for seeking divorce compared to the wife's six, this amounts to unequal treatment that cannot and should not be sustained in view of the Constitutional guarantee of equality of treatment to all Indian citizens. The Court held that, even assuming there is some substance in the grievance that Section 10 as it stands discriminates regarding grounds of divorce between a Christian husband and a wife, the Court had no power to introduce into the Section a ground which the legislature did not contemplate. The Court observed:

> Even assuming that Section 10...is considered to be discriminative against the Christian husband, it is not open to us to read into Section 10 any ground other than the ground provided by the legislature. In view of the matter it is unnecessary to contend that the Section is discriminatory of rights between a Christian husband and wife. There may be several reasons why the law permits dissolution of marriage at the instance of the Christian husband only on the solitary ground of wife's adultery. Perhaps Christian women are never cruel to their husbands, for they are Christians. Assuming that there is at all a discrimination, the discrimination at all would be in favour of women, which is perfectly valid and permissible in view of Article

> 15(3)...Therefore we decline to go into the constitutional issue raised by [the husband's counsel].[41]

Besides the predictable reluctance of the Court to declare the discriminatory provision unconstitutional, the comment that, "perhaps Christian women are never cruel to their husbands," is not only surprising, but totally uncalled for. Human nature can never be religion-specific. In this case, the wife did not contend that she was not guilty of cruelty, but that cruelty as a ground is not available to the husband. But the Court, without going into the merits of the case, opined that Christian wives are perhaps never guilty of cruelty. Does this mean that, as the husband is entitled to seek dissolution on grounds of the wife's adultery, it is common for wives to lead adulterous lives? The judiciary should refrain from making such sweeping statements that are totally inconsistent with human behaviour, be it of the husband or the wife.

In *Ammini E J v Union of India*,[42] two petitions were filed by Christian women on the grounds that the provisions of Section 10, IDA violate the Fundamental Rights guaranteed to them and other similarly situated Christian women under Articles 14, 15 and 21 of the Constitution of India. Here, overruling the judgment in *Dwarka Bai v Nainan Matthews*[43] (discussed earlier), the Court held the impugned provisions to be void as they constitute sex-based discrimination. The Court held that, as far as the ground of adultery is concerned, the husband is in a much more favourable position as compared to the wife, since she has to prove adultery with one or the other aggravating circumstance. Such a discrimination based purely on sex will be against the mandatory provisions in Article 15 of the Constitution of India and a denial of equality before law guaranteed under Article 14 of the Constitution. The difference between the after effects of adultery committed by the husband and wife – namely, that the husband even by committing adultery does not bear a child as a result of such adultery and make it the child of the wife to be maintained by the wife, but the wife by committing adultery may bear a child as a result of such adultery and the husband will be liable to maintain that child[44] – cannot be a justification for differential treatment because it is a difference solely resulting from sex and that cannot be treated as a valid justification in the light of Articles 14 and 15 of the Constitution. The Court not only struck down these provisions of Section 10, IDA as violative of the equality provisions of the Constitution, but also held that they are arbitrary as they tie a woman to a marriage that is broken down irretrievably and, thus, violate the right to life of a Christian woman guaranteed under Article 21 of the Constitution. The Court said that it would be a "humiliating and oppressed life without dignity and personal liberty and without the freedom to remarry and enjoy life in normal course. It would be a life curtailed in various fields and can legitimately be treated only as a life imposed by a tyrannical or authoritarian law on a helpless, deserted or cruelly treated Christian wife quite against her will which she is bound to lead till her death tormented always by the feeling that she is remaining as the wife of a man who has treated her cruelly, hated her and deserted her for no fault of her" [*sic.*].[45] With respect to the conflict of these provisions with Article 14, the Court said:

> Section 10 in so far as it compels a deserted or cruelly treated Christian wife to perpetually [*sic.*] tied down to a marriage which has for all practical purposes ceased to exist as a result of desertion and cruelty shown by the husband concerned is highly harsh and oppressive and as such arbitrary and violative of Article 14 of the Constitution of India. Whatever may have been the conditions in 1869 when the Act was enacted and which might have justified the incorporation of such provisions in the Act, it will be difficult to find any justifiable reason in support of the impugned provisions in the light of the provisions in Chapter III of the Constitution guaranteeing various fundamental rights especially Articles 14, 15 and 21. As it is only the Christians who cannot get a dissolution

> based on the desertion of the spouse while all other personal laws in India do recognise dissolution based on the desertion of one of the spouse, it would be discrimination based solely on religion and thus cannot be sustained in light of Article 15 of the Constitution.[46]

Keeping in mind Article 13 of the Constitution, the Court said that provisions in an enactment must pass the test of Constitutionality, notwithstanding the fact that it is based on religious principles.

Mother as a guardian in the father' lifetime

Under Hindu law (Hindu Minority and Guardianship Act, 1956) as well as the secular law of guardianship (Guardians and Wards Act, 1890), the natural guardian of a minor child is the father and "after him" the mother. The mother can be a guardian in the presence of the father only when the father is judicially disqualified to be a guardian: i.e., if he has ceased to be a Hindu or has finally and completely renounced the world by becoming a hermit. If he is alive and not disqualified judicially, the mother cannot be the guardian.

This inability of the mother to be a guardian in presence of the father was challenged as discriminatory in *Githa Hariharan v Reserve Bank of India.*[47] The problem arose when the bank account application forms of a minor child that were signed by the mother as the guardian were refused by the bank, which insisted that either the application be signed by the father or that the mother produce a certificate of guardianship from a competent authority in favour of the mother. In another case, that was heard along with *Githa Hariharan*, a woman approached the Court with a similar prayer, because her divorce petition was pending in court and her husband was repeatedly writing to the school authorities of their minor child to say that, as he was the natural guardian of the child, no decision should be taken with respect to the child without his consent. Both these mothers challenged the

Constitutional validity of Section 6 of the Hindu Minority and Guardianship Act, 1956 and Section 19(b) of the Guardians and Wards Act, 1890, as violative of the equality clause of the Constitution in as much as the mother of the minor is relegated to an inferior position on the ground of sex alone since her right as a natural guardian of the minor is made cognisable only after the father.

Although in matters of custody and guardianship, it is always the welfare of the child that is taken into consideration, in this case the Reserve Bank of India had rejected the mother's application even though she had acted with the father's concurrence. The Court said:

> If the word "after him" means only "after his life time", the section has to be struck down as unconstitutional as it undoubtedly violates gender equality principles.[48]

However, the Court noted that the Hindu Minority and Guardianship Act had come into force in 1956, i.e., after the promulgation of the Constitution and wondered if the Parliament wanted to transgress Constitutional limits or ignore the Fundamental Rights guaranteed by the Constitution which specifically prohibit discrimination on grounds of sex? Answering this question in the negative, the Court said:

> ...it is well settled that if on one construction a given statute becomes unconstitutional, whereas on the another [*sic.*] construction which may be open, the statute remains within the constitutional limits, the courts will prefer the latter on the ground that the legislature is presumed to have acted in accordance with the Constitution and courts generally lean in favour of the constitutionality of the statutory provisions.[49]

Holding that Section 6 of the Hindu Minority and Guardianship Act is capable of such construction as would retain it within Constitutional limits, the Court concluded that the words "after him" do not mean after the father's lifetime, but rather in the "absence of", thereby referring to the father's absence from the care of the minor's property or person for any reason whatever. If the father is wholly indifferent to the matters of the minor even if he is living with the mother or, if by virtue of a mutual understanding between the father and the mother, the latter is put exclusively in charge of the minor or if the father is physically unable to take care of the minor either because of his staying away from the place where the mother and the minor are living or because of his physical or mental incapacity: in all such situations the mother can act validly on behalf of the minor as the guardian. Such an interpretation will be the natural outcome of a harmonious construction of Sections 4 and Section 6 of the Hindu Minority and Guardianship Act, without causing any violence to the language of the Sections.

This modified interpretation enabled the mother to act as the guardian of the minor, but this limited concession strengthens her subordination. The refusal to declare the provisions discriminatory, despite the Court's conviction that they were, is not appropriate because if the father is willing to perform his duties, the mother cannot act as a guardian. Her situation remains as before, despite the modified interpretation of the Court.

Challenging multifarious family laws

In *Ahmedabad Women Action Group v Union of India*,[50] with writ petitions under Article 32 of the Constitution, the following reliefs were prayed for:

(i) To declare Muslim personal law, which allows polygamy, void on account of offending Articles 14 and 15 of the Constitution.

(ii) To declare Muslim personal law, which enables a Muslim male to give unilateral *talaq* to his wife without her consent and without resort to the judicial process of courts, void on account of offending Articles 13, 14 and 15 of the Constitution.

(iii) To declare the fact that a Muslim husband takes more than one wife an act of cruelty within the meaning of Section 2, clause

VIII(f) of the Dissolution of Muslim Marriage Act, 1938.

(iv) To declare the Muslim Women's (Protection of Rights on Divorce) Act, 1986 void on account of infringing Articles 14 and 15 of the Constitution.

(v) To further declare the provisions of Sunni and Shia laws of inheritance, which discriminate against females as compared to males of the same status regarding shares, void on account of sex-based discrimination.

In the same case, the challenges regarding various Hindu laws were as follows:

(i) To declare Sections 2(2), 5(ii) and (iii), 6 and the explanation to Section 30 of the Hindu Succession Act, 1956 as void on account of offending Articles 14 and 15 read with Article 13 of the Constitution of India.

(ii) To declare Section 2 of the Hindu Marriage Act, 1955 as void on account of offending Articles 14 and 15 of the Constitution.

(iii) To declare void Sections 3(2), 6 and 9 of the Hindu Minority and Guardianship Act, 1956 read with Section 6 of the Guardians and Wards Act, 1890.

(iv) To declare void the unfettered and absolute discretion allowed to a Hindu spouse to make testamentary disposition without providing for an ascertained share to his or her spouse and dependant.

With respect to Christian law as was operative in India at that time, the same case sought a declaration that Sections 10 and 34 of the Indian Divorce Act, 1869 and Sections 34-46 of the Indian Succession Act, 1925 were void.

At the outset, the Supreme Court held that these writ petitions do not deserve disposal on merits, inasmuch as the arguments advanced wholly involved issues of State Policy with which the Court will not ordinarily have any concern. It has been observed by the Supreme Court that the remedy in such cases lies elsewhere, and not by knocking at the doors of the courts.[51]

The Court had a similar response in *Maharishi Avadesh v Union of India*,[52] where the prayer was:

(i) To issue a writ of mandamus to the Union of India to consider the question of enacting a common civil code for all citizens of India.
(ii) To declare the Muslim Women (Protection of Rights on Divorce) Act, 1986 as void on account of being arbitrary and discriminatory and in violation of the Fundamental Rights and Articles 14, 15, 38, 39, 39-A and 44 of the Constitution of India.
(iii) To enact Shariat Act in respect of those adversely affecting the dignity and right of Muslim women and against their protection. [*sic.*]

The Court very emphatically said that these are all matters for the legislature. Even though what the petitioner had sought was a declaration and direction from the Court to be issued to the legislature, the Court nevertheless held that it cannot legislate in these matters and the writ petition was dismissed.

Maintenance to Divorced Muslim Women

Under classical Muslim law, the wife's entitlement to claim maintenance from her husband is conditional upon her being faithful to him and obedient to his reasonable commands. Upon divorce, the general and prevalent view is that the husband's liability to maintain his wife extends only during the period of *iddat*,[53] after which the responsibility of her maintenance falls upon those of her relatives who otherwise would inherit her property in that order. Matters became complicated soon after the well-known case of *Mohd Ahmed Khan v Shah Bano Begum*,[54] with the Supreme Court pronouncing that a divorced Muslim woman can claim maintenance from her husband under the secular provisions of the Code of Criminal Procedure, 1973 (CrPC). A political and religious backlash to this judgement saw the enactment of the Muslim Women's (Protection of Rights on Divorce) Act, 1986. The Act lays down that:

(i) A Muslim divorced woman is entitled to a reasonable and fair provision and maintenance within the period of *iddat*. In addition, her right to claim *mahr* or dower and all the properties given to her by her relatives, friends, husband and husband's relatives are protected. If the above benefits are not given to her at the time of divorce, she is entitled to apply to the Magistrate for an order directing her former husband to provide for such maintenance, the payment of *mahr* or dower or the delivery of the properties.

(ii) Where a Muslim divorced woman is unable to maintain herself after the period of *iddat*, the Magistrate is empowered to make an order for the payment of maintenance by her relatives who would be entitled to inherit her property upon her death according to Muslim law in proportion to which they would inherit her property. Upon the inability of such relatives to pay their share on the grounds of insufficiency of funds, the Magistrate would direct other relatives who have sufficient means to pay the shares of these relatives as well. But where a divorced woman has no relatives or the relatives do not have the means to pay the maintenance or other relatives who have been asked to pay the shares of the defaulting relatives also do not have the means to pay the defaulting relatives' share, the Magistrate would order the state Wakf Board to pay the maintenance ordered by him.

Apparent confusion[55] led these provisions to mean that a husband's liability extends only during the period of *iddat*. Also, the Act clearly provided that CrPC provisions would be available to the wife only if the husband and the wife together, by a joint affidavit, consent to being governed by the criminal court and not otherwise. Thus, the popular understanding of these provisions was as follows:

(i) The husband is under a legal obligation to pay maintenance to his wife only for the period of *iddat* and not beyond that.

(ii) Unless the husband himself, with an affidavit, consents to being governed by the secular provisions of the CrPC, the wife on her own cannot approach the criminal courts to claim maintenance.

Patently against the rights of divorced women and yet strangely entitled, the Muslim Women's *Protection of Rights on Divorce* Act [emphasis added], the Act's Constitutional validity was challenged in several cases. In the landmark *Daniel Latifi v Union of India*,[56] the Act was challenged on the grounds that:

(i) As the CrPC is an enactment providing for a quick and summary remedy to neglected Indian women who are in need of maintenance, to deny the same to a Muslim woman would result in her being led into destitution or vagrancy and this would be a negation of the concept of social justice enunciated in Article 21 of the Constitution.

(ii) The Act was un-Islamic, unconstitutional and had the potential of suffocating Muslim women as it undermines the secular character which is the basic feature of the Constitution.

(iii) There is no rhyme or reason to deprive Muslim women from the applicability of the provisions of Section 125, CrPC[57] and, consequently, the present Act must be held to be discriminatory and violative of Articles 14 and 21 of the Constitution.

(iv) This deprivation also creates a distinction between Muslim women and non-Muslim women who, though identically placed, can approach the court under the CrPC, and such discrimination would make the Act unconstitutional, as there is no rationale in depriving a Muslim woman from availing the remedies under Section 125, CrPC, notwithstanding the fact that the conditions precedent for availing of the said remedies are satisfied.

The Government of India defended the enactment and contended that:

(i) The Act does provide for a reasonable and fair provision and maintenance to be made and paid to the Muslim divorced woman by her former husband during the period of *iddat*, but it also makes clear that the maintenance cannot be for life, but would be only for the period of *iddat*; when that fact has clearly been stated in the provisions, the question of interpretation as to whether it is for life or for the period of *iddat* does not arise.

(ii) Personal law is a legitimate basis for discrimination if at all and therefore the Act does not offend Article 14 of the Constitution.
(iii) If the legislature, as a matter of policy, wants to apply Section 125, CrPC to Muslims, the same legislature can, by implication, withdraw such application and make some other provisions in that regard. The Parliament can amend Section 125, CrPC so as to exclude them and apply personal law and the policy of Section 125, CrPC is not to create a right of maintenance *de hors* the personal law.
(iv) In the Shah Bano case, it was held that a divorced woman was entitled to maintenance from her husband even after the *iddat* period and that is how Parliament also understood the *ratio* of that decision. To overcome the *ratio* of that decision, the present Act was enacted and, thus, it is not in discord with personal law.

The All India Muslim Personal Law Board also contended that:

(i) The Parliament enacted the impugned Act respecting the personal law of Muslims and that in itself is a legitimate basis for making a differentiation.
(ii) A separate law for a community on the basis of personal law applicable to such community cannot be held to be discriminatory.
(iii) The personal law is now being continued by a legislative enactment and the entire policy behind the Act is not to confer a right of maintenance, unrelated to the personal law.
(iv The object of the Act itself was to preserve personal law and prevent inroads into the same.
(v) The Act aims to prevent the vagaries and not make a Muslim woman destitute and, at the same time, not penalise the husband.
(vi The impugned Act resolves all issues bearing in mind the personal law of the Muslim community and the fact that the benefits of Section 125, CrPC have not been extended to Muslim women.

Justice Rajendra Babu, while interpreting the enactment, noted that the main provisions relating to maintenance of divorced women were as follows: "a divorced woman shall be entitled to a reasonable and fair provision and maintenance to be made and paid to her within the *iddat* period by her former husband". He said that there were two expressions used in the Section, namely, "reasonable and fair provision" and "maintenance", and both are distinct. The Parliament seems to indicate that it intended that the divorced woman gets sufficient means of livelihood after the divorce and, therefore, the word "provision" indicates something that is paid in advance for meeting some needs. Thus, at the time of the divorce, the husband is required to contemplate the woman's future needs and make preparatory arrangements for meeting those needs. "Reasonable and fair provision" may include provision for her residence, food, clothes and other articles. It actually means that the husband has to make a fair assessment of the needs of the wife, present and future, even beyond the period of *iddat* and, based on those needs, calculate a sum or valuable property and pay her during the period of *iddat*. The expression "within" should be read to mean 'during' or 'for'. Thus, the "reasonable and fair provision and maintenance" is not limited to the period of *iddat*, but extends to her whole life, unless she gets remarried. Within the *iddat* period does not mean that the liability extends during this period, rather, it indicates the time during which the husband has to make the payment.

If, during the *iddat* period, the former husband has not paid her a reasonable and fair provision and maintenance or *mahr* due to her or has not delivered the properties given to her before or at the time of marriage by her relatives or friends or the husband or any of his relatives or friends, the woman still has the remedy of approaching the criminal court under the CrPC and the Magistrate would be empowered to direct the errant husband to make payment to her. "Within" means 'on or before' and not 'beyond' and, thus, it means that before the expiry of the *iddat* period, the husband is bound to make and pay maintenance to the divorced wife and, in addition, make a fair provision for her to take care of her future needs.

While upholding the validity of the Act, the Court concluded:

(i) A Muslim husband is liable to make reasonable and fair provision for the future of the divorced wife, which obviously includes her maintenance as well. Such a reasonable and fair provision extending beyond the *iddat* period must be made by the husband within the *iddat* period.

(ii) Liability of a Muslim husband to his divorced wife is not confined to the *iddat* period.

(iii) A divorced Muslim woman, who has not remarried and who is unable to maintain herself after the *iddat* period, can proceed against her relatives (including her children and parents) who are liable to maintain her in proportion to the properties which they inherit upon her death according to Muslim law. If any of the relatives are unable to do so, the Magistrate would direct the Wakf Board established under the Act to do so. Thus, the Act does not offend Articles 14, 15, and 21 of the Constitution of India.

An extremely intelligent interpretation, this judgement not only changed the understanding of the entire law relating to the maintenance of a divorced Muslim woman, but also adequately secured her rights and very effectively checked the attempted evasion of financial responsibilities by Muslim men.

Daughters as coparceners under Hindu Law

Under classical Hindu law relating to the Mitakshara Hindu joint family, sons had a right by birth in the Mitakshara coparcenary, while daughters could not be coparceners. Even at the time of the enactment of the Hindu Succession Act, 1956, the legislature retained the concept of Mitakshara coparcenary with only sons as coparceners. In 1985, the state of Andhra Pradesh introduced unmarried daughters as coparceners, soon followed by an identical enactment in Karnataka: the Karnataka Hindu Succession (Amendment) Act, 1994. However, this Act allowed only unmarried daughters to become coparceners, which meant that those females who, on the date of promulgation of the Act, were unmarried became coparceners, but those daughters who were married on the day the Act came into force, could not become coparceners.

In *Nanjamma v State of Karnataka*,[58] the Karnataka Hindu Succession (Amendment) Act, 1994 was challenged as violative of the Constitutional guarantees of equality on the grounds that it did not treat all daughters equally and discriminated against a married daughter by excluding her from being a coparcener. The petitioner prayed that the words, "to a daughter married prior to" in Section 6A(d) of the Act be declared unconstitutional, contending that daughters married prior to the commencement of the Act are wrongly deprived of their coparcenary rights. According to the petitioner, daughters are daughters and differentiation made on the basis of their marital status is unreasonable.

Dismissing the contention and upholding the Constitutionality of the Act, the Court said:

> ...the daughters married prior to the commencement of the Amendment Act were deprived of the right to claim the share in coparcenary property as was available to an unmarried daughter or a daughter married after the enforcement of the said Act. The alleged discrimination cannot be termed to be either unreasonable or irrational and without basis. The two types of married daughters as contemplated by the offending portion of the section are well defined classes in themselves. Justification for classification in the instant case appears to be on the basis of social necessity keeping in view the prevalent system. The object of excluding the married daughter and the cases of partition already effected from the application of the Act appeared to be reasonably intended to avoid reopening of partition already effected in the family and the settled rights of brothers and sisters. Extending the benefit to a married daughter, married prior to the commencement of the Act would be likely to unsettle things which stood settled long back in the family and

> may even affect third parties who might have acquired valid rights and title in the property on the basis of settled rights or partitions.[59]

The Court upheld the Constitutionality of the Act, saying it was satisfied that there was a definitive nexus between classification made and the object which had been intended to be achieved by the legislature by making a provision in the form of the enactment.

Inheritance laws

Absolute ownership to Hindu females under the Hindu Succession Act, 1956

Under classical Hindu law, men were perceived to be legitimate and absolute owners of property, but a Hindu woman could not own the property as its full owner. Her rights over property were, by and large, in the nature of a limited owner, terminable upon her death or remarriage. The power of alienation of the property was restricted only to cases of legal necessity or for performance of indispensable religious duties. With an intention to remove this age old discrimination against women and promote their economic emancipation, Section 14 of the Hindu Succession Act, 1956 provided:

> **Property of a Hindu female to be her absolute property**: Any property possessed by a female Hindu whether acquired before or after the commencement of this Act would be held by her as full owner thereof and not as a limited owner.

This Section removed the statutory disability imposed on a Hindu woman to hold property as a full owner. However, its Constitutional validity was challenged in *Pratap Singh v Union of India*,[60] on the grounds of hostile discrimination against men, as it benefited only one section of the community – namely, women – notwithstanding the fact that men already were in an advantageous position and needed no statutory help or declaration for the same. In this case, upon the death of a Hindu male, his two widows and an adopted son took possession of his property. One of the widows relinquished her share in favour of the adopted son, while the other continued in possession of her one-third share. After consolidating his share to around two-thirds of the total property, the adopted son wanted the share of the other widow as well and filed a suit against her seeking a declaration that she had no right or title in her share. After the commencement of the Hindu Succession Act, 1956, the widow, as the full owner of the property, bequeathed the same to her relative. The adopted son contended that she had no right to make such a bequest as she was the limited owner of the same and also challenged the Constitutional validity of Section 14 of the Act that converted limited estates into absolute estates.

The adopted son's contention that Section 14 of the Act benefited only women and, thus, was hostile towards men and, therefore, violative of Article 14 of the Constitution was dismissed by the Court in view of Article 15(3) of the Constitution, which permits the State to enact special provisions in favour of women and children and overrides the Constitutional provision that the State shall not discriminate on grounds of sex alone. The Court also observed that Section 14 of the Hindu Succession Act, 1956 was enacted to remedy to some extent the plight of Hindu women who could not claim an absolute interest in the property inherited by them from their husbands, but could only enjoy it as limited owners thereof, with all the restrictions attached to the widow's estate under Hindu law. Expressing surprise, the Court said that there was hardly any justification for Hindu males to raise any objections to the beneficial provisions contained in the Act on the grounds of hostile discrimination and dismissed the petition.

Schemes of succession for male and female Hindu intestates under the Hindu Succession Act, 1956

Under the Hindu Succession Act, 1956, two different schemes of succession are provided on the basis of the sex of the intestates. For a Hindu male, it is primarily his relatives who inherit the property; none of his wife's relatives can be his heirs.[61] But if a Hindu female dies, the entire category of "heirs of the husband" not only inherits her property, but is accorded precedence over her own parents and siblings.[62]

The Constitutional validity of the provisions providing for these two separate schemes of succession was challenged in *Sonabai Yeshwant Jadhav v Bala Govinda Yadav*[63] as violative of Articles 14 and 15 of the Constitution and, therefore, *ultra vires* of the guarantee of equal treatment. In this case, upon the death of a Hindu man, his wife inherited his property and, upon her death, the son of a cousin brother of the husband laid claim over the property. The contention of the petitioner was that, as none of the relatives of the wife can inherit the property of a Hindu male, a provision that permits the "heirs of the husband" to inherit the property of a Hindu female was not only unreasonable, but also discriminatory and unconstitutional.

The Court said that the primary question involved was whether, in the case of a Hindu female dying intestate, by preferring the category of "heirs of the husband" to her parents, an irrational and arbitrary classification is made only on the ground of sex against the citizens of the state. Upholding the Constitutional validity of the impugned provision, the Court dismissed the suit and observed that:

> ...the Constitution does not posit totally unguided non-classified equality, as equal protection under the laws is not an abstract proposition. Laws are intended to solve specific problems and achieve definitive objectives and hence absolute equality or total uniformity is impossible of achievement. The governing principles of Article 14 operate upon the field that amongst the equals the

> law should be equal and be so administered. Discrimination is forbidden between classes and persons who are substantially similarly circumstanced. If the persons or groups are rationally classified and such classification bears the testimony of long standing position of personal law, then surely law can reach them differently and such different treatment would not result in discrimination. If the classification is founded on intelligible differentia and has rational relation to the object the legislative provision is intended to achieve, then such a challenge can hardly merit acceptance.[64]

Tracing the origins of Hindu society and the schemes of succession, the Court observed that the rules of succession and inheritance, when the marriage of the woman was in approved form under classical law, were based on the concept that the valid marriage results in unity of the spouses, i.e., wife and husband together formed one union. In recognition of that position, when succession opened to wife's property, the class known as "heirs of the husband", when no other immediate heirs were available, was permitted to succeed. This was the logical result of initial unity, in which the husband and the wife came to be interwoven by the tie of marriage. Recognition and reference to the heirs of the husband was just a logical necessary step to continue that unity in which the female had merged by marriage and was an integral part of such a family. However, conferment of full ownership upon a Hindu female with regard to the property acquired by her and, thus, putting her on par with other owners of the property in a Hindu family, is not intended to affect either her position as the wife in the family or the character of the family or property in her hands. With specific reference to succession to the property of a female, the Court noted:

> ...the supportive principle of the provisions is sustaining unity of the family and for that the entitlement to the property carved out in favour of closer relations than remote. Choose the core group and permit remote ones to come in only in case of its want, is the

> principle. Even the main scheme of succession 15(1) provides that when a Hindu woman dies intestate her property has to devolve upon her sons and daughters and her husband (all closely related blood relatives), secondly upon the heirs of husband (showing the principle of the close knit family unity with the husband), thirdly upon the mother and the father (indicating the second group of related family) and fourthly upon the heirs of the father and lastly upon the heirs of the mother (other distant related group). This scheme itself throws light upon the principles on the basis of which choice and arrangement of different classes of heirs is made, namely closer blood relations is preferred to the distant one, having reference to the family where succession opens.[65]

The Court concluded that there was hardly any manifest or remote evidence to indicate that any sex preference is legislated by this measure. On the other hand, as the beneficiaries were both male and female heirs, just because the words of statute use the phrase "heirs of the husband" to indicate upon whom the property should devolve, such terminology does not lead to the conclusion that this has enacted preference only on the ground of sex:

> The true principle is that a community governed by the given personal law itself forms a recognised class within the Constitutional contemplation and that itself offers a reasonable class of persons for testing the given legislation and the same has to be examined in the background of the principles by which such class is governed by the tenets of their personal law. If those principles are otherwise reasonable in the context and the history of the given system of personal law, then the challenge like the present one is hardly sustainable.[66]

Upholding the Constitutional validity of the provisions, it dismissed the petition without even addressing the issue of whether relegating the parents of a Hindu female intestate to an inferior position in comparison to even a remote relative of the husband can be justified or not. Even otherwise, the reasoning and the decision of the Court does not appear to be correct as its justifications can be summarised as follows:

(i) After marriage, the wife merges with the husband and together they form one union.
(ii) As a logical result of this unity, the husband's family becomes her family and his blood relations take preference over her own blood relations.
(iii) As a single scheme of succession is provided for female intestates, there is no discrimination between daughters based on marital status.

These arguments of the Court cannot be sustained as in all patriarchal societies, and not merely Hindu society, upon marriage, a husband and wife form an exclusive union and a woman is regarded as a member of the family of the husband; yet, none of the other family laws strip a married woman of her true identity and treat her as a foreigner to the natal family as does Section 15 of the Hindu Succession Act, 1956. For all other religious communities, where too the wife inherits from both her father and her husband, her property is never classified in light of the source of its acquisition and there is no interposition of her husband's heirs in preference to her own parents.

The Court's observation that a husband and wife merge in one union where the marriage is in approved form under the classical Hindu law also suffers from grave infirmity. Succession laws apply irrespective of the form of marriage. The only qualification is that the marriage should be valid. After that, whether the form of solemnisation was *shastric*, approved or unapproved, or customary or even if the marriage was solemnised in court, is irrelevant and succession laws would apply uniformly. The principles of the Hindu Succession Act, 1956 cannot have a varied application depending upon whether the marriage of the deceased was solemnised in approved form or in court. A fully secular solemnisation in court, with not an iota of religious observance, would still give rise to the application of the same inheritance principles that, in the view of the court, are based on the merger of the husband and the wife into one. Further, with the legislative permissibility of the dissolution of marriage and the remarriage of widows, the unity of spouses has lost its permanency (even if we accept those arguments of merger) and, in succession, a scenario imposing age old orthodox norms by the judiciary is most unwarranted.

Finally, it is incorrect for the Court to conclude that the legislature has provided a single scheme of succession, irrespective of the marital status of the woman. In operation, the succession laws for an unmarried and a married woman are fundamentally different. In the former case, the property goes to her blood relatives, as it should, but the moment the woman gets married, the legislative obsession with her transportation from her natal family to the matrimonial home and the presumed superiority of her in-laws over her blood relations is clearly reflected in making the entire clan of the husband her heirs and relegating her parents to an inferior placement. The woman may never have seen her husband's relatives, but in the event of her death, her parents who raised her are expected to step aside and the husband's relatives, who may never have been on the scene before her death, can legally claim her property, leading to unnatural, illogical and discriminatory consequences.

Succession rights in agricultural property

In India, the bulk of property is agricultural property which is governed by laws that vary from state to state. Patently discriminatory in their content, several of these laws completely eliminate a daughter from inheriting agricultural property, while others relegate her to a very inferior position. Unfortunately, the judiciary blatantly refuses to come to the aid of women, expressing its helplessness and taking shelter behind possible future consequence, while in reality, its attitude indicates its succumbing to the pressure of a patriarchal society which perpetuates the conservation and control of material assets in male hands only.

In *Madhu Kishwar v State of Bihar*,[67] the provisions relating to succession of tenurial land in the Chhota Nagpur Tenancy Act, 1908 were challenged as discriminatory against women. According to the provisions of this Act, tenurial rights in land are owned only by men and not by women, although it is a practical reality that both men and women till the land. After the death of a man, tenure rights are inherited only by his male descendants and, upon their failure, by male collaterals. If none of the male relatives is present, the property becomes village property, even in the presence of female representatives of the deceased. In this case, two tribal women challenged the discriminatory provisions of the Act as violative of the equality provisions of the Constitution, as not only were the provisions gender discriminatory, but they also took away the livelihood and only means of sustenance of these women. The moment the male members who held the land died, the male collateral would take possession of the land by forcibly dispossessing them. As the denial of the right of succession would amount to deprivation of their right to livelihood under Article 21 of the Constitution, the Act was also challenged as violative of the same.

Disagreeing with the submissions of the petitioners and upholding the Constitutional validity of the Act, the Court said:

> Rules of succession are indeed susceptible of providing differential treatment not necessarily equal. Non uniformities would not in all events violate Article 14. We refrain from striking down the provisions as such on the touchstone of Article 14 as this would bring about a chaos in the existing state of law. However laudable, desirable and attractive the result may seem it has happily been viewed by our learned brother that an activist court is not fully equipped to cope with the details and intricacies of the legislative subject and can at best advice and focus attention on the state policy on the problem and shake it from its slumber, goading it to awaken, march and reach the goal [*sic.*]. For in whatever measure be the concern of the court, it compulsively

> needs to apply, somewhere and at sometimes, brakes to its self motion described in judicial parlance as self restraint. Thus under the circumstance it is not desirable to declare the customs of tribal inhabitants as offending Articles 14, 15 and 21 of the Constitution and each case must be examined when full facts are placed before the courts.[68]

Holding the provisions within the ambit of the Constitution, the Court held that after the death of the last male member in the family capable of holding tenurial rights, the ownership would not pass to the females, but to the male relatives/collaterals and, in their absence, to the entire village. However, the females would still have the right to cultivate the land and enjoy the produce for their lifetime. The male relatives/collaterals who inherit the tenurial rights would not be entitled to take possession until the death of the women.

Fixation of ceilings

Time and again, laws dealing with fixation of ceilings of agricultural land have been challenged unsuccessfully as violating Constitutional principles of equality. In *Ambika Prasad Mishra v State of UP*,[69] the Uttar Pradesh Zamindari Abolition and Land Reforms Act, 1950 was challenged. The petitioners contended that the Act discriminated against major unmarried daughters by not providing extra land to their father as it did for the sons and also discriminated between the husband and wife in fixation of ceilings by regarding only the husband as the tenure holder, even if the wife was its real owner.

Admitting that land reform enactments did not treat Indian women fairly, the Court said:

> We wonder whether the Commission on Status of Women or the Central Government has considered this aspect of sex discrimination. Adult damsels should not be left in distress by progressive legislations geared to land reforms. This criticism may have bearing on the ethos of the community and the attitude of

> the legislators but we are concerned here only with the constitutionality of the provisions.

Despite having said this, however, the Court held that, "these legal sentiments and jural value must not run riot and destroy provisions which do not discriminate between men and women but merely organise a scheme where life's realism is legislatively pragmatised. Such a scheme may marginally affect gender justice but does not abridge, even a wee bit, the right of women. If land holding and ceilings thereon are organised with the paramount purpose of maximising surpluses without manning women's ownership no submission to destroy this measure can be permitted using sex discrimination as a means to sabotage what is socially desirable".[70] The Court said that these land-related legislations were in the nature of social welfare legislation and cannot be declared void on grounds of gender discrimination. Ironically, the judgment was delivered by Justice Krishna Aiyyar, usually known for his gender sensitive views.

The exclusion of women as tenure holders was explained away as a legislative device for simplifying procedural dealings and the judgment stated that, when all is said and done, married women in our villages do need their husbands' services and speak through them in public places. Further, the Court said that large land holders cannot be allowed to outwit socially imperative land distribution by putting female discrimination as a mask. The challenge was dismissed.

Unfortunately, both judgements – *Madhu Kishwar* and *Ambika Prasad* – have strengthened women's subordination, furthered gender injustice and are an exact antithesis to the Constitutional goals of gender parity.

Conclusion

The response of the courts to the challenges of family law provisions displays a conflict of judicial opinion which can be summarised as follows:

(i) The courts have held that family laws are not "laws" within the meaning of the Constitution and, therefore, they need not grapple with their Constitutionality.

(ii) The courts have admitted that family laws have to pass the Constitutional validity test, but have refused to adjudicate the issue themselves. They have said that even if family laws are discriminatory, the remedy does not lie with the judiciary, but rather, with the legislature.

(iii) The courts have held that certain provisions of family laws are differential in their character, but are not discriminatory as they are based on a reasonable classification and do not offend the Constitutional principles of parity.

(iv) The courts have held that provisions of family laws are amenable to different interpretations and, to make them Constitutional, have proceeded to give a modified interpretation, different from the interpretation hitherto given, so that a harmonious construction is possible between the impugned provisions and the basic provisions of the Constitution.

(v) In some cases, the courts have come to the conclusion that being unconstitutional, the impugned provisions of family laws should not be allowed to continue on the statute books and have declared them void.

The Constitution of India is the basic law of the land and as every legislation derives its validity from the Constitution, a legislation can never be inconsistent with basic Constitutional provisions. The Constitution itself provides that no law, ordinance, rule, byelaw, etc., inconsistent with its basic provisions can be sustained in law. Therefore, the duty of the courts is to ensure that laws inconsistent with the basic provisions of the Constitution are not allowed to continue on the statute books as their continuation would make Article 13 and the guarantees of parity meaningless. No other statutory authority besides the judiciary has the power to declare discriminatory provisions as violative of Constitutional provisions and, therefore, void. The courts are, therefore, under a Constitutional duty always to take Constitutional challenges seriously, assess the implications and effects of the impugned provision in both theory and practice and either craft a harmonious interpretation of the impugned provision or declare it void. Upholding Constitutional principles is the primary duty of the courts and taking shelter behind imagined consequences of increased litigations, dissensions and unpleasantness in the family or possibilities of socio-political backlash is not only improper, but also extremely unfortunate. Stray exceptions notwithstanding, an analysis of the Constitutional challenges to discriminatory provisions of family laws has till now proven to be disappointing, with courts displaying an unwarranted reluctance and sometimes even helplessness to adopt a correctional attitude and failing to discharge their primary duty to uphold the principles of the Constitution.

Notes

[1] Article 13 of the Constitution of India reads:

Laws inconsistent with or in derogation of the Fundamental Rights—(1) All laws in force in the territory of India immediately before the commencement of this Constitution, in so far as they are inconsistent with the provisions of this Part, shall, to the extent of such inconsistency, be void. (2) The state shall not make any law which takes away or abridges the rights conferred by this part and any law made in contravention of this clause shall, to the extent of the contravention, be void. (3) In this Article, unless the context otherwise requires—

(a) "law" includes any Ordinance, order, bye-law, rule, regulation, notification, custom or usage having in the territory of India the force of law;

(b) "laws in force" includes laws passed or made by a Legislature or other competent authority in the territory of India before the commencement of this Constitution and not previously repealed, notwithstanding that any such law or any part thereof may not be then in operation either at all or in particular areas. (4) Nothing in this Article shall apply to any amendment of this Constitution made under Article 368.

[Editor's Note: The Constitution of India is available online at: http://indiacode.nic.in/coiweb/welcome.html]

[2] Examples of such pre-Independence legislations include the Child Marriage Restraint Act, 1929 and the Sind Leti Act, 1939 (prohibiting the giving and taking of dowry). Post-Independence legislations include the Bihar Dowry Restraints Act, 1950, the Andhra Pradesh Dowry Prohibition Act, 1958 and the Dowry Prohibition Act, 1961.

[3] However, the first legislative step banning polygamy for Hindu men was taken in Bombay in 1946 and a conviction under that Act resulted in the accused challenging its Constitutional validity.

[4] AIR 1952 Bom 84.

[5] The accused argued that, in so far as both these personal laws allow polygamy but not polyandry, they discriminate against women only on the ground of sex and, if that is so, the provisions of the personal laws permitting polygamy offend Article 15(1) of the Constitution and, as such, are also void to that extent under Article 13(1) of the Constitution. In other words, after the commencement of the Constitution, bigamous marriages under Hindu as well as Muslim law became void and Hindu and Muslim men who entered into such marriages became liable to be punished for committing bigamy. Yet, the impugned Act specifically provides for punishment of Hindus alone and, in so doing, discriminates against Hindus solely on the ground of religion. The grievance was that the impugned Act should have provided for punishment of both Hindus and Muslims who contract bigamous marriages.

[6] AIR 1952 Bom 84, at p. 91.

[7] AIR 1952 Bom 84, at p. 90.

[8] AIR 1952 Bom 84, at pp. 92–93.

[9] AIR 1952 Bom 84, at p. 93.

[10] AIR 1952 Bom 84, at p. 94.

[11] AIR 1959 Manipur 20.

[12] Though the accused did not specifically plead violation of Article 25 of the Constitution, he argued nevertheless that matters relating to marriage are part of Hindu religion and that, under Article 25 of the Constitution, every citizen has a right to profess, practice and propagate his religion untrammeled by State interference. The argument questioned the power of the State to legislate on matters essentially falling under religion.

[13] AIR 1952 Mad 193.

[14] See also *Lakshmindra Theertha Swamier v Commr. Hindu Religious Endowments, Madras* [AIR 1952 Mad 613].

[15] AIR 1972 AP 156.

[16] AIR 2007 Chh 64.

[17] *Brajendra Singh v State of MP* [AIR 2008 SC 1056].

[18] *Malti Roy Chowdhary v Sudhindranath* [AIR 2007 Cal 4].

[19] AIR 1991 Kant 186.

[20]AIR 1991 Kant 186, at p.187.
[21]AIR 1991 Kant 186, at p. 188.
[22]AIR 1983 AP 356.
[23]AIR 1983 AP 356, at p. 373.
[24]AIR 1983 AP 356, at pp. 369–370.
[25]AIR 1983 AP 356, at p. 370.
[26]The remedy of restitution of conjugal rights was abolished in England by Section 20 of the Matrimonial Proceedings and Properties Act, 1970.
[27]AIR 1983 AP 356, at p. 374.
[28]AIR 1984 Del 66.
[29]AIR 1984 Del 66, at pp. 71–73.
[30]AIR 1984 Del 66, at p. 75.
[31]AIR 1984 Del 66, at p. 78.
[32](1984) 4 SCC 90.
[33](1984) 4 SCC 90, paragraph 14.
[34]The IDA was amended in 2001 and the grounds of divorce were brought more or less on par with those available under the other enactments. Now, common grounds exist for spouses irrespective of their sex. The Act has also been renamed the Divorce Act, 1869. Like its predecessor, the Divorce Act applies only to Christians.
[35]Prior to its amendment, Section 10 of the IDA read as follows:

When husband may petition for dissolution—Any husband may present a petition to the District Court or to the High Court, praying that his marriage may be dissolved on the ground that his wife has since the solemnisation thereof, been guilty of adultery.

When wife may petition for dissolution—Any wife may present a petition to the District Court or to the High Court, praying that her marriage may be dissolved on the ground that since the solemnisation thereof, her husband has exchanged his profession of Christianity for the profession of some other religion, and gone through a form of marriage with another woman;

Or has been guilty of incestuous adultery;

Or of bigamy with adultery;

Or of marriage with another woman with adultery;

Or of rape, sodomy or bestiality; or of adultery coupled with such cruelty as without adultery would have entitled her to a divorce a *mense et toro*;

Or of adultery coupled with desertion without reasonable excuse, for two years or upwards.

[36]AIR 1953 Mad 792.
[37]AIR 1953 Mad 792, at p. 800.
[38](1994) 5 SCC 704.
[39](1994) 5 SCC 704, at p. 708.
[40]AIR 2001 Bom 208.
[41]AIR 2001 Bom 208, at pp. 209–210.

[42]AIR 1995 Ker 252.
[43]AIR 1953 Mad 792.
[44]Under Section 488 of the Code of Criminal Procedure, 1973 (CrPC), read with Section 112 of the Indian Evidence Act, 1872.
[45]AIR 1995 Ker 252, at p. 270.
[46]Ibid.
[47](1999) 2 SCC 228.
[48](1999) 2 SCC 228, at paragraph 9.
[49]Ibid.
[50](1997) 3 SCC 573.
[51](1997) 3 SCC 573, at p.575. The apparent hint of the Court was that the remedy lay with the legislature.
[52]1994 Supp (1) SCC 713.
[53]Under classical Muslim law, *iddat* is the period during which a woman whose marriage has been dissolved either by divorce or by death of the husband must wait before she can remarry.
[54]AIR 1985 SC 945.
[55]Confusion existed among both jurists and the judiciary with respect to the availability of CrPC provisions to a divorced Muslim woman in the absence of an affidavit filed by the parties. The predominant view was that the husband is under no obligation to provide maintenance to his divorced wife beyond the period of *iddat* and would also not be subject to CrPC provisions. Judicial interpretations in this regard were conflicting and, in several cases, the courts denied women maintenance beyond the period of *iddat*.
[56](2001) 7 SCC 740.
[57]Section 125 of the CrPC obligates male members of the family to provide maintenance to dependents in the family, including wives and children.
[58]1999 AIHC 3003 (Kar)
[59]1999 AIHC 3003 (Kar), at paragraph 5.
[60]AIR 1985 SC 1695; (1985) 4 SCC 197.
[61]For details, see Section 8 and the Schedule of the Hindu Succession Act, 1956.
[62]For details, see Section 15 of the Hindu Succession Act, 1956.
[63]AIR 1982 Bom 156.
[64]AIR 1982 Bom 156, at p. 163.
[65]AIR 1982 Bom 156, at p. 166.
[66]AIR 1982 Bom 156, at p. 170.
[67]1996 (5) SCC 125.
[68]1996 (5) SCC 125, at p. 135.
[69](1980) 3 SCC 719.
[70](1980) 3 SCC 719, at p. 729.

6 Nepal: From Equality to Gender Justice[1]

Sapana Pradhan Malla

Background

While the government of a country is often understood to be the prime agent for ensuring the security and stability of the country and its citizens, a constitution is understood to provide a legal framework defining relations between each arm of the State, as well as its relation with the citizens. Politics and law are, therefore, inherently connected in achieving the sovereignty of a State. It is, therefore, often surprising that a country like Nepal, which has seen drastic changes in both the above-mentioned features, has still succeeded in upholding its sovereignty and integrity as a nation.

Legal developments in Nepal have been inherently intertwined with its political developments and yet the law has been the backbone through every transition. While the people's movement, which culminated in the overthrowing of monarchy in April 2006, has been hailed as the prime deciding factor in Nepal's democracy thus far, it was not the first of its kind. Nepal has witnessed several revolts in the past – during 1950, 1979 and 1990 – on several grounds, most commonly that of tackling feudalism and the ever-unstable monarchy which had been in a near constant state of internecine conflict.

It is also important to note that the first ever codified legal document of Nepal was not its Constitution, despite the unification of all territories previously under autonomous rulers by Prithvi Narayan Shah. Nepal's laws were not codified until several decades later, in 1910, under the first Prime Ministership of Janga Bahadur Rana, when the Country Code or the *Muluki Ain* was formulated. Both the Shah and the Rana dynasties having been followers of Hinduism, the *Muluki Ain*, though inspired by the Napoleonic Code in France, was based on the Hindu scriptures, in particular the *Manu Smriti*, and exists to date as the basic framework for all civil and criminal legal action within the country.

The first Constitution of Nepal was formulated in 1948 under Rana Padma Shamsher. In subsequent years, Nepal witnessed a series of six constitutions, formulated during different political times, each a larger step towards democracy compared to its predecessors. However, this process of Constitutional reform did not essentially ensure a strong system of governance; neither did it ensure effective application of the principles enshrined within it. With regard to women's rights, while several attempts were made, through Constitutional provisions, to incorporate and expand the principles of equality and non-discrimination on the basis of sex, the language, by and large, remained masculine and some of the provisions remained glaringly discriminatory against women. Democracy and its birth in Nepal had failed to consider and incorporate gender issues. One of the primary reasons for this failure could well be the lack of adequate participation of women in the revolutionary and restructuring processes.

After 12 years of insurgency and discontent in the country, in 2006, the "second people's movement" attempted to reinstate democracy and end monarchy in absolute terms. 14,000 citizens had been killed over the years, accompanied by a high incidence of disappearances of people, exploitation of children and suppression of voices of Non-Governmental Organisations (NGOs). On the other hand, this revolution had a large impact on women. Women's participation was visible and effective, including as part of the Maoist cadres. The need for addressing women's issues was never greater in all the years of Nepal's existence as a sovereign state.

The Comprehensive Peace Accord (CPA) was signed on November 21, 2006 between the Government and the Communist Party of Nepal (Maoist), as a collective effort of seven political parties. Subsequently, the state restructuring process started focusing on institutional reform, with the enactment of a new Constitution through the Constituent Assembly (CA). An Interim Constitution was formulated on the basis of the CPA, declaring Nepal to be an "independent, indivisible, sovereign, secular, inclusive and a fully democratic State".

As it formulates its new Constitution, Nepal faces the immense challenge of living up to the ideals of inclusiveness for which thousands of lives have been sacrificed in the last decade. In terms of gender equality, the primary challenge since the people's movement has been in ensuring visibility of women's voices in the current state restructuring process. Though the strategy of ensuring gender equality thus far had been one of court interventions and judicial activism, more recently there has been a focus on strengthening the political processes and direct intervention through the country's foremost law-making body: the Constituent Assembly.

This paper attempts to trace the movement for gender equality and gender justice, through the past decades of Nepal's struggle for political and legal stability and through monarchy to democracy and theocracy to secularism.

Status of women

The total population of Nepal is 23,151,423, of which women constitute 50.05%, i.e., 11,587,502.[2] Despite this strength in numbers, women continue to face discrimination on the basis of sex and gender in various spheres of life. The overall literacy rate of women is only 42.49%, compared to the male literacy rate of 65.08%.

Hindu women and women belonging to indigenous ethnic groups such as *Rai, Limbu, Gurung*, etc., each have different community laws, customs, norms by which they are bound and also suffer from different modes of oppression. Women from indigenous groups enjoy more egalitarian rights, with equal or more access and control of resources, relatively higher degree of social mobility and freedom within the private sphere. However, their participation in the public sphere is negligible due to the dominant ideology of *Bahunbad* (Bahunism).[3] In contrast, Hindu women have no autonomy within the private sphere, but enjoy limited positions in the public sphere. Their oppression stems from the concepts of hierarchy, the caste system, traditional thoughts about food and the high value placed on chastity.

Economic Status

The dominant Hindu religion and culture have popularised a belief that women should be dependent on men for income. Men are considered the sole breadwinners of the family and women are viewed as being only domestic and maternal. "Women's work" is confined to the household from the very beginning of their life cycle. Though the National Census 2001 took some steps to include the contribution of domestic labour in its assessment of economic activities, generally women's domestic labour goes unnoticed and unpaid. Women who are engaged in paid employment are concentrated in agriculture, carpet industries, as domestic servants or other wage labour activities.[4]

According to the Three Year Interim Plan (2007–2010) of the Government of Nepal:

> Gender Development Index and Gender Empowerment Index are found to be 0.452 and 0.391 respectively. Labor participation is 48.9 percent for females, and 67.6 percent for males. Most of the women are involved in informal, subsistence-oriented, *domestic* (home-based), and (unpaid) *non-wage earning* work. The weekly contribution of male and female to external economic activities is

> 42.6 and 36.3 hours respectively. On the other hand, weekly male and female contribution to household economic activities is 46.5 and 42.5 hours respectively. Similarly, weekly labour contribution of male and female to non-economic household activities is 9.7 and 25.1 hours respectively. The total weekly male and female involvement in economic and non-economic activities is found to be 98.8 and 103.9 hours respectively.[5]

Complicated economic disparity is increasing the number of poor women. Women's ownership of a house is only around 11%. This system leads to discrimination against the girl child in food distribution, the provision of clothing, healthcare, education and entertainment. This is because the female child is viewed as having no lasting value to the family.[6]

Socio-cultural status

Patriarchy persists and the dominance of Hindu religion and culture has resulted in women being treated as second class citizens. Of the various communities within Nepal, Hindu women often are the most oppressed.[7] Some of the socially backward practices that have contributed to the vulnerable status of women – such as child marriage, violence in marriage, dowry, *chhaupadi, deuki, badi,* and *jhuma* – are still prevalent in Nepalese society. Finally, regional differences, caste and class also affect the status of women.

Political status

Nepalese women have been involved in political movements since the 1950s. However, as they were excluded from participating in local or national politics under the law, their voices were not heard in the country's political system. Later, even when they were represented in politics, they were unable to occupy key posts and/or influence policy decisions. Factors that created barriers included: the dominant ideology of patriarchy, male chauvinism, criminalisation of politics, lack of equal property rights, restrictions on women's mobility and domination of men in all the political parties and the media.

After the second people's movement, the issues of inclusion of women in politics have been emphatically raised by women's rights activists, civil society members and women's wings of political parties. The Interim Parliament proclaimed to ensure one-third representation of women in the State mechanism. The Interim Constitution has also ensured women's representation in the CA.

The Constituent Assembly Members Election Act, 2007 requires that candidacy lists consist of at least one-third women. In the CA elections of 2008, 32.8% of CA seats (197 out of 601) were filled by women who were elected (191) or nominated (6). This is a remarkable representation in the parliamentary history of Nepal. However, given the fact that women constitute half the population of Nepal, the successes so far have only extended to one-third representation.

Though the present Vice-President of the CA is a woman, there is an acute paucity of female leadership in higher public positions, including in the judiciary, civil services, other government bodies as well as in constitutional bodies and in diplomatic positions at the national level.

The Local Self-Governance Act, 1997 reserved 20% seats for women in local government. Here too, only 10% women can be seen in the decision-making structure of political parties.

Constitutions, equality and non-discrimination

Previous Constitutions

The evolution of Constitutional language through the years depicts the gradual and steady change of Nepal's policy towards women and gender equality.

The first Constitution, having been formulated in 1948, delegated all powers of the State to the Shree Tin Sarkars, vesting the authority to carry out the administration of the country in Padma Sham Shere and, later, to the King. This tradition of vesting all authority of the State in male inheritors of the monarchy was followed until Nepal was declared a republic state by the Interim Constitution of Nepal 2007.

While there was no special mention of women or discrimination on the basis of sex, a general guarantee of equality under the Constitution of 1948 was provided in Article 4:

> Subject to the principles of public order and morality this Constitution guarantees to the citizens of Nepal freedom of person, freedom of speech, liberty of the press, freedom of assembly and discussion, freedom of worship, *complete equality in the eye of the law*, cheap and speedy justice, universal free compulsory elementary education, universal and equal suffrage for all adults, security of private property as defined by the laws of the State as at present existing and laws and rules to be made hereunder. [Emphasis added]

The Constitution of 1951 provided a slightly improved structure of equality and non-discrimination, which was retained in essence through every successive Constitution. In Article 14, it stated:

> **Equality before law**
> His Majesty's Government shall not deny to any person equality before law or the equal protection of the laws within the territory of Nepal.

And, thereafter, in Article 15:

> **Discrimination on grounds of religion, race, caste, sex, etc.**
> (1) His Majesty's Government shall not discriminate against any citizen on grounds only of religion, race, caste, sex, place of birth or any of them.
> (2) Nothing in this section shall prevent His Majesty's Government from making any special provision for women and children.

In Article 16, it also incorporated the right to equal opportunity for all citizens in appointments and employment under His Majesty's government, even allowing reservations in favour of any backward class of citizens.

With specific reference to women, the Constitution of 1951 guaranteed equal rights of men and women to adequate means of livelihood [Article 5(a)], equal pay for equal work [Article 5(d)] and protection for women against heavy work in acknowledgement of their physical weakness [Article 5(e)]. In a display of substantive progress, under Article 8, the Constitution specified provisions for securing just and humane conditions of work and for maternity relief. Furthermore, in Article 11, the Constitution guaranteed special care in the promotion of the educational and economic interests of weaker sections of society and their protection from social injustice and all forms of exploitation. Lastly, having introduced a parliament and a system of general elections for the first time, the Constitution provided that, "no person shall be ineligible for inclusion in any such roll for any such constituency on grounds only of religion, race, caste, sex or any of them", thereby ensuring women's right to vote.

In its Preamble, the Constitution of 1959 explicitly declared for the first time that the monarchy in Nepal be followers of the Hindu religion and required the King to be an "adherent of Aryan culture and Hindu religion". Although this Constitution guaranteed the right to religion, it also stated that every citizen must practice the religion of their choice in keeping with and respecting the established traditions within the country.

While the code of equality formulated under the Constitution of 1951 – in terms of equality before the law, non-discrimination on the basis of sex and equal opportunity in employment – was retained, in a regressive step, the Constitution of 1959 did not reflect the provisions on adoption of special measures for women and children that were provided under the Constitution of 1951. However, in

Article 3(2), it introduced a prohibition of trafficking in human beings, slavery and forced labour. Most importantly, under Article 9, the Constitution of 1959 introduced the right to Constitutional Remedies, thereby facilitating court action protecting women's rights.

Nepal was declared a Hindu State for the first time under the Constitution of 1962. The issue of citizenship was introduced for the first time under this Constitution as well [Article 7]. It acknowledged the citizenship of a child either of whose parents was born in Nepal. However, Article 7(c) stated that a woman marrying a Nepali citizen could become a citizen, but disregarded the right in reverse whereby a man marrying a Nepali woman may choose to take Nepali citizenship. This provision was maintained in all the Constitutions formulated thereafter.

Article 17(2)(f) of the Constitution of 1962 reintroduced affirmative action through the enactment of laws for the protection of the rights and interests of women. This Constitution also introduced several other provisions particularly dedicated to women: recognition of women's organisations as separate entities, elimination of child marriage, traditional practices and bigamy and provision of free and compulsory primary education for all that may include women.

The most democratic Constitution thus far is that of 1990. The Preamble of this Constitution states that, "the source of sovereign authority of the independent and sovereign Nepal is inherent in the people and therefore...desire to conduct the government of the country in consonance with the popular will". In keeping with the Preamble, multi-party democracy was considered as the primary strength of the country.

However, the acquisition of citizenship was further restricted in this Constitution and was more discriminatory towards women in comparison to the Constitution of 1962. Under Article 9, eligibility for citizenship at birth was restricted to descent from a Nepali father only. The citizenship of a child with unknown parents was deemed to be Nepali until the father of the child was found, overlooking the identity or presence of the mother. While a gender neutral provision acknowledging both maternal and paternal descent of a child seeking citizenship after residence for two years in Nepal was incorporated, the provision was never applied.

Article 11(5) guaranteed equal pay for equal work. However, the right to privacy [Article 22] protected "the privacy of the person, house, property, document, correspondence or information of anyone", thereby having a detrimental effect on the rights of women in the private sphere.

Expanded provisions under the Directive Principles and Policies of the State required the State to ensure the participation of women in the task of national development by making special provisions for their education, health and employment [Article 26(7)] and to ensure the welfare and protection of helpless women [Article 26(9)].

Political representation of women in the National Assembly, newly formed under this Constitution, was ensured through the proportional representation of three women members amongst 35 members to be elected by the House of Representatives [Article 46(1)(b)] and reserving 5% candidacy for women in elections to the House of Representatives [Article 114].

Interim Constitution of 2007

The Interim Constitution of 2007 was one of the first successes towards effective and comprehensive articulation of women's human rights in the structure of the country's governance. This was mainly attributed to the larger participation of women in the Constitution writing process, as shown in the graph below (p. 190).

The Preamble of the Interim Constitution proclaims the adoption of a multi-party democracy and the progressive restructuring of the State with an aim to resolve existing problems of the country relating to class, caste, region and gender.

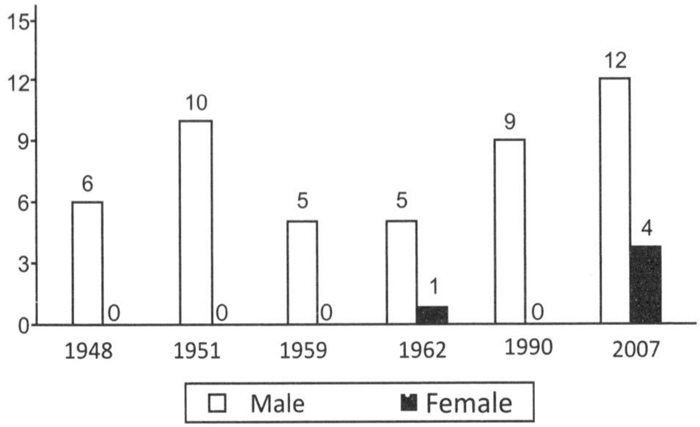

Women's representation in Constitution Writing

Citizenship rights were considerably reformed to allow both women and men to pass citizenship on to their children [Article 8(2)(b)]. However, Nepali women are still not entitled to pass on citizenship on to their non-Nepali husbands [Article 8(6)].

While the Interim Constitution retained the equality code of previous Constitutions, the guarantee of non-discrimination was extended to the application of laws as well as to the actions of the State [Article 13]. In addition, the right to social security was guaranteed to women in accordance with the law [Article 18(2)]. Article 20 was introduced specifically for the protection of the rights of women: prohibiting discrimination in any form on the basis of gender [Article 20(1)]; guaranteeing the right to reproductive health and other reproductive matters [Article 20(2)]; providing that no physical, mental or other form of violence can be inflicted on a woman [Article 20(3)]; and guaranteeing equal inheritance rights for sons and daughters to ancestral property [Article 20(4)]. Article 21 guaranteed the "proportional inclusion" of women in State structures on the basis of economic, social and educational backwardness.

Article 29 guaranteed the right against exploitation, including exploitation on the basis of custom, tradition and convention or in any manner. It also prohibits human trafficking, slavery, bonded or forced labour.

Article 33 identified the responsibilities of the State, including the responsibility to carry out inclusive, democratic and progressive restructuring of the State in order to address the problems related to women (amongst others) and to eliminate all discriminatory laws.

The Directive Principles of the State guaranteed the adoption of special measures, including provisions to prevent economic exploitation and as well as economic disparity of any caste, sex, tribe, origin, etc [Article 34(4)].

Regarding representation in decision-making bodies, the Interim Constitution mandated one-third candidacy of women in the CA [Article 63] and required representation of women in the National Human Rights Commission (the only Constitutionally mandated commission) [Article 131].

Act to Amend Some Nepal Acts for Maintaining Gender Equality, 2006 (hereafter, "Gender Equality Act")

Non-implementation of the Constitutional guarantees of equality and non-discrimination was plainly visible in the remaining framework of laws within the country.

In an effort to provide an impetus to the demands for the amendment or elimination of discriminatory provisions under laws, regulations and policies, in 2000, the Forum for Women Law and Development (FWLD) conducted a pioneering study, *Discriminatory Laws in Nepal and Their Impact on Women: A Review of the Current Situation and Proposals for Change.*[8] This study revealed 118 Clauses/Sections/Rules, two Rules in their entirety and 67 Schedules/Annexes/Forms in 54 different legislations, including the Constitution, which contained gender discriminatory provisions. The main areas of discrimination against women were found in relation to nationality, property, trafficking, sexual abuse, education, employment, health (including reproductive health), marriage and family and legal procedures and court proceedings. The study depicted the multifaceted impact of discriminatory laws on women, restricting their options for development in virtually every sphere of their lives. In addition, these discriminatory laws deprived women from education and health facilities and increased their vulnerability to be trafficked and sexually abused. The study highlighted other impacts of discriminatory citizenship laws: creation of second class citizens, statelessness, difficulties in acquiring passports, deprivation from employment opportunities, difficulties in transferring property, separation from family and residence and problems in selecting residence, etc. Using the study's findings, many Public Interest Litigations (PILs) were filed and advocacy was conducted for the reformation and effective implementation of law.

Though triggered by the FWLD study, as well as directives issued by the Supreme Court, in response to PILs, for the amendment of discriminatory provisions, there were several other factors that also contributed to the enactment of the Gender Equality Act. The initiation of action in the State took place with the formation of a high-level Committee in August 2001 to prepare amendment proposals. The Committee updated the list of discriminatory laws and also prepared proposals for amendments. Simultaneously, FWLD, in coordination with different networks, also prepared amendment proposals. Upon submission of the same, the House of Speaker issued a directive to the Ministry of Women, Children and Social Welfare for the registration of the amendment bill based on civil society initiatives.

FWLD published updates of its study in 2004, 2006 and 2007. The 2006 study examined the Constitution, 281 Acts and 278 Rules. It revealed 173 Clauses/Sections/Rules, two Rules in their entirety and 102 Schedules/Annexes/Forms scattered in 83 different legislations, including the Constitution, which discriminated against women. The study also took into account indirect discrimination and gender discriminatory language.[9]

As a result of concerted lobbying by concerned women stakeholders, political leaders, parliamentarians and civil society actors to repeal or amend gender discriminatory laws on the basis of the FWLD studies, the House of Representatives, reinstituted after the historic people's movement, endorsed a landmark Proposal to Eliminate all Forms of Discrimination Against Women on May 30, 2006. This proposal led, in turn, to the Gender Equality (Amendment) Bill being approved by the House of Representatives on September 28, 2006. The Certification of the Bill took place on November 3, 2006.

The Bill, now the Gender Equality Act, has proved to be an important step in the elimination of discrimination against women. The Act has repealed or amended 56 discriminatory provisions under various laws and has also incorporated some additional provisions to acknowledge and protect women's rights.

Some of the major discriminatory provisions (particularly influenced by religious and traditional definitions of women's role in society) which were amended include:

- The provision relating to the grounds for divorce in the case of no children within 10 years of marriage was eliminated.
- Marital rape was included as a ground for divorce. The definition of rape as a criminal offence was also broadened to include marital rape.
- Mothers were granted the first right to guardianship of a child, if the child was a minor.
- The provision that deprives a mother from the guardianship of children in the instance where she enters a second marriage was removed.
- The provision that a daughter shall return the share of paternal inherited property once she is married was repealed.
- A woman was now entitled to use her movable and immovable property freely, as opposed to the previous provisions that required the gaining of consent from the husband or family before exercising her rights over more than half of the immovable property.

- It was provided that *any person* of the family shall be the head of the household, as opposed to the previous provision that assumed only the father or husband as the head of a household.
- It was provided that the consent of the first wife should be taken before entering into polygamy under conditions prescribed by the law.
- The difference in prescribed age for men and women to enter into court marriages has been amended to 20 years of age for both.
- The provisions relating to a claimant in the line of succession under various provisions have been amended to ensure gender equality.

CEDAW and its applicability in Nepal

The Convention on the Elimination of All Forms of Discrimination against Women (CEDAW) was ratified by Nepal in April 1991. As per Section 9 of the Nepal Treaty Act, 1991, all conventions and treaties to which Nepal is a signatory are accorded the force of binding law. In *Reena Bajracharya v HMG/Nepal*,[10] the Supreme Court upheld Section 9 of the Treaty Act, stating that it provides a higher status to the Conventions to which Nepal is a party, as opposed to the domestic law, thereby making the implementation of these Conventions easier and more efficient. However, as per the new jurisprudence developed by the Supreme Court, Conventions cannot overrule the Constitution.[11] The exact status of international conventions vis-à-vis domestic jurisprudence is, therefore, unclear at present.

However, it is encouraging to note that, despite a general ignorance of CEDAW amongst most law enforcers and government bodies, the Supreme Court of Nepal has been extremely successful in acknowledging and upholding its principles. It is indeed the Supreme Court that has, time and again, displayed splendid judicial activism in law reform based on Nepal's obligations under CEDAW. One of the major reasons for this is the recognition of PILs under the

Constitution of 1990 – a feature that has been retained till now.

For a long time in Nepal, equality and non-discrimination were understood to be synonymous. Therefore, the Constitutional code on equality initially centred on prohibiting inequality by public acts or actors, principally prohibiting the enactment of unequal laws and policies. However, the problematic line between public and non-public inequality has been increasingly contested and is gradually changing.[12] Statutory equality aims to equalise relations among individuals as members of social groups defined on specific social grounds, such as sex, age or race, in specific spheres of civil society, typically education and employment. A more comprehensive definition of discrimination, provided by CEDAW,[13] is yet to be translated into domestic law. The Supreme Court of Nepal has issued a directive to use Article 1 of CEDAW for the interpretation of all domestic laws and policies until a new and specific provision or law defining discrimination is enacted.[14]

An analysis of the decisions of the Supreme Court in PILs reveals that, out of the 38 cases relating to sex-based discrimination, the Court has issued directive orders in 42% of the cases. In 26% of the cases, the Court has not found the laws in question discriminatory. In 21% of the cases, the Court has declared discriminatory laws *ultra vires* and in 11% of the cases, the Court has recognised special measures taken for women to be inconsistent with the principle of equality.[15]

Declaring those laws *ultra vires*, the Court not only reinforced the principle of the supremacy of the Constitution as the law of the land, but also validated the treaty jurisprudence of CEDAW. The Court has also played a catalytic role, especially when there was a vacuum created by the lack of a parliament and laws that were directly discriminatory against women could not be amended. Progressive judgements by the Court in such situations enabled women to exercise their rights equally. *Mira Gurung v Department of Immigration*[16] is the first case where the

Supreme Court stated that particular visa provisions led to unequal treatment and discriminatory practices on the grounds of sex against Nepalese wives with foreign husbands as compared to Nepalese husbands with foreign wives and that, therefore, they were in contravention of the right to equality. In *Reena Bajracharya and Others v HMG*,[17] the Supreme Court declared as *ultras vires* the rule of early retirement for women employees of the Royal Nepal Airlines Corporation, considering it discriminatory and inconsistent with the principle of equality. In *Sapana Pradhan Malla for FWLD v HMG/Nepal*,[18] the Court held as *ultra vires* the discriminatory provision relating to rape under the Country Code (*Muluki Ain*) that provided for lesser punishment for those guilty of the rape of a prostitute. In this case, the Supreme Court also referred to CEDAW's General Recommendation Number 19 and the Beijing Platform for Action.

Providing women's right to equality in property and guaranteeing the right to self- determination, in *Lily Thapa v Office of Prime Minister and Council of Ministries*,[19] the Supreme Court noted that a man faces no restrictions on his use of immovable property on the grounds of his marital status (unmarried, married or widower), whereas women face restrictions in exercising the same rights over their immovable property on the grounds of their marital status. Furthermore, the law also requires the husband to give consent for women to use their own property. This provision imposes unreasonable restrictions against women and, thus, it was considered discriminatory. To ensure that women, irrespective of their marital status, are able to continue to exercise their rights over property that has been inherited from their natal family, specially if it is intestate property, in *Meera Dhungana for FWLD v Office of Prime Minister and Council of Ministries*[20], the Supreme Court declared null and void Section 12A of the Chapter on Succession of the Country Code, which concerned the return of paternally inherited property by a daughter after her marriage.

In *Meera Dhungana for FWLD v the Office of Prime Minister and Council of Ministers,*[21] the petitioner challenged Section 1(1) of the Chapter on Husband and Wife of the Country Code, which allowed the husband to seek a divorce if a government recognised medical board affirmed the wife's inability to conceive. Moving beyond the underlying Hindu belief that regards procreation as the sole purpose of marriage, the Supreme Court held this provision discriminatory and declared it *ultra vires* to the Constitution.

Non-recognition of the identity of a child through the mother was also challenged in the Supreme Court. In *Tek Tamrakar v HMG,*[22] the Supreme Court declared the words "among the males" appearing in Section 4(1) of the Birth, Death and Other Personal Events (Registration) Act, 1977, *ultra vires* the Constitution and declared it to be ineffective. Invoking the doctrine of severability, the Court determined that the law allowing only the senior-most male members of the family to register birth and death was against the right to equality guaranteed under Article 11 of the Constitution.

Regarding a woman's right to inheritance, in *Meera Dhungana v Ministry of Law and Justice,*[23] the Supreme Court noted that a son has a right to property as a birthright, whereas in the case of an unmarried daughter this is conditional upon her completing the age of 35. However, according to the Court, taking into consideration the other provisions relating to partition, the provision under Section 16 of the Chapter on Property of the Country Code, 1963 did not seem discriminatory against the daughter. The Court further said that if Section 16 were to be declared unconstitutional, then the daughter would have a right in the father's property as well as the husband's property. The Court feared that the son would be entitled only to the father's property and hence the situation would be discriminatory against the interest of the son. Although the Court issued a directive order to introduce an appropriate Bill in parliament, it asked the Government to take into consideration the patriarchal nature of the society, the social structure and the fear of positive discrimination against men, thus showing its patriarchal bent of mind.

Even after the legalisation of abortion, Sections 28, 28A and 32 of the Chapter on Homicide in the Country Code provided for a higher punishment for a pregnant woman performing an abortion beyond the conditions stipulated in the law, as opposed to the punishment for a person whose action causes an abortion. In *Sapana Pradhan Malla for FWLD v HMG, Nepal*,[24] the Supreme Court, in delivering its verdict on the writ petition, recognised Sections 28 and 28A as discriminatory against women and issued a directive order to the Government to introduce an appropriate Bill in parliament amending the provision in order to address the inconsistency in punishment awarded for performing abortion through choice rather than coercion.

The issue and the need for criminalisation of marital rape were raised in *Meera Dhungana for FWLD v HMG/Nepal.*[25] In this case, the petitioner challenged Section 1 of the Chapter on Rape (which provided the definition of rape) as violating Article 11 of the Constitution on the basis of having excluded marital rape from its ambit. The Supreme Court said:

> It cannot be said that any person who commits the heinous and inhuman crime of rape against a woman should be immune from criminal liability simply because he is her husband. Such husband has to be made liable to punishment for the offence he has committed...[A]s a punishable offence, there is a difference in consequences of rape committed by a third person and by a husband, and the present law only deals with the consequences of rape committed by a third person. There is a gap of legal provisions in the situation of rape of one's own wife, such as providing immediate relief by allowing the wife to live separately from or to divorce the rapist husband, and for prescribing the degree of offence in case of child marriage...[T]he Ministry of Law, Justice and Parliamentary Affairs should introduce a Bill to bring necessary amendments with regard to the highlighted gaps and to make complete legal provisions for justifiable and

> appropriate solutions in an integrated manner with regard to marital rape, taking into account the special situation of the marital relationship and position of husband.

In *Advocate Sarmila Parajuli and others v HMG*[26], the issue was to create a safe and healthy working environment. In this case, the Supreme Court held that any type of sexual abuse is violence against women and that State Parties are obliged to take legislative and other measures to eliminate such discrimination. The Court issued a directive order to the Government to take necessary initiatives to make an appropriate law relating to sexual harassment.

In *Dil Bahadur Vishwokarma & others v HMG, Prime Minister and Council of Ministers*[27], realising that socio-cultural practices are not only barriers to women's equality, but also violate women's right to life, freedom and dignity, the Supreme Court directed Government authorities, including the Cabinet Secretariat, to promulgate appropriate laws to ban *chhaupadi*, a discriminatory practice against women prevalent in the country. This practice requires that while menstruating and during and after childbirth, girls and women must leave their homes and live in cowsheds instead. The petitioners contended that *chhaupadi* is an inhuman and degrading practice against women and that illiteracy is the main reason for *chhaupadi* still being followed.

Regarding the practice of witchcraft, the Supreme Court referred to various human rights instruments and held that the Government of Nepal has an obligation to ensure a dignified life for all Nepalese women. Nevertheless, many women have suffered inhuman treatment due to the unscientific and superstitious belief in witchcraft that still prevails in the country. Such ill treatment of women clearly falls within the ambit of criminal activities and the existing laws cannot be assumed to be sufficient and appropriate to handle such crimes against women. Therefore, the Court ordered the Government to promulgate a law specifically to punish criminal activities committed against women in the name of witchcraft. In addition, the Court issued an order to the Government to conduct awareness programs to eliminate such traditional and superstitious beliefs.

In *Chandra Bajracharya for Misha Khala v Parliament Secretariat et al*[28] and *Sapana Pradhan for FWLD v Ministry of Law and Justice,* discriminatory legal provisions in penal law, adoption law and in matters relating to succession (legacy), discrimination in punishment, divorce and remarriage were challenged. In the above cases, the Court acknowledged the influence of Hindu jurisprudence and gender discriminatory religious codes on the legal system.

Unfortunately, in several cases, the Supreme Court did not recognise equal rights to citizenship through women and validated patriarchal norms of citizenship through male line descent.[29] In *Chandra Kant Gyawali v HMG/Nepal,*[30] the Court held that the Constitutionality of a Constitutional provision cannot be tested and that the rule of harmonious construction must be applied because Articles 9 and 11 of the Constitution are separate and independent of each other and the right to equality guaranteed under Article 11 is not absolute. In addition, the Court stated that the supremacy of Convention applies only in case of other laws and a treaty cannot supersede a Constitutional provision. Similarly, in *Achyut Prashad Kharel v HMG et al,*[31] the Supreme Court observed that the demand for conferring citizenship to children born to an unwed mother is against the moral fabric of society and the dignity of the nation. Thus, instead of upholding basic and inalienable human rights, such judicial attitudes reinforce patriarchal values. On a positive note, however, in *Tek Tamarakar for Pro Public v HGM, Council of Ministers,*[32] the Supreme Court made it mandatory for the Government to award citizenship to every child found within the Kingdom whose parents are unknown.

Shyam Krishna Maskey v HMG/Nepal[33] is a unique case where the plaintiff went to the Supreme Court to curtail women's right to inheritance in cases of divorce. The Court's verdict narrowed down the new amendment provision that allowed women the right to claim partition of the husband's property in a divorce proceeding, on the basis of a fear that, in such instances, women who remarried would be beneficiaries of multiple properties. The Court also noted that the economic status of the spouse needs to be taken into consideration for providing such a right.

Taking a progressive position, in *Prakash Mani Sharma for Pro-Public v Office of Prime Minister and Council of Ministries*,[34] the Supreme Court held that Section 1 of the Chapter on Property under the Country Code (*Muluki Ain*) gives equal rights to the daughter to get one share in inherited property and, having received such share, she has the full right to enjoy, use, sell or dispose of the property according to her will. However, Section 16 of the Chapter on Property not only places restrictions on the daughter to enjoy, use, sell or dispose of the property, it also compels her to return the remaining property once she gets married. In this manner, a daughter's absolute and vested partition right becomes conditional on her marital status. Due to this provision, the goal of the Eleventh Amendment of the Country Code – to provide equal partition rights to daughters – is vitiated and it ultimately results in discrimination as defined by Article 1 of CEDAW. The Supreme Court issued directive orders to the Government to review the whole Chapter, including Section 16, from the equality rights perspective, as a first step in removing discrimination against women.

FWLD's analysis of these judicial trends in 2000 indicted a lack of consistency in the judicial approach towards women's equality issues. While the judiciary is sympathetic towards women, its level of gender sensitisation is still not satisfactory and it is influenced by the "protectionist approach" rather than the "substantive approach." However, this trend is changing with time.

In its concluding comments to the First Periodic Report on CEDAW by Nepal, the CEDAW Committee has expressed its concern about the Supreme Court's interpretation of discriminatory laws and the Court's views on culture and tradition. However, in its Concluding Comments to the Second and Third Periodic Reports on CEDAW, the CEDAW Committee has also complimented the judiciary for its landmark decisions.

Undoubtedly, court intervention in several PILs has facilitated the development of a normative framework of equality and non-discrimination and has protected the rights of women. Though the process of law making is not speedy, the legal position of Nepalese women has been substantively changed through judgements. For instance, the Country Code Eleventh Amendment is an outcome of judicial intervention, in addition to the long struggle of Nepalese women and civil society organisations and the commitment expressed by political parties, members of Parliament and women political leaders to the quest for equality. It has recognised, albeit in a limited manner, a daughter as the heir of the family. It has protected the rights of married, divorced and widowed women. It has legalised abortion, increased the age of marriage to 18 years with parental consent and 20 years without parental consent, increased the punishment for rape, criminalised paedophilia and given limited acceptance to the daughter and daughter-in-law as tenants.

The previous understanding of the impossibility of guaranteeing absolute equality has been reinterpreted in *Chandra Gyanwali v HMG, Prime Minister and Council of Ministers*.[35] Here, the Supreme Court noted that although absolute equality cannot be guaranteed and protective discrimination can be continued, inequality and unfairness cannot be practiced and state action has to be reasonable and justifiable. However, such jurisprudence is yet to be elaborated in more cases in a clear framework with an understanding of the implications of the sameness approach, protectionist approach and corrective approach.

As mentioned earlier, the Supreme Court has given directives to the Government to declare *chhaupadi* a social evil, to form a study team to identify the instances of such evil practices and to launch awareness programmes for its eradication. In *Reshma Thapa v HMG and Council of Ministers*,[36] a similar direction has been made to eliminate the practice of witchcraft. However, unless a system is developed for a collaborative effort to implement such decisions through strong monitoring mechanisms, implementation is impossible. Although such decisions recognise law as an instrument and indicator of change, they also reiterate that law and society must go together. Adequate resources have to be allocated for the practical realisation of the rights. Such a conceptualisation of rights has to be adopted by all the organs of Government who have a duty to guarantee *de jure* and *de facto* rights, so that the rights holder can claim and realise such rights in their life.

In *Radheshayam Parajuli v HMG/Nepal*,[37] the Supreme Court validated the principle of special measures incorporated in the Constitution of 1990 on the basis of CEDAW. It quashed a writ petition challenging a special provision and held that this special provision that allows women to file for divorce directly to the District Court, is not discriminatory against men. The Court said that special measures are necessary for the advancement of women and in line with Article 11(3) of the Constitution. Similarly, in *Sita Acharya v Public Service Commission*,[38] the Supreme Court declared Section 18 of the Nepal Health Service Act, 1997, which requires a one-year probation period for newly appointed employees, to be inapplicable to women employees, on the grounds that the Civil Service Act, 1992 has special provisions that provide a shorter probation period of six months for women employees in Government service. In delivering the judgment, the Supreme Court referred to Articles 3, 4(1) and 4(2) of CEDAW and the proviso to Article 11(3) of the Constitution, which obligates the Government to implement temporary special measures to achieve *de facto* equality between men and women.

However, a critical question on the legality of special measures was raised in *Proddhos Chetrtri v Office of Prime Minister and Council of Ministries*.[39] In this case, the Supreme

Court invalidated the reservation initiative taken by Tribhuvan University Teaching Hospital as unconstitutional as it was based only on a policy and not on any specific law as required by the Constitution. At the same time, however, the Court recognised the need to take measures for the advancement of backward communities by enacting a law so that permanent and institutional arrangements could be made as per the spirit enshrined in the proviso to Article 11(3) of the Constitution. The Court issued a directive order to enact a law for the development of women and "backward communities", with a specific demarcation on the basis of economically, socially and educationally backward.

Similarly, in *Basundhara Thapa v Cabinet Secretariat*,[40] the petitioner challenged Section 7(3) of the National Foundation for Development of Indigenous Nationalities Act, 2058. According to this provision, women are eligible for a member position for two years only as compared to men who can hold the member position for four years and are eligible for re-nomination. In its defence, the Government stated that it enacted such a provision as a special measure to benefit all women, as shorter terms and the ineligibility of re-election would create more vacancies providing opportunities to a greater number of women. Disagreeing with the Government's arguments, the Supreme Court declared that the challenged proviso is discriminating against women.

The Supreme Court's judicial activism can also be seen in these cases where the Court has issued guidelines until laws are enacted to respect and protect rights guaranteed by CEDAW: in *Sapana Pradhan Malla v Government of Nepal*,[41] the Court issued guidelines to protect the confidentiality of victims of violence against women and children and HIV and AIDS affected people. In *Prakash Mani Sharma v Ministry of Women*,[42] a guideline has been issued to protect women working in dance bars from exploitation. In *Sunil Babu Pant v Government of Nepal*,[43] the Court has issued directives to recognise the identity of third gender.

Major laws enacted or amended in the past few years for the protection and promotion of the rights of women on the basis of CEDAW principles are the Human Trafficking Act, 2007; Foreign Employment Act, 2007 and the National Commission on Women Act, 2006.

Ensuring gender equality through a secular Constitution

Democracy, the rule of law and freedom of religion are preconditions in the current call for a new Constitution. Diverse approaches to secularism provide a variety of prescriptions in the relationship between a democratic State and the religious freedom of its citizens.

While the Interim Constitution of 2007 has recognised secularism as its basic principle, in reality Hinduism continues to dominate all cultural and traditional practices. As an integral part of inclusive Constitution drafting, the present Government adopted a policy of collecting grassroots public opinion from citizens in all 75 districts of Nepal. This exercise revealed that secularism is generally considered synonymous with anti-Hinduism. The reasons for such sentiments seemed to stem from the fact that secularism was introduced by the erstwhile interim parliament and not the current Constituent Assembly, which is seen as the appropriate forum due to its inclusive nature. Therefore, the adoption of secularism in Nepal is perceived in the grassroots as a political decision and not a people's decision. This is of supreme concern since the guarantee of religious freedom cannot be well implemented if secularism is not internalised by the people of the country. At the same time, however, it is interesting to note that dalit groups in the country have provided unconditional support for the transition into a secular nation as they have been discriminated against and excluded from State benefits and services due to the caste system created by Hinduism.

In addition, the competing concerns of religious minorities demanding autonomy of practice (in the form of following personal laws) and the recognition of customary practices under the law, threaten the process of ensuring equality for women within the private sphere. Such demands are not only supported, but also actively forwarded by women belonging to the aforesaid religious communities. Women belonging to indigenous groups have also been demanding recognition of traditional and cultural practices under the law.

Given these sentiments, the primary challenge is to ensure that women's human rights are upheld, irrespective of religious or cultural edicts within the country. It is also a challenge to ensure that the demand for substantive equality for women under the forthcoming Constitution is not eclipsed by the increasing demands for affirmative action on the basis of caste, religion, minorities on the basis of geographical barriers, disabilities, etc. It is, therefore, essential to ensure that women's human rights are acknowledged as a cross-sectional right on the basis of multiple discriminations faced by women. It is also important to ensure that discrimination on the basis of cultural, religious and traditional practices is strictly prohibited.

Studies reveal that women continue to be discriminated in the following areas under law:

- Nationality (Citizenship): As a result of the notion of dependent nationality of women and the non-recognition of women as independent citizens due to social, cultural and religious influences, the Constitution, Citizenship Act, Citizenship Regulations and Passport Rules continue to discriminate against women. In conferring citizenship to children, the new law requires that children born from foreign husbands have to be born in Nepal and be permanent residents of Nepal.[44] Only upon the completion of these two conditions, can children acquire naturalized citizenship. According to the present Constitution, women of foreign nationality who marry Nepalese citizens can acquire Nepalese citizenship after initiating the process of renouncing their former citizenship. However, a man of foreign nationality who marries a Nepalese woman is not entitled to acquire Nepalese citizenship by virtue of the marriage.[45] In addition, passport forms mention wife and children only as accompanying persons.[46]

- Property: Economic justice is a crucial goal for women in Nepal. Since women are economically dependent on their families, they are forced to live in abusive relationships and endure both physical and mental violence.[47] Taking this into consideration, the Interim Constitution of 2007 has guaranteed equal rights of the son and the daughter in ancestral property.[48] However, although the Country Code amendment recognises equal rights of women in property in keeping with the Constitutional guarantee, married daughters continue to be excluded from the right to inheritance and intestate property. They are not considered as coparceners and fall behind in the line of succession.[49] Nepalese law has stated that bigamy is illegal, but the law itself recognises *all wives* as equal shareholders in the husband's property.[50] Separated women who remarry are still required to return property inherited from their previous husband.[51] Unmarried daughters are eligible to file an application for inheritance only after the sons and married daughters fall even further behind in the line of succession.[52]

With regard to savings in the event of the death of the nominee, the provision of succession is discriminatory as unmarried daughters fall behind sons in the line of succession and married daughters fall even further behind.[53] Wives of all male police personnel can receive pension upon the accidental death of their husbands; however, in the case of women police personnel, the Government has the power to decide whether their husbands are eligible to receive such pension.[54]

Widows of teachers or staff of Tribhuvan University may receive pension benefits only after the recommendation of the Executive Council of the University.[55] Widows of government employees are discriminated against in the case of allowances: a widow of a government employee is not entitled to the family allowances and gratuity if she was not living together with her husband at the time of his death. Hence, a widow, even if she has not taken her share of the husband's property or is not divorced, is deprived of such allowances.[56]

- Sexual Offences: Article 29 of the Interim Constitution of 2007 guarantees the right against exploitation to all its citizens. In addition, it specifies that no one shall be trafficked in or be held in slavery or servitude.[57] As mentioned earlier, the Supreme Court has recognised marital rape as an offence and issued a directive order to introduce a Bill for providing immediate relief by allowing the wife to live separately from or to divorce the rapist husband.[58] After the enactment of the Act to Amend Some Nepal Acts for Maintaining Gender Equality, 2006, marital rape has been recognised as a crime, but the punishment for marital rape is negligible as compared to that of rape outside of marriage.[59] The Supreme Court has also recently issued a directive order to amend the law on marital rape which is discriminatory with respect to punishment.[60]

  The law relating to incest is based on religion and customs and is impractical in various situations. For instance, according to the existing law, if a person marries a widow within the relation of brother-in-law, it constitutes an offence[61], but it is an accepted norm in society to marry one's sister-in-law.
- Education/Women and Employment: The Interim Constitution has guaranteed the right to employment as a fundamental right of all Nepalese citizens. Similarly, laws have been amended or enacted to ensure the right to education to all Nepalese citizens. Despite that, the literacy rate of women is remarkably lower than that of men. *De facto* realisation of the right to education is a crucial task in the context of Nepal.

Army Police Regulation discriminates against women by requiring them to be unmarried or widowed in order to be eligible to apply for a job and also restricts women from marriage during the training period.[62] Consequently, women who are married are not eligible to enter Armed Police Services. The previous Foreign Employment Act was directly discriminatory against women, but the Foreign Employment Act, 2007 has ensured the right to equality with respect to foreign employment. Even so, women continue to face challenges and discriminatory behaviour with respect to foreign employment.

- Health (including reproductive health): The Interim Constitution guarantees that, "every woman shall have the right to reproductive health and other reproductive matters" as a fundamental right.[63] Despite that, maternity leave provision in various laws is highly inconsistent: some laws prescribe 52 days, others 60 or 98 days, while in some legislations there are no provisions for maternity leave.[64] In 2003, the Supreme Court held that the Constitution of Nepal, CEDAW and the Convention on the Rights of the Child protect the right to reproductive health and issued a directive order to provide for measures to ensure adequate maternity leave in line with international human rights instruments, especially the International Labour Organization's Maternity Protection Convention, 2000, which provides for 14 weeks of maternity leave.[65] However, due to a lack of implementation of judgements, discriminatory provisions continue to remain.

In addition, as per existing abortion law, if a woman miscarries as a result of an act of anger or malevolence of another person, the punishment for the accused is up to six months imprisonment or a fine of up to Rs. 1000, depending on the stage of the pregnancy and knowledge about the pregnancy.[66] However, if a woman undertakes an abortion in other circumstances, she can be imprisoned for up to five years, depending on the stage of the pregnancy.

- Marriage and Family: Various Nepalese laws relating to marriage and family rights are inconsistent with the rights guaranteed by international human rights instruments and the right to equality guaranteed by Article 13 of the Interim Constitution. The Chapter on Husband and Wife of the Country Code mentions that if a married woman remarries, the earlier marriage is automatically terminated. This provision is discriminatory because if the husband remarries, his earlier marriage is not automatically terminated. In this latter instance, the wife has to apply for divorce citing bigamy.[67]

  Bigamy is somewhat encouraged by the law in that it allows a man to remarry without divorcing his first wife in the following circumstances: the first wife becomes infected by an incurable sexually transmitted disease; she becomes incurably insane; she becomes crippled and cannot not walk or is blind in both eyes; a medical board recognised by the Government certifies that she is infertile; she is living separately after taking her share of the husband's property.[68]

  Although bigamy is illegal, the second marriage is not void and becomes legal after the completion of the minimal punishment of imprisonment ranging between one to three years and the payment of a fine between Rs.5,000-25,000.[69] Moreover, the second wife and her children also have a share in the family property, thus affecting the right to property of the first wife.[70]

  The limitation provided by law to file a suit in a case of polyandry is one year.[71] However, in the case of bigamy, it is only three months.[72] Clearly, then, discrimination prevails in the same nature of activities done by men and women.
- Legal and Court Proceedings: Court proceedings play a very important role in accessing justice and obtaining legal remedies. However, under previous regulations, women's names were not required in legal documents such as petitions, replies and appeals submitted in court. The

format of the summons, *subpoenas* and notices issued by the court also required the names of the father or husband of the person to whom such orders were issued.[73] While the law was amended in letter through the Gender Equality Act, this is yet to be realised in practice.[74]

While external attempts at amending the law through active lobbying with members of the current Constituent Assembly continue, the ongoing process of drafting the Constitution within the CA itself is also being used as a strategic means of incorporating gender friendly language, specific gender concerns and provisions for empowerment.

Lobbying by the women's rights movement successfully ensured a minimum of 50% candidacy of women through proportional representation for the 2008 election towards the formation of the Constituent Assembly. This stipulation succeeded in acquiring candidacy of women from all sections of marginalised communities as can be seen in the table below:

Cross-sectional candidacy of women in the Constituent Assembly		Percentage of representation
Minimum stipulated representation of women		50.0%
Madhesi	Female	15.6%
	Male	15.6%
Dalit	Female	6.5%
	Male	6.5%
Adivasi, Janajati	Female	18.9%
	Male	18.9%
Backward Classes	Female	2.0%
	Male	2.0%
Others	Female	15.1%
	Male	15.1%

This stipulation on proportional representation in candidacy helped in ensuring a total of 32.8% representation of women within the CA. While 12.5% representation within this constituency of women was ensured through direct elections, 49.71% of women were elected through proportional representation in candidacy and 6% of the total numbers of women were nominated.

For functional purposes, the Constituent Assembly – as the main legislative body of the country – has been divided into four main factions: the first, identified as Legislative Procedures, is responsible for the regular parliamentary affairs of the country with a total of 10 committees; the second is the 10 Thematic Committees responsible for providing concept papers for the drafting of the Constitution; the third, the three Procedural Committees responsible for ensuring proper and effective execution of the work of the CA through public opinion gathering, capacity building and resource management; and lastly, the main Constitutional Committee responsible for the final drafting of the Constitution.

Since the establishment of the CA, women representatives have made various attempts to mobilise themselves towards strengthening their voices in the legislative process. The first stage of lobbying for gender rights was witnessed during the formulation of Rules and Procedures for the CA. This process was also utilised by women parliamentarians to negotiate and ensure proportional representation in each of the Committees mentioned above. Representation in the 14 Committees responsible for the formulation and drafting of the Constitution is shown in the table (on p. 212):

An attempt was also made to create a formal Women's Committee as one of the thematic committees, but this was unsuccessful. In lieu of the Women's Committee, a Women's Caucus was formed within the CA. This Caucus consists of all women representatives, irrespective of their political affiliations. Thus far, the Women's Caucus has been successful in exerting pressure on the political parties to

Name of the committee	Total number of members	Number of women members	Percentage
Fundamental Rights and Directive Principles	43	15	34.88
Protection of Fundamental Rights of Minority and Marginalised	41	16	39.02
Restructuring of State and Distribution of State Power	43	12	27.9
Form of Legislative Body	43	14	32.55
Determination of Form of Government of State	43	12	27.9
Judicial System Committee	43	16	37.2
Structure of Constitutional Bodies Determination	40	15	37.5
Natural Resources Distribution, Financial Rights and Public Revenue	43	9	20.93
Determination of the Base of Cultural and Social Solidarity	41	19	46.34
National Interest Preservation	42	9	21.42
Committee on Citizen	36	12	32.33
Public Opinion Collection and Coordination	43	16	37.21
Capacity Building and Resource Management	38	17	44.73
Constitutional Committee	63	15	23.81

ensure 33% participation of women representatives as chairpersons in the various committees. As a result of such intensive lobbying, 38% of the total number of committee chair posts is currently held by women.

The Rules and Procedures of the CA prescribe that the drafting of the Constitution shall be completed by May 2010.[75] In pursuance of the same, the various thematic committees have been vested with the responsibility of creating concept papers on each theme as well as formulating draft language for the relevant sections of the Constitution. Thus far, concept papers along with draft language have been submitted on four thematic issues. As prescribed in the Rules and Procedures, these submissions were left open to comments and opinions on a voluntary basis from all members of the CA within a stipulated period of time.

It is interesting to note that, amongst the constituency of CA members who submitted their opinions and suggestions to the above-mentioned thematic drafts, women constituted approximately one-third of the respondents. Of the 156 members who responded to the submission of the National Interest Preservation Committee, 52 were women (33%). Of the 162 members who responded to the submission of the Protection of Fundamental Rights of Minority and Marginalised Committee, 53 were women (33%). 10 experts were invited from outside the CA to provide their opinions on the said draft. Out of these, two experts were women. Of the 166 members who responded to the submission of the Committee on Determining the Base of Cultural and Social Solidarity, 59 were women (36%). Here, however, out of 18 experts who were invited from outside the CA to provide their opinions, only two were women. Finally, out of the 133 members who responded to the submission of the Committee on Determining the Constitutional Bodies, 46 were women (35%). Once again, out of 28 external experts invited to provide their opinions, only five were women.

While women's participation in decision-making bodies is being considered a primary strategy in current times, it is also important to acknowledge that such a strategy alone may not ensure the respect, protection and fulfilment of women's human rights.

Women themselves are often unaware of the rights that are inherent or need to be protected. While the representation of women in the CA has led to the recognition of various inter-sectionalities of inequality and discrimination, the same is negated by some of the radical political parties which fail to acknowledge differences of experiences within the community of women and the varying levels of vulnerability and exploitation faced by them. The race for establishment and hierarchy of political ideology often results in the essentialisation of women's concerns, thus sidelining the understanding of women's human rights promoted by CEDAW. The most common error committed in such situations is seen in the demands for legal provisions for protecting women instead of their rights.

These problems are then manifested in recommendations that have been seen to emerge from the Constituent Assembly. Concept papers prepared by each of the four Committees have often failed to consider women's concerns of multiple discrimination, violation of rights by private actors and, most importantly, have fallen short of addressing the concerns of women through the cross categories of religious rights and protection of rights relating to cultural and traditional practices. The challenge before the Women's Caucus is to introduce and ensure cohesive understandings of gender equality and non-discrimination amongst all women members of the CA, irrespective of political affiliation.

Further, in order to sustain the level of participation in decision-making bodies, it is important to engage with the structural formation of political parties themselves. Even though the State's primary agenda is inclusiveness, democracy, republicanism and federalism, barely any inclusion is seen in the decision-making structures of the political parties and women are often left out of the political hierarchy within individual parties. Law and politics are not women-centric.

Finally, in policy making, women continue to face obstacles despite their substantial representation in the Constituent Assembly. For instance, strategic lobbying within the CA has provided momentum to the finalisation of the much awaited Domestic Violence Bill. A sub-committee on domestic violence has recently finalised the Bill, which is presently awaiting enactment through the formal approval of the larger legislative body.[76] At the same time, there is major resistance from male members of the CA regarding the reformation of the law on nationality allowing Nepalese women to pass on citizenship to their husband of foreign nationality. This resistance is being justified on the pretext of disallowing the creation of open borders and the increase in population within Nepal. In reality, however, one can see that the identity of a woman is still considered to be created through men within families, along with the prevailing notion of dependant nationality for women. Despite general unity of women on this issue, the fight for equality has to be fought with increased vigour and determination at the highest level of policy-making. It is only then that the principles of secularism and equality will meet in application.

Notes

[1] Editor's Note: This paper was written in October 2009 and, therefore, does not reflect more recent political and legal developments in Nepal. Readers are encouraged to consult other sources for the most current information on ongoing developments in the country.

[2] *Nepal in Figures, 2003*, Kathmandu: Central Bureau of Statistics (2003).

[3] *An Update of Discriminatory Laws in Nepal and their Impact on Women*, Kathmandu: Forum for Women, Law and Development (2006).

[4] *An Update of Discriminatory Laws in Nepal and their Impact on Women* (2006), *op.cit.*

[5] *Three Year Interim Plan 2064/65–2066/67*, Government of Nepal, National Planning Commission (July 2007).

[6] *An Update of Discriminatory Laws in Nepal and their Impact on Women* (2006), *op.cit.*

[7] *An Update of Discriminatory Laws in Nepal and their Impact on Women* (2006), *op.cit.*

[8] *Discriminatory Laws in Nepal and Their Impact on Women: A Review of the Current Situation and Proposals for Change*, Kathmandu: Forum for Women, Law and Development (2000).

[9] *An Update of Discriminatory Laws in Nepal and Their Impact on Women* (2006), *op.cit.*

[10] NKP 2057 B.S., vol. 5, p. 376.

[11] *Chandra Kant Gwyawali v HMG Nepal* [Writ No. 3368/2057; Decided on 2058.10.25 (unreported)].

[12] *Sex Equality – Approaches and Judicial Intervention*, A Special Volume publication for the 50th anniversary of the Supreme Court (2006).

[13]Article 1 of CEDAW states: "For the purposes of the present Convention, the term 'discrimination against women' shall mean any distinction, exclusion or restriction made on the basis of sex which has the effect or purpose of impairing or nullifying the recognition, enjoyment or exercise by women, irrespective of their marital status, on a basis of equality of men and women, of human rights and fundamental freedoms in the political, economic, social, cultural, civil or any other field."

[14]*Prakash Mani Sharma for Pro-Public v Office of Prime Minister and Council of Ministries* [Writ No. 31 of 2061; Decided on 2062.8.30]

[15]Sapana Pradhan Malla, "Role of Supreme Court in Sex Equality Cases" in *Bar Special Bulletin* (2006).

[16]NKP 2051 B.S., p. 68.

[17]NKP 2057 B.S., p 376.

[18]Writ No. 56 of 2058 B.S. (unreported).

[19]Decided by the Supreme Court on 2062.8.30 B.S. (unreported).

[20]NKP 2061 B.S., p. 377.

[21]NKP 2062, vol. 1, p. 6; Decision No. 7635.

[22]Writ No. 121 of 2060; Decided on 2062.5.30.

[23]NKP 2052, p. 462.

[24]NKP 2062, vol. 1, p. 10; Decision No. 7478.

[25]Writ No. 55 of 2058; Decided on 2059.1.19 .

[26]NKP 2061, vol. 10, p. 1312.

[27]Writ No. 3303; Decided on 2062.1.19 (unreported).

[28]NKP 2053, p. 537.

[29]*Benjamin Peter v Department of the Immigration* [NKP 208, vol. 11, p. 749; Decision No. 4413]; *Chabi Piters v HMG Nepal* [NKP 2049, vol. 5, p. 443; Decision No. 4533].

[30]NKP 2058, p. 615.

[31]Writ No. 3404 of 2061.

[32]NKP 2062, vol. 6, p. 680; Decision No. 7550, decided on 2062.5.30.

[33]NKP 2061, vol. 10, p. 1254.

[34]Writ No. 31 of 2061; Decided on 2062.8.30.

[35]NKP 2061, vol. 11, p. 1418; Decision No. 7459.

[36]NKP 2062, vol. 2, p. 205; Decision No. 7498.

[37]Writ No. 3692/056.

[38]Writ No. 3975; Decided on 2058.5.29 (unreported).

[39]NKP 2061, vol. 7, p. 901.

[40]NKP 2060, vols. 5 and 6, p.389.

[41]Writ No. 3561/2063; Decided on 2064.9.10.

[42]Writ No. 2822/2062; Decided on 2065.8.11.

[43]Writ No. 917/2064; Decided 2064.9.6.

[44]Article 8(7) of the Interim Constitution of 2007.

[45]Article 8(6) of the Interim Constitution of 2007 and Section 5(1) of the Nepal Citizenship Act, 2006.

[46]Application Forms of Passport and Passport Rules, 1970.

[47]*An Update of Discriminatory Laws in Nepal and their Impact on Women* (2006), *op.cit.*

[48]Article 20(4) of the Interim Constitution of 2007.

[49]Section 5 of the Chapter on Women's Exclusive Property of the Country Code, 1963.

[50]Section 4 of the Chapter on Partition of the Country Code, 1963.

[51]Section 4 of the Chapter on Husband and Wife of the Country Code, 1963.

[52]Rule 101(2) of the Civil Services Rule, 2050.

[53]Rule 11(3) of Postal Savings Bank Regulations, 2033; Rule101(2) of Civil Services Rules, 2050; Section 99(2) of the Nepal Health Service Rules, 2055; Rule 58(3) of Armed Police Rules, 2060; Rule 86(2) of Cabinet Secretariat Administration Rules, 2050; Rule 59(2) of Rules of Service of the Tribhuvan University Teachers and Staff, 2050.

[54]Rule 107(5) of Police Rules, 2049.

[55]Rule 57(1) of Rules of Service of Tribhuvan University Teachers and Staff, 2050

[56]Rule 98(2)(a) of the Civil Service Rules 2050 (1993); Rule 95(2) of the Nepal Health Service Regulations, 2055.

[57]Article 29(3) of the Interim Constitution of 2007.

[58]*Meera Dhungana for FWLD v HMG/Nepal* [Writ No. 55 of 2058; Decided on 2059.1.19].

[59]Section 3(F) of the Chapter on Rape of the Country Code, 1963.

[60]*Jeet Kumari Pangeni et al v Government of Nepal et al*, 2064.

[61]Nos. 3 and 4 of the Chapter on Incest of the Country Code, 1963.

[62]Rules 4(3)(h) and 4(4) of Regulation relating to Army-Police 2001.

[63]Article 20(2) of the Interim Constitution of 2007.

[64]Section 65 of Rules Relating to Staff of the Office of Auditor General, 2050 (1994); Section 106 of Education Regulation, 2059 (2002); Section 59 of Civil Service Rules, 2050 (1993); Section 105 of Armed Police Rules, 2060 (2003); Section 34 of Labour Regulation, 2050 (1993); Section 35 of Labour Regulation Relating to Tea Estate, 2050 (1993); Section 51 of Nepal Health Service Regulation, 2055 (1998); Section 244 of Local Self Government Regulation, 2056 (1999); Section 16 of Regulation Relating to Working Journalist, 2053 (1996); Section 8 of Act Relating to Remuneration, Terms and Condition of the Judges of the Supreme Court, 2026 (1969); Section 14 of Act Relating to Remuneration, Terms and Condition of the Attorney General, 2052 (1995); Section 15 of Act Relating to Remuneration, Terms and Condition of the Office Holders of Constitutional Bodies, 2053 (1996).

[65]*Advocate Prakash Mani Sharma et al v HMG/Nepal et al* [Writ No. 88/ 2059; Decision dated September 11, 2003].

[66]No. 32 of the Chapter on Homicide of the Country Code, 1963.

[67]No. 2 of the Chapter on Husband and Wife of the Country Code, 1963.

[68]No. 9 of the Chapter on Marriage of the Country Code, 1963.

[69]No. 9 of the Chapter on Marriage of the Country Code, 1963.

[70]No. 4 of the Chapter on Partition of the Country Code, 1963.

[71]No. 6 of the Chapter on Adultery of the Country Code, 1963.

[72]No. 11 of the Chapter on Marriage of the Country Code, 1963.

[73]Rules 14, 19 and 41 of District Court Regulations, 2052; Rule 6 of Labour Court Regulations, 2052; Rule 16 of Appellate Court Regulations, 2055.

[74]*A Study on Discriminatory Laws Against Women, Dalits, Ethnic Minorities and Persons with Disabilities*, Kathmandu: Forum for Women, Law and Development (2009)

[75]Editor's Note: This deadline was not met.

[76]Editor's Note: The Bill has since been enacted.

7 Women's Rights Protection in China

Guo Jianmei and Li Ying

China has established a legal framework to guarantee women's rights and interests with legislative documents ranging from the *Constitution of the People's Republic of China* to *Law of the People's Republic of China on the Protection of Rights and Interests of Women.* All of them stipulate legal protection for women's rights and interests, either from the perspective of general principles or specific practice. Laws, regulations and policies in various localities through village committees and communities also have laid down special provisions for protecting women's rights; for example, over twenty provinces and municipalities have identified their *Implementation Provisions on Law on the Protection of Rights and Interests of Women*; Hunai Province released China's first local regulation on the prevention and prohibition of domestic violence; and the Ministry of Labor and Social Security has developed a retirement policy well-targeted to female specialists. Arguably, China has evolved a full-fledged legal framework for women's rights protection, owing to its advanced legislative concepts and philosophy. However, the general principles or the declarative and advocating wordings enshrined in many laws lead to their inoperability to some extent. Moreover, there is still a legislative void and some inadequacy when it comes to specific provisions; while given existing legal and judicial gaps, the inadequacy and absence of law enforcement have cropped up as major problems and barriers in the process of safeguarding women's rights.

Therefore, we maintain that, given the "equality" stated in the laws is actually no more than a legal term, it is still an uphill battle to attain the substantive equality proposed in CEDAW and related international conventions.

This essay will introduce the basic legal framework of women's rights protection in China, and focus on the legal protection of women's household property, bodily and labour rights. These rights have a great bearing on women's basic right to survival and development and represent the core human rights for women. In the second part, it will introduce the practice of the Center for Women's Law and Legal Service at Peking University in promoting gender equality. Several typical cases will give illustrate our efforts in challenging legal policies and stereotyped mindsets, when it comes to gender equality and anti-sex discrimination.

I. WOMEN'S RIGHTS PROTECTION IN CHINA

The basic legal framework for protecting women's household property, bodily and labour rights may be represented diagrammatically as below:

A. Constitution

The Constitution of the People's Republic of China is the fundamental law with superior legal effectiveness. In the *Amendment to the Constitution of the People's Republic of China* (2004), it states that "the State respects and guarantees human rights"; "human rights", incorporated into the Constitution for the first time, represented a milestone in China. Through Article 48, women in the People's Republic of China enjoy equal rights with men in all spheres of life—political, economic, cultural and social—and family life. The State protects the rights and interests of women, applies the principle of equal pay for equal work, and trains and selects cadres from among women. Constitutionally, it confirms that women enjoy equal rights with men and emphasises that

- CONSTITUTION
  - Law on the Protection of Rights and Interests of Women (Basic Law)
    - Household Property Rights
      - Marriage Law and its Regulations
      - Succession Law and its Regulations
      - Land Contract Law
    - Bodily Rights
      - Domestic Violence
        - Women's Law
        - Marriage Law
        - Criminal Law
        - Local Regulations and Other Provisions
      - Sexual Abuse and Harassment
        - Women's Law
        - Criminal Law
        - Local Regulations and Other Provisions
    - Labour Rights
      - Labour Law
      - Labour Contract Law
      - Employment Promotion Law
      - Other Regulations and Policies

women shall enjoy the right of equal pay for equal work, and the same political rights as men. In marriage and family life Article 49 states that, "Marriage, the family, and mother and child are protected by the State. Violation of the freedom of marriage is prohibited. Maltreatment of old people, women and children is prohibited."

Arguably, the Constitution establishes the legal ground for gender equality. However, since there is no constitutional court[1] in China, and general courts do not accept cases related to constitutional appealing, a judicial review mechanism is needed if laws, legislation and law enforcement are unconstitutional. The Constitution, in this sense, is merely a superior law for declarative and advocating purposes.[2]

B. Law on the Protection of Rights and Interests of Women

The Law of the People's Republic of China on the Protection of Rights and Interests of Women was promulgated in 1992 and amended with the approval of the National People's Congress in August, 2005. As a fundamental law designed to protect women's rights, it also serves as a specialised law; for the first time its amendment legalises gender equality as basic State policy. It also provides that various institutions for women's rights will be improved gradually in order to eliminate all forms of discriminations against women.

The law stipulates women's rights in six areas, namely: political rights; rights and interests relating to culture and education; rights and interests of labour and social security; rights and interests relating to property; rights of person; and rights and interests relating to marriage and family. Compared to the 1992 version, the 2005 amendment has made numerous breakthroughs: apart from establishing gender equality as basic State policy and eliminating all form of discrimination against women for the first time, the amendment states that in the political aspect, women shall comprise an appropriate proportion of district and village committees (Article 11); in the field of culture and education, "parents or other guardians must perform their duty of ensuring that female school-age children or adolescents receive compulsory education" (Article 18); in the field of labour, no unit may dismiss female staff and workers by reason of sex discrimination when it comes to implementing the retirement system (Article 27). In addition, it specifies that domestic violence in the Marriage Law(Article 46); the prohibition of female sexual harassment is proposed for the first time (Article 40); and it prescribes the relief measures that victims of domestic violence and sexual harassment can avail of when required. These are discussed in detail later.

Unfortunately, the specific rights enshrined in the *Law on the Protection of Rights and Interests of Women* are too general to be applied in judicial practice. Many grassroots courts seldom quote this law when handling cases relating to women's rights and interests, leading some legal experts to call it a "Sleeping Beauty". However, as a specialised and basic law that aims to protect women it is of irreplaceable significance and value and has been vigorously promoted by both women's rights experts and practitioners through publicity, educational campaigns, training and judicial practice. After all in women rights protection in China.

C. Other Related Laws

1 Women's rights in marriage and family life, and property rights

Stipulations regarding women's rights in marriage and family life and their property rights can be found in many related laws and regulations. The first and foremost among them is *Marriage Law; Succession Law* focuses on women's rights and interests in property inheritance; *Land Contract Law* is directed at women's right to land contracts and their other land rights and clearly states that women enjoy equal land rights with men. The *Law on the Protection of Rights and Interests of Women* reconfirms the related stipulations.

(i) Marriage Law

Marriage Law was amended in 2001 based on the 1980 version, and exemplifies social progress and new a legislative philosophy. Women's marriage, family and property rights are stated as follows:

- The marriage system featuring "equality between man and woman" (Article 2) clearly defines equal status in a family (Article 13).
- Jointly possessed property is at the disposal of both spouses, an equal footing (Article 17).[33] Article 17 of the 2001 Marriage Law Revisions provides that the following properties incurred during the existence of marriage shall be jointly owned by both husband and wife:
- A husband may not apply for a divorce when his wife is pregnant or within one year of the birth of a child, or within six months after suspension of pregnancy (Article 34). This restriction shall not apply should the wife apply for a divorce, or when the people's court deems it necessary to accept the husband's divorce application.
- At the time of divorce, the disposition of the property in the joint possession of the husband and wife is subject to agreement between the two parties. In cases where an agreement cannot be reached, the people's court shall arrive at a judgment based on consideration of the actual circumstance of the property and on the principle of caring for the rights and interests of the wife and child or children. (Article 39).

In this connection, the *Law on Protection of Women's Rights and Interests* contains detailed stipulations: a woman shall enjoy equal rights with her spouse in possessing, utilising, profiting from and disposing of the property jointly possessed by them according to law, which shall not be affected by the income status of either party. Items of property acquired during their marriage are in their separate possession according to a couple's written agreement. If one party performs more duties in rearing their children, looking after their elders and assisting the other party in work, he or she shall have the right at the time of divorce to request compensation from the other party who shall compensate accordingly. (Article 47).[4]

Besides this, at the time of divorce, this law also enshrines the principle of "caring for the rights and interests of the wife and child or children, in terms of real estate disposition and the child's or children's custody".

The highlight lies in *Article 46 of Marriage Law* which sets out the divorce compensation system. It provides that "a no-fault party shall have the right to make a request for damage compensation under any of the following circumstances bringing about divorce", such as domestic violence, bigamy, or cohabitation. This stipulation was one of the highlights in the amended Marriage Law, but it is seldom applied in practice, due to its infeasibility, difficulty in evidence demonstration and limited compensations. Moreover, *Several Specific Opinions of the People's Court on Handling the Property Division in Divorce Ca ses* issued by the Supreme People's Court emphasises, the principle of gender equality and caring for the legitimate rights and interests of women and children.

(ii) Succession Law

The right to inheritance is an important property right for citizens. In a patriarchal feudal society like old China, women had no inheritance rights and this mindset still lingers in the remote villages of today's China. After the founding of People's Republic of China in 1949, the Chinese government's insistence on gender equality was also embodied in the right to inheritance. In particular, the *Succession Law* promulgated in April 1985 legalised an equal right to inheritance for men and women, thus advancing the protection of women's property rights. Major stipulations related to women's right to inheritance are as follows:

- Males and females are equal in their right to inheritance (Article 9).
- The estate of the decedent shall be inherited as follows: First in order: spouse, children and parents. Second in order: brothers and sisters, paternal grandparents, maternal grandparents (Article 10).

  Widowed daughters-in-law or sons-in-law who have made the predominant contribution to maintaining their parents-in-law shall, in relationship to their parents-in-law, be regarded as successors first in order.

  The right to inheritance thus knows no gender.
- Besides, the *Marriage Law* and *Law on Protection of Rights and Interests of Women* state that "husband and wife shall have the right to inherit each other's property"; "parents and children shall have the right to inherit each other's property."

In the *Law on Protection of Rights and Interests of Women*, women's equal right, with men, of succession to property shall be protected by law. Among the statutory successors in the same order, women shall not be discriminated against. Widowed women have the right to dispose of the property inherited by them, and no one may interfere with the disposition thereof (Article 34). Widowed women who have made the predominant contribution in maintaining their parents-in-law shall be regarded as statutory successors first in order, and their rights of succession thereto shall not be affected by inheritance in subrogation (Article 35).

(iii) Land Contract Law

Restricted by a traditional mindset, educational level and their status in the family, Chinese rural women have fewer choices in employment and development than rural men, and tend to be more attached to land. However, patriarchal ideology seems to place them in an inferior position when it comes to land rights. Hence, *Land Contract Law* and related laws have made specialised provisions to protect their rights.

- *Land Contract Law*, as a specialised law, states that the land rights of rural women are guaranteed. Article 6: In undertaking land contracts in rural areas, women shall enjoy equal rights with men. The legitimate rights and interests of women shall be protected in contract. No organizations or individuals may deprive them of their right to land contractual management, which they are entitled to, or infringe upon such rights. Article 30: During the term of contract, if a woman gets married and undertakes no contract for land in her new residence and the party giving out the contract may not take back her originally contracted land ÿand where a divorced woman or a woman bereaved of her husband still lives in her original residence, or does not live in her original residence but undertakes no contract for land in her new residence, the party giving out the contract may not take back her originally contracted land.

  Besides, the law also stipulates the corresponding legal responsibility of violators of rural women's land rights. Article 53: Any organization or individual who infringes upon the contractor's right to land contractual management shall bear civil responsibility. Article 54 (7): Where the party giving out the contract commits one of the following acts, it shall bear such civil responsibilities as desisting from the infringement, returning the original articles, restoring the original state, forestalling damages, eliminating dangers and compensating losses; depriving women of the right to land contractual management that they enjoy according to law or infringing on such right.
- Article 39 of *Marriage Law* amended in 2001: The rights and interests enjoyed by husband or wife in the operation of land under a contract based on the household shall be protected according to law.
- The amendment to *Law on Protection of Rights and Interests of Women* adopted in 2005 also clearly protects the land rights of rural women. Article 32: Women shall enjoy equal rights with men in the contracted management of rural

land; distribution of proceeds of collective economic organizations; use of land requisition and occupation compensations and use of house sites. Article 33: No organization or individual may trespass on a woman's rights and interests in the rural collective economic organization on the ground that she is not married, is married, is divorced or has lost her spouse. The corresponding liability is stated in Article 55: Where a woman's rights and interests in the rural collective economic organization are damaged under the excuse that she is not married, is married, is divorced or has lost her spouse, or in the event that the husband settles at the domicile of his wife, the equality of the husband and the child (children) in enjoying the same rights and interests as those enjoyed by the members of the local rural collective economic organization is infringed upon, the town (township) people's government shall mediate the case in accordance with the law. The victim may also file an application with the rural land contracting arbitration institution for arbitration or lodge a lawsuit in the people's court, and the people's court shall accept the case in accordance with the law.

Besides, *Notice on Protection of Land Contract Right of Rural Women* jointly issued by Communist Party of China Central Office and the General Office of the State Council in May 2001 provided the legal ground for its application. Some localities have also mapped out local rules and policies for protecting the land and related rights of rural women.

2 *Women's right of person*

(i) Laws and regulations on domestic violence

Currently, there is no specialised law against domestic violence in China; however, existing laws and regulations have embodied the legislative spirit and essence for protecting women's right of person.

- ★ *Constitution*: Citizen's right of person is sacred and inviolable.
- ★ The amended *Marriage Law:* domestic violence is incorporated for the first time. The laws has made a clear statement regarding domestic violence in its general provisions, divorce relief measures and legal liability. Especially in the chapter on *Relief Measures and Legal Liability*, several articles set out relief channels for victims and legal liability for attackers. By doing so, all dimensional relief measures (self-help, administrative relief, judicial relief, community relief) and legal liability systems against domestic violence have taken shape.
- *Amendment to Law on Protection of Rights and Interests of Women*: Article 46: Family violence against women is prohibited. The State shall take measures to prevent and stop family violence. The public security, civil affairs, judicial administrative departments, urban and rural grassroots self-governing organizations and social organization shall, according to their respective functions, prevent and stop family violence and help women victims. Article 58: If anyone engages in sexual harassment or family violence against a woman, and if his act constitutes a violation of the public security administration, the victim may require the public security organisation to give the violator an administrative punishment or may initiate civil action in the people's court.

  Arguably, the prevention and prohibition of domestic violence is stipulated, both in principle and substantive terms, which serves as the legal basis for competent authorities to handle domestic violence cases.
- In other legislations on civil action, *General Principles of the Civic Law of the People's Republic of China* states that "citizens shall enjoy the rights of life and health". (Article 98) and that "The main methods of bearing civil liability shall be: cessation of infringements; compensation for losses; extension of apology."(Article 134).

- In terms of legislation on criminal offence, the violator is accountable for criminal liability if domestic violence is as serious as a criminal offence. Female victims of domestic violence can resort to *Criminal Law of the People's Republic of China*. To be specific, there are Article 232: intentional killing; Article 234: intentional injuring; Article 236: raping; and Article 260: abusing. In terms of public security administration, Article 43 of *Law of the People's Republic of China on Public Security Administration Punishments* states that "anyone who blows any person or intentionally injures the body of any person shall be detained for not less than five days but not more than ten days, and shall be fined not less than 200 yuan but not more than 500 yuan. If the circumstances are lenient, he (she) shall be detained for not more than five days or shall be fined not more than 500 yuan."

What merits our attention is that the judicial department is exploring the protection order for women victims. In March 2008, China Institute of Application Law Studies of Supreme People's Court released *Guide to Handling the Marriage Case Related to Domestic Violence*. These guidelines cover the definition of domestic violence, handling principle, evidence, property division, child's custody and visiting, mediation, and so on. The regulation governing bodily protection measures for victims of domestic violence is one of the highlights of this *Guide*. It reads: "Victims of domestic violence can request the court for bodily protection. The court can issue 15 days emergency protection or long term protection ranging from three to six months. Its implementation is monitored by the court. Otherwise, violation of the order will be sanctioned. The public security authority will be notified and carry out the duty of protection." The release of regulations on a protection order (similar to overseas practice) is a breakthrough in protecting victims of domestic violence.

(ii) Laws and regulations on sexual harassment and abuse

Sexual harassment insults women's dignity and violates their right of person. Sexual harassment in the workplace makes the working environment more hostile and even forces victims to lose jobs. Thus, it is detrimental to the victim's labour rights.

China's legislation on the prevention and prohibition of sexual harassment is much too general. The newly amended *Law on Protection of Rights and Interests of Women* states for the first time that "sexual harassment of women is banned. Victims shall be entitled to complain to the entity or the relevant organs" (Article 40). However, it is yet to specify a definition of domestic violence, assign responsibilities and duties on employers to prevent and prohibit sexual harassment, and stipulate civic liability for compensation when sexual harassment occurs.

Currently, those who harass women will take the legal liability, including civic, administrative and criminal liabilities. *The Amendment to Law on Protection of Rights and Interest of Women in 2005* states: "If anyone commits sexual harassment or family violence against a woman to violate this Law, and if his act constitutes a violation of the public security administration, the victim may require the public security organ to give the violator an administrative punishment or may initiate a civil action in the people's court" (Article 58). *Law on Public Security Administration Punishments* stipulates that "anyone who acts indecently towards any person or deliberately exposes his body at a public place shall be detained for not less than five days but not more than ten days if the circumstances are absolutely vile" (Article 44).

Apart from administrative responsibility stated in *Law on Public Security Administration Punishments* (Article 44), sexual abuse mainly involves a legal liability for criminal offences. If sexual abuse is as serious as a crime, the criminal will take the liability. Female victims may resort to the following articles: Article 232: intentional killing; Article 234: intentional injuring;

Article 236: raping; Article 237: molesting and abusing women. The Criminal Law also states that if the girl is less than 14 years old the rapist is subject to severe punishment.

(iii) Women's labour right

Women's labour right includes their rights to survival and development, making it one of their most important rights. China has no specialised labour law for women, but protective provisions for their rights can been found in various laws and regulations, as well as stipulations, such as:

(a) Labour Law

This law, enacted in 1995, has laid down the following principles for equality between men and women: *Section 12*. Labourers shall not be discriminated against in employment, regardless of their ethnic community, race, sex or religious belief; *Section 13*. Females shall enjoy equal rights with males in employment. It shall not be allowed, in the recruitment of staff and workers, to use sex as a pretext for excluding females from employment or to raise recruitment standards for them, except for types of work or posts that are unsuitable for them as stipulated by the State.

Special protective principles for female labourers are found in *Chapter VII Special Protection for Female and Juvenile Workers:*

Section 58: The State shall provide female workers and juvenile workers with special protection.

Section 59: It is prohibited to employ female workers to engage in work in pit-mines, or work with Grade IV physical labour intensity as stipulated by the State, or any other work deemed avoidable for female workers.

Section 60: Female workers shall not be deputed to engage in work high above the ground, under low temperatures, or in cold water or work with Grade III physical labour intensity as stipulated by the State during menstruation.

Section 61: Pregnant female workers shall not be deputed to engage in work with Grade III physical labour intensity as stipulated by the State or in any other work that should be avoided during pregnancy. Workers in or beyond their seven months pregnancy shall not be required to extend their working hours or to work night shifts.

Section 62: After childbirth, female workers shall be entitled to no less than 90 days of maternity leave with pay.

Section 63: Female workers, while breast-feeding their babies less than one year old, shall not be required to engage in work with Grade III physical labour intensity as stipulated by the State or other labour that they should avoid during this period, nor should they extend their working hours or work night shifts.

(b) Labour Contract Law

This law was promulgated in June 2007, and took effect on January 1, 2008. Its legislative purpose is to improve the labour contract system, clearly identify the rights and obligations of both parties to the labour contract, and protect the legitimate rights and interests of labourers. However, it has aroused hot debate after being enacted, for many enterprises and scholars argue that the law is over-protective for labourers, but cost-ineffective and threatening on the part of enterprises. Labor Contract Law has no special regulatory articles for female labourers except for Article 42: the employer shall not dissolve a labour contract with a female employee under circumstances like pregnancy, maternity leave or breastfeeding.

(c) Employment Promotion Law

This law was adopted in August 2007, and took effect on January 1, 2008. As a law designed to promote employment and protect labour rights and interests, it is not very gender-sensitive in terms of women's employment rights. There are only two points related to women's employment promotion: first, in its third principle, workers seeking employment shall not be subjected to discrimination based on ethnicity, race, gender, religious belief, etc; second, in Article 27 of the chapter on *Fair Employment*, the State shall ensure that women enjoy labour rights equal to those of men. When an employer recruits employees, it shall not refuse to recruit women or increase the threshold for recruitment of women under the pretext of gender. When an employer recruits female employees, it shall not stipulate in the employment contract any clause which prevents female employees from getting married or bearing children.

(d) Regulations on female employee's labour protection and prohibition

Regulations on Female Employee's Labour Protection is a specialised and protective department regulation well-targeted to the special physical features of female employees which took effect in 1988. Arguably, it has played an important role in protecting the legitimate labour rights of female labourers, particularly their special physical rights and interests. Some special protections are as follows:

(i) Lowering the basic salary or terminating a contract is disallowed if female employees are on pregnancy, maternity or breastfeeding leave.

(ii) It is prohibited to direct female employees to engage in work in pit-mines, or work with Grade IV physical labour intensity as stipulated by the State, or in any other work that female employees should avoid.

(iii) Female employees shall not be directed to engage in work if they are pregnant or on maternity and breastfeeding leave.

Regulations on the labour scope where female employees are prohibited, in line with the requirements on female employer's labour protection, was released by the then-Ministry of Labour in January 1990. It specifies the labour scope where female employees are prohibited and where they are not allowed to work during menstruation, pregnancy or breastfeeding.

Given that these two regulations have been in force for twenty years, the legislative department has recently embarked on their amendment and promoted them as administrative regulations, in line with China's tremendous socio-economic changes.

As a specialised NGO engaged in women's rights protection, we have three legislative principles to propose for *Regulation on Protection of Female Employers*: First, standards for female employee's labour protection should be aligned with those in the International Labour Convention; second, the State's responsibility should be incorporated in concrete measures for female employee's rights protection; third, female employees should be protected in a moderate manner. According to the ILO's research on gender differences in the past fifteen years, distinctions among labourers are mainly caused by individual factors rather than by physical differences between the sexes. More and more labour experts hold that legislation on women's protection tends to be overprotective, because its formulation is based on assumption and stereotyped thinking rather on than scientific evidence. Such legislation then becomes an obstacle to women's employment and hampers their development.

(e) Other governing regulations and policies

China has a large labour law system comprising numerous departmental regulations or governing documents. Since Labour Law and related laws only lay down principles, local and departmental regulations and documents (or policies) have to be developed and implemented when it comes to application and governing details.

Regulations targeted to women's labour right at local levels can be numbered, and many of them are policies related to retirement. For example, *Provisional Regulations of the State Council on Retirement of Senior Experts* [No 141 Document Issued by the State Council (1983)]; *Notice of the State Council on Extending the Retirement Ages of Some Backbone Teachers, Doctors, and Technological Professionals* [No 142 Document Issued by the State Council (1983)]; *Notice on the Issue of Retirement Age of Female Cadres* jointly issued by the

Organization Department of CPC Central Committee and Ministry of Labour and Personnel; and *Notice on the Issue of Retirement Age of Female Cadres with the Title Above Township (Division) Head* jointly issued by the Organization Department of CPC Central Committee and Ministry of Personnel. These policies have extended the retirement age of some women (senior intellectuals and women cadres above the title of division head) to the same as that of men, but they are poorly implemented. Currently, different retirement ages for men and women was are important problem, responsible for employment discrimination in China.

II OUR PRACTICE

A. Brief Introduction to the Center for Women's Law and Legal Service, Peking University, China

Established in 1995, our center is China's first NGO specialising in providing legal aid services to women. We are committed to protecting women's rights and promoting gender equality By means of free legal consultation, litigation, investigation, law publicity, education and training, and legal advocacy, the Center is deeply involved in women's rights protection and social development. We break new ground in civil legal aid for women in China, which enables us to carry weight both at home and abroad.

Our Center focuses on women's labour rights, family and marriage rights, property rights, and rights of person. Specifically, these cover sex discrimination and sexual harassment in the workplace, non-local women workers' rights and interests, domestic violence, women's property rights at the time of divorce, and land rights of rural women, etc. We have handled more than 2600 cases related to women's rights, provided legal consultations to nearly 7000 visitors, and proposed more than 70 legislative and policy changes. Through various approaches like case-handling and litigation for public benefits, we have not only provided substantive assistance to the female victims of rights violation, but also actively promoted women's comprehensive rights. Apart from legislative advocacy, we have explored and challenged the problems of legislative inadequacy and deficiency and law enforcement, including outdated and stereotyped mindsets, as part of our effort to promote the development of women's rights protection in China.

B. Case Studies[5]

Our goal and essential strategy is to review and improve women's rights from a legal perspective. Well-targeted to the hot spot and difficult issues in the field of women's rights, the cases we have dealt with through research, publicity and advocacy serve as a gateway to promoting gender equality and non-discrimination, and improving legislation and enforcement. The following cases illustrate our strenuous efforts in promoting the gender equality over the past fourteen years.

1 Promoting the same retirement age for men and women: the challenge to institutional sex discrimination

In China, men and women have different retirement ages. The legal ground for this policy can be traced back to No. 104 Document issued by the State Council in 1978, which stipulated that "men retire at the age of 60 years; female cadres at the age of 55 years; and female workers at 50." Regulatory as it is, this provision document has been regarded as the superior legal document for retirement in China for the past thirty-one years and is in effect till today.

When No.104 Document was released, China was at in early stages of reform and opening up. At that time, workers depended on physical exertion, but women were not suitable for long term manual work, given their physical characteristics and needs of caring for children. Arguably, this legislation was intended for their protection. However, as the socio-economic landscape in China has undergone such tremendous change, this protective regulation has been very discriminatory. Since female cadres and female workers retire at different ages, it has been charged with double discrimination (gender and status); besides, it runs counter to gender equality enshrined in the Constitution and in state policy.

Since the late 1990s, our Center has begun promoting the same retirement age for men and women. It not only aims to protect women's equal labour rights, but also challenges institutional discrimination. Here are our practices:

(i) Litigation: in all, 29 cases have been handled, most of which were collective cases filed by hundreds of litigants, involving nearly one thousand people. These cases were influential, because they related to personnel policies and the entire work unit, regional sector or systems where litigants worked.

(ii) Proposing a review of laws that are unconstitutional. On the eve ofWomen's Day in 2006, our Center proposed the anti-constitution review to the National People's Congress, aiming to challenge the stipulation in No.104 Document issued by the State Council in 1978 that "men and women retire at different ages". This was the first time that an NGO asked for legal review mechanisms in this regard. *China Women's Newspaper* reported the news, and it was later quoted by dozens of newspapers and magazines at home and abroad; *Nanfang Weekly* also commented editorially on it. As a result, some ministries began to abide by the principle of same retirement age, but the legislation remains unchanged.

(iii) Investigation. From late 2007 to early 2008, our Center conducted investigations on same retirement age in Zhangjiang Province, Shanghai City and Shaanxi Province respectively, and put out a report which analysed the early retirement of China's women specialists, on the basis of cases we had handled.

(iv) Promotion of local legislation. In December 2008, Beijing solicited public opinions on the draft of *Beijing's*

Implementation Rule of the Law on Protection of Rights and Interests of Women. Its Article 23 states that "the working age of women cadres whose title is above the head of division and senior women intellectuals shall be extended so as to achieve equality between men and women". This aroused heated discussion nationwide, among which were some dissenting voices. Given that the adaptation of this Article would help influence the legislative process on same retirement age, both nationally and provincially, our Center, together with three other women's organizations, submitted our legislative proposal to Beijing People's Congress Legal Work Committee and Beijing Municipal Legal Work Office. In addition we posted and publicised it online, which attracted huge public attention.

2 Sexual harassment in the workplace: litigation practice and promotion of legislative improvement

As mentioned earlier, sexual harassment in the workplace is an infliction on women's bodily rights, dignity and working rights. Existing laws and regulations in China are far too general, therefore one of our priorities has been to address this shortcoming. In this regard, we adopt a bottoms-up approach to improve legislation through a series of litigations, challenging legislative inadequacy and voids, and helping corporations establish anti-sex harassment mechanisms.

(i) *Litigation practice*. Since the amendment regarding the prohibition of "sexual harassment of women" was made to the *Law on Protection of Rights and Interests of Women* in 2005, our Center has handled six cases of national influence, and drawn public attention to the prevention and prohibition of sexual harassment in the workplace. Given that sexual harassment has yet to be legally defined and is hard to prove, it is difficult to win such cases. Here is a successful and typical one, in which litigant Wang accused her boss of sexual harassment and won her case with the assistance of our Center.

Ms. SUN (under a disguised name): Female, 28 years old, single.

Mr. AN: Male, 28 years old, married.

Both of them work in the same work unit. AN is the head of the department where Sun works.

On June 21, 2004, AN invited six associates (including Sun) to dinner after work. During dinner, they all drank some beer. Sun could not drink, so she asked for early leave. AN offered to send Sun home. In the taxi, Sun was forced down on the seat and forcibly kissed by AN. Embarrassed as she was and awed by AN's status, she only managed to push AN away rather than cry out. After several such assaults, Sun was too drunk to struggle. AN addressed Sun with obscene words and demanded to have sex with her. AN's molestation did not stop till the taxi pulled over at Sun's apartment. AN followed Sun out of the taxi and kissed and fondled Sun forcibly in the passage.

After this, Sun often woke up at night and could not sleep. She was afraid of dealing with people, of going to work and coming across AN. She was later diagnosed with depressive disorder caused by her horrible experience. Since she was too scared to see AN again, she had no choice but to quit a job she liked and had to travel a long way to work in a suburb with meagre payment. With our assistance, Sun sued AN for sexual harassment with liability.

The court conducted a non-public trial and decided on April 20, 2007 that AN's obscene words and harassment had offended Sun's dignity and were liable for Sun's mental disorder. AN had to apologise to SUN in the work unit and pay 15,000 yuan as compensation for her disorder.

(ii) Promoting the establishment of corporate anti-sexual harassment mechanisms. Overseas practices have proven that prevention is more effective than punishment; the best way to do this is to establish related mechanisms of anti-sexual harassment in corporations, including specific rules, complaint and case acceptance mechanisms, punishment mechanisms, education and training. Starting in 2007 our

Center, in partnership with the American Embassy, UNIFEM task force on gender issues, and ILO explored ways to establish such mechanisms.

In 2007, our Center co-operated with the China Textile Industry Association and held training programmes in several large textile enterprises. In August 2008, we helped established the very first pilot mechanism in Heibei Hengshui Alcohol Corporation, which was reported by the media and drew wide public attention. In March 2009, we extended the pilot programme to Beijing. Cuiwei Corporate, and Xijiao Hotel took the lead in establishing such mechanisms, which served as role models in China.

3 Domestic Violence: Wang's Case

Wang (female) got to know and fell in love with Chen when they were college students. After graduation, Chen was assigned to work in Beijing. Wang followed him there and tied the knot in 1999. Over the past ten years of their marriage, Wang has been insulted and hurt by Cheng, as evidenced by the following facts: Chen denies their marriage and Wang as his wife, and claims that he is single before his parents; often abuses and threatens Wang for no reason; controls the family's income and spending; restricts Wang from making friends with other people and has hurt her so violently that Wang has twice reported him to the police. However, the police made no report of her complaint. In August 2008, Wang called the police again after being beaten by Chen. The police asked Chen to promise in writing that he would abstain, and pay her medical fees. Wang received minor injuries but was not judicially accredited. What saddens her the most is that Chen refuses to cohabit without giving any reason, that is to say, Wang has had a ten-year marriage with no sex life. Under such circumstances, Wang became sorrowful and unhappy, and was unable to work normally, except at some simple duties. As a result, she was diagnosed with serious mental depression.

In December 2008, Wang approached the court and asked for a divorce, pleading that Chen was guilty of domestic violence and should compensate her 50,000 yuan. Our Center provided her with legal aid. The court began the trial of this case on April 22, 2009, but the judgement has yet to be announced.

Going by the definition of domestic violence prevention and control, Wang suffers from a typical case. According to this definition, widely-used internationally, any behaviour causing bodily, mental or sexual infliction or property damage among family members amounts to domestic violence. To be specific, Wang's experience of suffering physical and verbal abuse and no sex life without good and viable reason can be regarded as domestic violence. On the pretext and for the purpose of controlling the victims, the offender violates the victims' basic rights, damages their dignity and traumatises them seriously.

Under the existing legal framework, however, the prospect of Wang's successful rights protection is not that hopeful, for the following reasons:

a) Domestic violence is narrowly defined in the laws. According to Judicial Interpretation ONE of Marriage Law issued by Supreme People's Court, domestic violence is defined as: the behaviour of the violator causing certain physical and mental injuries to family members by beating, bundling and hurting them, and restricting their liberty. Economic control and restrictions on making friends are yet to be listed as domestic violence, as is the denial of sex. Besides, there is no clear-cut stipulation on mental violence.

b) Accordingly, in current judicial practice, most courts and judges in China *seldom* define mental and sex-related violence as domestic violence or order violators to make the corresponding compensation.

c) Considering that gender-insensitive judges might adopt very strict accreditation standard in their trials, only ***long-term*** and *repeated* behaviours that lead to serious physical damage of victims had been regarded as domestic violence, which runs counter to the definition of Judicial

Interpretation ONE of Marriage Law issued by the Supreme People's Court. The consequence is that cases of minor physical injury are dismissed and victims are denied the justice and assistance of a legal approach.

d) In current judicial practice, even if domestic violence is accredited in the judgement of a divorce case, the compensation tends to be far from adequate for victims.

Wang's shocking case illustrates how serious mental and sex-related violence is. It tells us that if existing laws and current judicial practice continue to ignore such violence, some seriously injured and traumatised victims might be denied effective relief. It goes against our commitment to legally protecting women's rights and safeguarding justice and fairness, as well as our common aspiration for a society free from domestic violence. Therefore, it is imperative for us to reflect on existing legal terms and judicial practice, and to advocate for reform in these two aspects.

4 Land rights for rural women

Let's examine a case first:

Five married-out women, including Hai and Zhu, are members of a villagers' group in Tongcheng, Anhui Province. Their group is located between the city proper and the township. After they got married, their land was not taken back; they continued to pay the taxes and fees for the land every year, in line with the rules and regulations. With accelerated urbanisation, their land was taken over and compensated for. In January 2001, a plan for the distribution of land expropriation fees was drawn up by several village heads and representatives, depriving the married-out women of their rights to compensation. When another round of compensations was disbursed, those married-out women were determined to claim their rights. They went to the competent departments, from village council to district committee, from the municipal women's federation to the provincial agricultural committee, but in vain. In despair, they resorted to our Center for help through various channels. We offered them legal aid.

In June 2005, the married-out women filed a lawsuit in Tongcheng People's Court, but were dismissed with the excuse that after getting married they were no longer local residents. However, through our efforts and media coverage, the court finally accepted their case.

In August 2005, the Tongcheng court began its trial. On the day the court trial was held, the village committee assembled more than one hundred villagers to participate. During the trial, the defendant, the head of villagers' group, displayed a tough attitude and instigated the villagers present there to protest and exclaim, "no land for married-out women". On August 22, the court passed its first judgement it ruled that the villagers' group had made an invalid plan and would have to pay compensation to the five married-out women. The village refused to pay and continued abusing the women. At the end of 2005, the women requested mandatory enforcement, and in April 2006, the five married-out women eventually got their due compensation, eight months after they won their case.

Land is the farmer's source for livelihood and development. The land rights issue and related rights violations for married-out and divorced women like Han has become a national problem. What is commonly seen in rights violations are the following: villagers' self-governance body often deprives women of their rights under the pretext of rules and regulations developed by themselves, including land contract and operation rights; distribution rights to economic proceedings from village's collective economic organization; and the right to compensation for land expropriation. Many women are rendered helpless and in despair because of inaccessible relief channels, the inaction of administrative departments and dismissals by the court.

It is deeply felt by us that the difficulty in handling cases related to the land rights of rural women lies in judicial, administrative and enforcement problems and, in the final analysis, in barriers set by stereotyped mindsets and outdated tradition. To begin with, there is the complete absence of gender sensitivity. For example, the land contract right stipulated in *Land Contract Law* is household-based. Although it guarantees the household land contract and operation rights, to a large extent, it ignores the rights of rural women who live non-locally due to marriage. Then judicial practice and law enforcement are also gender-insensitive. Their passive indifference to rights violations of women who have lost their land is a result of their lack of awareness of equal rights enjoyed by women, of the social significance of women's rights protection, and of how important women's issues are in the process of building a genuinely free and harmonious society.

Next is the hangover of a traditional mindset. A "male-centered" ideology is deeply rooted in the minds of villagers, leaders of village councils, grassroots courts and competent departments. When proceedings distribution is concerned, this mindset changes into so-called legalised rules and village conventions; as for legal relief to women victims, this converts into incompetent enforcement by government departments. The growing rural economy and the nature of land rights confirmed in *Property Rights Law* might drive people to seek huge profits, as a result of which women's rights violation might get even worse.

We believe that the crux of the issue of rural women's land rights lies in how we challenge a stereotyped mentality and outdated tradition. Cognition determines action. If the mentality is changed, action will follow. What is required is patience and greater effort in publicity, advocacy, education and training.

Notes

1 In China there are the Basic People's Court, the Intermediate People's Court, the High People's Court, and the Supreme People's Court.

2 China does not have a Constitutional Court, so cannot hold legislation as invalid for being unconstitutional. China's legal system consists of its Constitution, laws, administrative regulations, local regulations, and ministry and local rules. Article 88 of China's Legislation Law states:

The limits of power for altering or annulling laws, administrative regulations, local regulations, autonomous regulations, separate regulations or rules are as follows:
(1) The National People's Congress has the power to alter or annul any inappropriate laws enacted by its Standing Committee, and to annul any autonomous regulations or separate regulations which have been approved by its Standing Committee but which contravene the Constitution or the provision of the second paragraph in Article 66 of this Law;
(2) The Standing Committee of the National People's Congress has the power to annul any administrative regulations which contradict the Constitution and laws, to annul any local regulations which contradict the Constitution, laws or administrative regulations, and to annul any autonomous regulations or separate regulations which have been approved by the standing committees of the people's congresses of the relevant provinces, autonomous regions or municipalities directly under the Central Government but which contravene the Constitution or the provision of the second paragraph in Article 66 of this Law;
(3) The State Council has the power to alter or annul any inappropriate rules of the departments and of local governments;
(4) The people's congress of a province, autonomous region or municipality directly under the Central Government has the power to alter or annul any inappropriate local regulations formulated or approved by its standing committee;
(5) The standing committee of a local people's congress has the power to annul any inappropriate rules formulated by the people's government at the same level;
(6) The people's government of a province or autonomous region has the power to alter or annul any inappropriate rules formulated by people's governments at the next lower level; and
(7) The authorizing organ has the power to annul any of the regulations formulated by an authorized organ that transcends the authorized limits of power or contravenes the authorized purpose, and when necessary, may revoke the authorization.

3 Article 17 of the 2001 Marriage Law Revisions provides that the following properties incurred during the existence of marriage shall be jointly owned by both husband and wife:
a. wages and bonuses;
b. any income incurred from production or management;
c. any income incurred from intellectual property;
d. any property inherited or bestowed, with the exception of those as mentioned in Article 18 (c) of this law;
e. other property that shall be jointly owned. Both husband and wife shall have equal rights in the disposal of jointly owned property."

Article 19 of the same provides that "Husband and wife may come to an agreement whether the property incurred during the existence of marriage or prior to marriage to be owned by each party, to be jointly owned or partially owned by each party and partially owned by both parties."

According to Articles 17 and 19, China Marriage Law generally requires that property of married couples are considered jointly owned after a marriage. However, if both spouses make other agreements, they would be required to abide by their agreements instead of default law.

4 In the event both husband and wife agree to separately own the property they respectively obtain during the existence of their marriage and either of them has spent considerably more effort on supporting children, taking care of the old or assisting the other party in work, etc, this party shall be entitled to demand the other party to make compensations at the time of divorce, and the requested party shall make compensations. This article serves as protection for the party who spends considerably more effort in the support and care of family. Since this party is usually the female spouse, this article serves as a protection for women.

5 The cases discussed in the article are typical cases handled by our Center. Some of our clients asked to remain anonymous for privacy reasons, and we have an obligation to protect their privacy. Therefore, we do not provide the real names and the courts in which the cases were litigated.

Contributors

Zarizana Abdul Aziz

Zarizana Abdul Aziz is a director of Women Living Under Muslims Laws (WLUML), former President of the Women's Centre for Change, Malaysia and former member of the Malaysian Bar Council.

Abdul Aziz is actively involved in numerous human rights and women's rights activities in Malaysia and internationally. Her primary areas of interest and expertise are in law reform, particularly in relation to gender equality, violence against women, gender and Islam, family laws and the adoption of international human rights standards into domestic laws, as well as the relationship between culture and human rights.

Abdul Aziz has also acted as consultant/legal expert for several international bodies.

Sandra Fredman

Sandra Fredman is Professor of Law at Oxford University, Fellow of Exeter College, Oxford and a barrister. In 2000, she became the first woman professor in the Oxford law faculty and was elected a Fellow of the British Academy in 2005. She holds degrees from the University of Oxford and the University of the Witwatersrand, Johannesburg, South Africa.

Fredman was a scientific director of the EU Network of Legal Experts on the implementation of EU equality directives. She has been an expert advisor to the proposed Single Equality Bill in Northern Ireland, the Equality Review in the UK and the Arthurs Commission on the Canadian Federal Labour code.

Fredman has published widely in the fields of equality, labour law and human rights. Her published books include *Human Rights Transformed* (OUP, 2008); *Discrimination Law* (OUP, 2002); *Women and the Law* (OUP, 1997); *The State as Employer* (Mansell, 1988) with Gillian Morris and *Labour Law and Industrial Relations in Great Britain* (2nd ed, Kluwer, 1992) with Bob Hepple. Most recently, she edited *Age as an Equality Issue* (Hart, 2003) with Sarah Spencer and *Discrimination and Human Rights: The Case of Racism* (OUP, 2001).

Savitri W.E. Goonesekere

Savitri Goonesekere is emeritus Professor of Law, University of Colombo, Sri Lanka. She was formerly Vice Chancellor, University of Colombo, Sri Lanka and a member of the Expert Committee (Treaty Body) monitoring the UN Convention on Elimination of All Forms of Discrimination against Women from 1999 to 2002. A member of several regional and national bodies on women's issues, she has held fellowships in universities in the US and UK. She currently serves as a member of the UN Trust Fund for Victims of Torture. Goonesekere has contributed to advocacy and law reform initiatives in Sri Lanka and has also acted as a consultant for several international agencies working on law and human rights projects in the Asian region. She has published widely on family law, women and children's rights, human rights, law and development issues.

Indira Jaising

Indira Jaising is the Director of Lawyers' Collective Women's Rights Initiative. She is the first woman to be designated Senior Advocate (1986) and the first woman to be appointed Additional Solicitor General of India (2009). Throughout her legal career, Jaising has focused on the protection of the human rights of women, successfully defending several landmark cases on discrimination against women.

The driving force behind the drafting of, lobbying for and enactment of the Protection of Women from Domestic Violence Act, 2005, Jaising was also instrumental in the drafting of the Sexual Harassment of Women at Work Place (Prevention, Prohibition and Redressal) Bill, 2006.

Jaising was nominated to be a member of the CEDAW Committee in January 2009.

Jaising is the recipient of the Padma Shri, the third highest civilian honour in India (2005).

Guo Jianmei

Guo Jianmei is Founder Director of the Centre for Women's Law Studies and Legal Aid at the Peking University School of Law, the premier legal centre for women in China. Her groundbreaking work on promoting women's human rights in China has resulted in major changes in laws and policies. She has participated in the drafting of the *Law of the People's Republic of China on the Protection of the Rights and Interests of Women*.

Renowned internationally for her grounding breaking advocacy and legal work for the under-privileged in China, Guo Jianmei was one of the women nominated by the project, *1000 Women for the Nobel Peace Prize 2005*. She has received the Global Women's Leadership Award for Human Rights presented by the United States' Vital Voices Global Partnership (2007) and the Mathew O. Torbriner Public Services Award presented by the San Francisco Legal Aid Society Employment Law Center (2007).

Sapana Pradhan Malla

Sapana Pradhan Malla is an Advocate at the Supreme Court of Nepal and Member of the Constituent Assembly/ Parliament of Nepal.

Malla is one of the pioneer advocates for issues of stigma and discrimination in Nepal. She has extensive experience in women's human rights, HIV/AIDS, legal advocacy, law reform, Public Interest Litigation and has worked with many international agencies and NGOs on women's rights implementation strategies. Her cases challenging unequal rape laws and inheritance laws are widely cited as instances in which CEDAW's anti-discrimination clause was successfully used to dismantle discriminatory laws affecting women in Nepal. Malla has also been involved in drafting the Trafficking in Persons and Transportation (Control) Act, 2007, Domestic Violence (Offence and Punishment) Act, 2009 and the draft bill on HIV and AIDS.

Malla is a recipient of the Gruber and Patricia Women's Right Award in 2008 for her contributions towards advancing women's rights in Nepal.

Poonam Pradhan Saxena

Poonam Pradhan Saxena is presently a Professor at the Faculty of Law, University of Delhi, India. She specialises in family law and succession, women and law and property law. She is a senior Fulbright scholar, a Shastri Indo Canadian fellow and a visiting faculty member at the University of Baltimore (USA). She has written six books including four volumes on Halsbury's laws of India, more than 50 articles that have been published in books, and in national and international law journals. She has presented papers at several international and national conferences.

Li Ying

Li Ying, a public benefits lawyer, is Deputy Director of the Centre for Women's Law Studies and Legal Aid at the Peking University School of Law, the premier legal centre for women in China.